Learning Interreligiously

Learning Interreligiously

In the Text, in the World

FRANCIS X. CLOONEY, SJ

FORTRESS PRESS
MINNEAPOLIS

LEARNING INTERRELIGIOUSLY
In the Text, in the World

Cover image: Photo of author with Hindu monks of the Swaminarayan community, taken on January 17, 2017, at the BAPS Shri Swaminarayan Mandir and Training Centre in Sarangpur, Gujarat, India. With permission.
Cover design: Laurie Ingram

Print ISBN: 978-1-5064-1771-4
eBook ISBN: 978-1-5064-4013-2

The paper used in this publication meets the minimum requirements of American National Standard for Information Sciences — Permanence of Paper for Printed Library Materials, ANSI Z329.48-1984.

Manufactured in the U.S.A.

Contents

Part II. In Dialogue

Author's Preface

Between November 2007 and December 2016, I regularly blogged at the *In All Things* site of *America*, the Jesuit journal of opinion. I had been invited as part of a start-up group in 2007, as *America* upgraded its web presence. Although I was given a free hand as to what I actually posted, unsurprisingly I was asked to attend particularly to matters of interfaith dialogue. Despite my heavy commitments to teaching and writing and, from 2010 onwards, added responsibilities as director of the Center for the Study of World Religions at Harvard University, I found the medium conducive, and continued to post blogs until I was informed in the fall of 2016 that posting at the website would henceforth be done in a more controlled fashion, largely by *America* staff members.

During that decade, I posted three hundred blogs, for a total of close to three hundred thousand words; my posts were rarely quick reads. My topics included interreligious happenings in the Catholic Church and, more widely, Vatican documents and related controversies involving theologians, reports on my occasional travels to Europe, India, East Asia, and Australia, provocative news items related to religion appearing in the American press, items related to teaching and programming at Harvard, and a few personal posts (e.g., the thirtieth anniversary of my ordination, the fortieth anniversary of my first trip to India, my father's ninetieth birthday, etc.). Occasionally, I posted a series of five or seven posts on a particular non-Christian text in relation to the themes and readings of the Christian liturgical calendar. I worked largely with Hindu materials familiar to me, but for reasons arising in the larger American context, I posted series beyond my expertise, such as on how Catholics can learn from the Qur'an or the Book of Mormon. Many of these posts received considerable comment online, positive and negative; some, hardly any notice at all.

Blogs are by their nature ephemeral, but I did feel that my posts were in a popular vein getting at issues germane to my teaching, first at Boston College and then at Harvard, and to my scholarly publications. I hoped to be able to invite my readers to think further and more deeply on issues pertaining to Catholic and Christian tradition, and to other religions, in history and today. I was finding in each post the opportunity to make the point that knowledge is fundamental to human and religious maturity, and expected of us by God; ignorance is a moral and spiritual failing that leads to escalating problems for individuals and society; much interreligious friction and hostility is due to ignorance; learning is a virtue and study a good spiritual discipline; whether one is a scholar or not, everyone can learn more than they know already, if they take the time; and such learning is very often a remedy for harmful ways of thinking and acting. My posts were, in other words, allied with my teaching, my writing, and my preaching on Sundays, and most often echoed Saint Paul's words, "Finally, beloved, whatever is true, whatever is honorable, whatever is just, whatever is pure, whatever is pleasing, whatever is commendable, if there is any excellence and if there is anything worthy of praise, think about these things. Keep on doing the things that you have learned and received and heard and seen in me, and the God of peace will be with you" (Phil 4:8–9).

I was pleased, then, when Dr. Jesudas Athyal approached me to ask if I would like to publish with Fortress Press and with his ready interest when I proposed publishing a selection of my blog posts. The hard part was to decide which ones were of relatively enduring value, not already too dated, but more likely to transfer reasonably well to the form of a printed collection. I decided to focus in two areas. First, I selected instances of my reading of the texts of other faith traditions (primarily Hindu), such as showed how I thought such texts enrich Christian faith, even if, when read closely, never "saying the same thing." In the first part of this collection, I follow the liturgical calendar common to most Christian churches—Advent to Pentecost, and a few from Ordinary Time—and perhaps these posts will help readers to think differently about those seasons. I then add two other notable readings, related to the holy Qur'an and the Book of Mormon. These posts add up to nearly fifty items.

In order to show that a focus on texts—ever my special focus—does not blind one to what is going on around us, in the second part of this book I collect another set of nearly fifty posts that deal with contemporary events, church issues, the death of important religious figures, signal advances in dialogue, and so on. These are given in chronological order. My hope is that they too will be of interest to the reader, as indicative of the progress—irreversible, despite setbacks—we are daily making in interreligious understanding and harmony.

The nature of blogs is their immediacy—quickly thought and quickly posted. While many of these pieces do benefit from my decades of theological and interreligious study, and my nearly fifty years of Jesuit life, nevertheless, without exception, they were written quickly and posted while still fresh. For this volume, I have honored and retained the quickness of the process. I have in some places slightly edited the blogs—to remove online links, clarify one or another reference, and so on—but I have chosen not to footnote them. As such, then, they remain provisional, meant to prompt the reader to further reading, not to make further study superfluous.

In their original form, as I have mentioned, these blogs were meant to elicit readers' reactions. While that cannot occur so easily or immediately in the case of a book, I do hope that they still prompt further reflection and confirm the point that while understanding is not the foundation of the spiritual life—love is—it is a very good thing to keep an open mind and insist on the importance of learning as intrinsic to the life of faith.

Francis X. Clooney, SJ
Cambridge, MA

PART I

Interreligious Readings

Krishna in Advent I

November 30, 2008

Cambridge, MA. I have been teaching a seminar on the *Bhagavad Gita*, reading it with two classical commentaries (by Ramanuja [eleventh century] and by Madhusudana Sarasvati [sixteenth century]) and two modern commentaries (by Mahatma Gandhi and by Bede Griffiths, the Catholic monk who lived for many years in an ashram in South India). The *Gita* itself is a rather short work, just over seven hundred verses, that is perhaps a bit more than two thousand years old. It is part of the very large epic *Mahabharata*, which tells of a great war between two sides of a princely family; the *Gita* begins just as the terrible final battle is about to occur. At the final moment, the leading warrior Arjuna hesitates in the face of the terrible slaughter that will surely follow and is overcome by grief as he considers the various awful possible outcomes. His charioteer is Krishna, a leading prince who does not personally fight in the war but has agreed to help Arjuna and his brothers in their battle; as the *Gita* tells us little by little, he is also the lord of the universe, divine savior come down to earth. His teaching constitutes the verses of the *Gita*, which leads Arjuna on an intellectual and spiritual journey that unfolds the meaning of self, duty, detachment and detached action, service, and love of God, so that he can recover himself and get up and fight, as is his duty.

While the entire *Gita* is a fascinating topic for study, I am thinking about it right now because today is the first day of Advent, when we begin to think in a prolonged, deeper way about the meaning of the birth of the Son of God in our midst. Advent, like other important times in the church year, is an occasion for learning from other religions, bringing our Christian expectations and intuitions to bear on their texts, images, and practices—and thereafter bringing what we learn from some particular religious tradition back into our reflection on Christian truths, values, and practices. This is the richer intelligent cultural exchange and learning, rooted in actual study and conversation. Pope Benedict has repeatedly reminded us that careful, contextual study—in culture—is superior to an unprepared effort to share on a neutral or purely religious level. We have minds, we must use them, even in the religious sphere, and so we must study.

Hence the "Krishna in Advent," focused on five verses near the beginning of chapter 4, where Krishna explains his coming into the world:

Many a birth have I passed through, and [many a birth] have you [Arjuna]: I know them all but you do not.

Unborn am I, changeless is my Self, of [all] contingent beings am I the Lord! Yet by my creative energy I consort with Nature—which is mine—and come to be [in time].

For whenever the law of righteousness withers away and lawlessness arises, then do I generate myself [on earth].

For the protection of the good, for the destruction of evildoers, for the setting up of the law of righteousness, I come into being age after age.

Who knows my godly birth and mode of operation thus as they really are, he, his body left behind, is never born again: he comes to Me.

(trans. R. C. Zaehner, Oxford University Press, 1969)

These verses, even more than most of the verses of the *Gita*, have occupied Hindu commentators and modern Western scholars, including Christian theologians. Many books have been written to compare and contrast Krishna and Christ and to ponder the differences between their births and activities in the world. (See, for instance, Steven Tsoukalas's essay "Krishna and Christ" in *Song Divine* and Jesuit Fr. Ishanand Vempeny's older book *Krishna and Christ*). Often, such reflection has had a win/lose edge to it: if there are too many similarities, the uniqueness of the Christ event gets lost from sight, and so distinctions must be made to show how the Christ event is more unique, more important, and more true. Our faith tells us it is more true, but we need not read with a competitive, must-win spirit.

While such concerns are quite understandable and important in the larger realm of Christian faith and theology, I suggest that we have much to learn by a more refined, narrower inquiry that is really simple: what is Krishna saying in these verses, what did Hindu theologians find in his words, and what do they mean for us? And so, this and two more entries to *In All Things* before Christmas: Today, (1) What is Krishna saying? and then, in two segments, (2) What did the great Hindu commentator Ramanuja think Krishna was saying? and (3) What therefore do we learn from the *Gita*, in this Advent meditation, about the coming of Christ?

So, for today, what is Krishna saying? Verse 5: Krishna identifies himself with the human condition—that we all are born into human bodies many times over. It is not that the fact that Krishna is born multiple times that distinguishes him from Arjuna, but that Krishna understands the cycle of births and remembers his previous births. Verse 6: Krishna describes himself in paradoxical language—he is transcendent and perfect, unchanging and unborn—and yet he comes into union with material nature, for the sake of birth, without losing his transcendent perfection. Verse 7: Krishna repeatedly responds to the situation on earth, the waning of that right order that is dharma and the arising of chaos and violence (in adharma). Verse 8: Krishna's interventions in the world are for the sake of good people and to destroy evildoers, and thus to restore the right order of things. This is a repeated activity, since in every age good and evil are in tension and conflict in our world. Verse 9: The key human response to this divine activity is to know what Krishna has done, in truth, since it is this knowing that leads to union with Krishna.

I hope my very brief comments state at least part of what Krishna is saying to Arjuna and thus give us something to think about: how in Jesus, God identifies himself with our human condition, yet without losing divine perfection; how God enters our world in order to side with those in need, against oppressors; how meditating on how Krishna does all of this enables us to come into union with Jesus, born among us.

Read the verses for yourself, of course, and read more of the *Gita* if you can. (There are innumerable translations, including excellent, more recent ones by Laurie Patton, Graham Schweig, and George Thompson; R. C. Zaehner's old edition has most helpful notes; and you can find many useful resources online). To know this about how God is and how God acts is the task we have in Advent, for the sake of a loving knowledge by which we approach him again. You may, of course, wish also to list difference (one birth vs. many births, for instance), but I hope you will not allow even important differences to make impossible the reflection to which the *Gita* invites us in Advent.

Krishna in Advent II

December 12, 2008

Cambridge, MA. My first reflection in this series made clear my hope that in this Advent season we can engage in interreligious, intercultural learning by considering, as an example, the teaching on the birth of Lord Krishna in the world, according to the *Bhagavad Gita*. I continue now with verses I cited in last week's reflection:

> Many a birth have I passed through, and [many a birth] have you [Arjuna]: I know them all but you do not. Unborn am I, changeless is my Self, of [all] contingent beings am I the Lord! Yet by my creative energy I consort with Nature—which is mine—and come to be [in time]. For whenever the law of righteousness withers away and lawlessness arises, then do I generate myself [on earth]. For the protection of the good, for the destruction of evildoers, for the setting up of the law of righteousness, I come into being age after age. Who knows my godly birth and mode of operation thus as they really are, he, his body left behind, is never born again: he comes to Me.

(4.5–9, Zaehner translation)

The verses are worthy of our reflection, and much is achieved just by reading them and thinking about them.

Yet, we would be missing something if we simply read the verses by themselves, as if there were no readers before us—pious and learned Hindus who took the *Gita* to heart over many centuries. A willingness to listen to believers in other traditions and to learn from their theological reflection is also part of the great intercultural exchange to which we are invited in the twenty-first century. To hear this wisdom, I turn today to Ramanuja (by tradition, 1017–1137, South India) and his reading of *Gita* 4.

Ramanuja, one of the great theologians of Indian history was, tradition tells us, a versatile figure—scholar, teacher, writer of philosophical and theological treatises and commentaries, reformer of temple ritual and daily order, and ardent proponent of love of God. One of the most intriguing and inviting stories about Ramanuja was that after long testing and delay, his teacher taught him the sacred Tiru Mantra, a brief prayer rich in meaning and efficacy, with the stipulation, imposed by his teacher, that he reveal it to no one else, under pain of hell. Ramanuja received the mantra humbly and with devotion and then went to the temple veranda, and from there proclaimed it to the crowds in temple courtyard. When his stunned teacher asked him why, Ramanuja is said to have replied with words to this effect: "To share this great grace with my community, I would gladly risk damnation."

In any case, Ramanuja wrote a commentary on the *Gita*, and in his reading of our verses from chapter 4, among many points, he made four key ones.

First, Krishna is clearly insisting that he was born, as Arjuna was born, even if "my birth" and "your birth" are in some way distinguished. There is no talk here of illusory births, merely appearances of being born.

Second, Ramanuja also insists that while humans are born over and again by the force of their bad karma, compelled, as it were, to reenter the world, Krishna freely chooses to be born whenever there is a need, but without any compulsion or imperfection.

Third, Ramanuja asks about the nature of Krishna's body and decides that Krishna had a real body but one made of perfect matter free from all the imperfections of other bodies: it was made not of *prakriti* (natural matter) but of a non-natural material (*a-prakriti*). While this clearly divides Krishna from others taking ordinary bodies, it is interesting to note that in Ramanuja's tradition, that non-natural matter appears again: it is the bodies that all those who reach liberation receive upon entrance into Krishna's heaven. What Krishna is at birth, all shall one day be.

These three points are all quite interesting because they point to ways in which Krishna's birth is like—and unlike—the birth of Jesus. It is not that Ramanuja believed in an illusory appearance of divine birth; rather, in a different religious and cultural context, he defended divine reality differently, on different grounds.

But a fourth and most interesting point deserves special mention. Why, Ramanuja asks, does Krishna bother taking on a human body at all, simply to "protect the good and destroy evildoers"? Could he not do this without bothering to take on a body, simply by the exercise of divine power? Here, Ramanuja does not offer our Christian answer, that the omnipotent God chooses to empty himself and share our lives, deaths, and sufferings. But he does offer a striking answer of spiritual depth: namely, the omnipotent Krishna came to earth and was present during the great battle that Arjuna faced, took on the great project of insuring the victory of righteousness, and taught the *Gita* in order that by such pretexts he might simply be present, accessible to human physical senses, nearby to those who would know and love him. A cosmic emergency occasions divine intervention, but it seems that to Ramanuja, Krishna would have found some reason to come among us anyway, so we could see him, hear him, be with him, touch him—and thus with our five material yet spiritual senses find God nearby and in our midst. This insight is not far from our Christian tradition's *felix culpa* insight: by a happy fault, Adam's sin was the cause for the great gift of God's physical presence in the world.

A Christian need not change their view of the incarnation in light of Ramanuja's insights into the reality, uniqueness, and loveliness of Krishna's divine birth. But our world is too small, and our well-being too fragile, for us to imagine that we cannot benefit from the wisdom of other believers in other traditions, particularly those who, like us, believe that God is among us. The unique, irreplaceable truth of Christ cannot be damaged by genuine, vulnerable appreciation for the wisdom and insight of Ramanuja into Krishna's birth.

Krishna in Advent III

December 19, 2008

Cambridge, MA. I return today for a third time to the theme of Krishna in Advent. In my first reflections on this theme, I highlighted famous verses from chapter 4 of the *Bhagavad Gita* and from the commentary on the verses by the medieval theologian Ramanuja. There is a lot going on in both the verses and in Ramanuja's comments on them, and much of it can be welcomed as insightful and wise by the Christian reader, helping us to think anew about the how and why of Christ's birth.

Thinking about Krishna in Advent marks a way of practicing what we preach: interreligious learning is not merely a matter of ideas or confessions of faith aimed at one another, but it is a true intercultural exchange. By attentive study, we find our way into the literature of another religious tradition, we learn from it, and we consider in respectful detail what is said and how it is said. While this kind of study does not lead to answers to life's enduring questions, it changes us little by little, and we find ourselves to be Christians who have genuinely learned from another religious tradition. While it may not be possible for a Christian simply to believe in Krishna, for instance, there is no reason why a Christian, pondering the meaning of Christ's coming this Advent season, cannot learn greatly from how Hindus have interpreted the coming of Krishna into the world.

For this final meditation on Krishna in Advent, I go back a few centuries before Ramanuja, drawing not on a Sanskrit text but on a verse from the *Tiruvaymoli* of Shatakopan, a ninth-century Hindu poet saint. *Tiruvaymoli* is a set of 100 songs, 1,102 verses in the Tamil language, a vernacular South Indian language that is the first

language of over seventy-five million Indians even today. In the thir-
teenth and fourteenth centuries, disciples of Ramanuja wrote commentaries on the verses of Tiruvaymoli, and I have for many years
enjoyed reading those commentaries, by Pillan, Nanjiyar, Periyavac-
chan Pillai, Nampillai, and other great medieval scholars. (Unfortunately, almost nothing by these commentators is translated; however,
for a sampling of verses by Shatakopan, see if you can find a copy
of A. K. Ramanujan's *Hymns for the Drowning*, a lovely selection of
verses from *Tiruvaymoli*, or, I dare to add, my 1996 book, *Seeing
through Texts*.)

In the third book of his songs, Shatakopan reflects on Krishna this
way:

> Griefless bright light, he is fire, abiding ever the same; grief abounds in
> human birth, but into it he came, so our eyes could see him; he causes
> griefs, this lord who made his divine state enter this world, griefless
> excellent marvelous Krishna—I praise him, and I sorrow no more.

(3.10.6)

The verse—lovelier in Tamil than in English, of course—makes a
series of basic points about Krishna's births: In his heavenly form, he
is all light, radiant and fiery, and in him there is no darkness. Though
perfect, he does not hesitate to come into our world, by a human
birth (as in *Gita* 4). He does this (as Ramanuja says) for the supreme
value of making himself accessible to human eyes. He does not abandon his divine nature but "brings it with him" when he enters the
world. He is excellent, amazing, even in human form, as heaven
comes to earth. All of this marks insights and values that should be
familiar to Christian readers, and we should not be jealous to learn
that a Hindu poet had such insights too.

The verse makes two additional points. First, we notice that "grief"
appears in each of the four lines. Krishna is "griefless" in his heavenly
form (line 1), but he is also (in line 4) still "griefless" in his earthly
form, after birth; he does not lose his transcendent equanimity in this
world, despite all that happens. Though griefless, he did not hesitate
to come into a world where grief abounds, where being born is to
begin experiencing grief (line 2); the implication is that his becoming visible is a remedy for the grief we otherwise experience in this
world. And finally, the commentators make a point of the fact that

(in line 3) Krishna is said, surprisingly, to be causing "griefs"—in the plural.

The commentators surely puzzled over this line, and they suggest that Krishna's coming into the world caused two kinds of grief: grief for evildoers, who are overcome, but also grief for those devoted to Krishna, souls who cannot bear to see him only briefly and on rare occasions, and so grieve out of love.

The second additional point is that right at the end of line 4, the poet reaches a state beyond sorrow—by meditating on Krishna portrayed in four ways in the four lines, his own state is changed as he voices words of praise and achieves his own journey beyond sorrow here on earth. Is it not true that by contemplation of what God has done for us, we discover our lasting joy?

What to make of this verse, then, as a Christian reader in Advent? I suggest again that we not allow ourselves to be distracted by the great theological questions but rather more simply embrace the option for a cultural dialogue that is rooted in study of this verse by Shatakopan, the Hindu poet, and a willingness to reflect on the verse and even bring it with us to prayer on Christmas Eve. It may help to hear Shatakopan's words along with words such as those of Evening Prayer at Christmas:

Blessed are you, Sovereign God,
our light and our salvation,
to you be glory and praise for ever.
To dispel the darkness of our night
you sent forth your Son, the firstborn of all creation, to be the Christ, the light of the world.

Rejoicing in the mystery of the Word made flesh,
we acclaim him Emmanuel, as all creation sings to you: Blessed be God, Father, Son and Holy Spirit.

And,

When peaceful silence lay over all,
and night was in the midst of her swift course:
from your royal throne, O God, down from the heavens, leapt your almighty Word.

It is clear that these words are *not* the same as what Shatakopan sang, and we are probably the better off for the difference. What we can

do, however, is pray with the words of the church after listening to
Shatakopan and taking his insights to heart. We need not be afraid.

Swami Yogananda's Wisdom on the Birth of Christ

December 22, 2009

Cambridge, MA. I marked the *Triduum* 2009 by drawing on Paramahamsa Yogananda's *The Second Coming of Christ*, reflecting on how he explained the meaning of Holy Thursday, Good Friday, and the resurrection. My point was in part that we do well to listen carefully to how people who are not Christian see Christ, since we can learn from their wisdom. I close the year similarly, with attention to how Yogananda values the birth of Christ in volume 1 of *The Second Coming*.

Yogananda first comments on how it was appropriate that the birth of Jesus was seen by peasants who were simple and, more importantly, pure of heart and bereft of large egos. (He mentions having personally met one such simple and clear-eyed person, the mystic Therese Neumann, famed for her meditations on the crucifixion and for bearing the stigmata.) The whole scene of the nativity, he says, makes this point: "As with the shepherds on the hillside, the shepherds of man's faith, devotion, and meditation will be bathed in the light of realization and lead those devotees who are humble in spirit to behold the infinite presence of Christ newborn within them."

In the face of the crass materialism surrounding Christmas—Yogananda speaks in the first part of the twentieth century—he says that he initiated for his followers a daylong meditation service to the worship of Christ: "The ideal is to honor Christ in spiritual meditation from morning till evening, absorbed in feeling in one's own consciousness the Infinite Christ that was born in Jesus." This meditation, he says, is the doorway to profound peace and joy.

He concludes that the peace of Christ, which is the gift of Christmas, "is found in the interiorized state of one's God-communion in meditation. Then, like an ever-full reservoir, it pours out freely to one's family, friends, community, nation, and the world." In Yogananda's view, he pleads that we take all this to heart: if we live this way, rooted in the ideals of the life of Jesus, "a millennium of peace and brotherhood would come on earth."

Indeed, we need to see anew our own lives and possibilities in light of Christ's birth: "A person who is imbued with God's peace can feel naught but goodwill toward all. The crib of ordinary consciousness is very small, filled to capacity with self-love. The cradle of goodwill of Christ-love holds the Infinite Consciousness that includes all beings, all nations, all races and faiths as one."

Yogananda has more to say on the Gospel accounts, but the preceding paragraphs suffice for this year. I recommend getting a copy of his *Second Coming*—two volumes, over one thousand pages—or asking for it in your library, since it really is a book from which we have much to learn.

In particular, his own Christmas practice is one we would do well to embrace: however busy we are in church or with family and friends, we are still called to contemplate in still silence and simple light the birth of Jesus, thus setting time aside in which we can absorb the light of Christ into our lives. In and through the familiar Christmas events, we too should be able to see the light of God shining in our darkness. Perhaps then we can rise to Yogananda's level of hope too, not letting sin and cynicism too heavily darken our view of the world. I can be more confident that my own personal, interior illumination will be my first, maybe best contribution to the transformation of our world, local and global.

Baby Krishna, Infant Christ at Christmas

December 17, 2011

Cambridge, MA. The semester is finally ending, and in a few days, my grades will be submitted and Introduction to Hindu Ritual Theory will be safely behind me. I hope now to add a few blogs this coming week, in light of the quickly arriving Christmas holiday—a few somewhat random insights and recommendations on the birth of Jesus in light of Hindu wisdom.

Prenote: As always and as with any comparative theme, we can assume at the start that Christ is unique, the incarnation is unique, his impact on the world is unique. Comparison is not about relativism. Good comparisons never mean that all religions are the same, or in this case, that *avatara* and incarnation are the same, or that Jesus is the same as Krishna, or those who believe in Krishna have nothing to gain from encounter with Jesus. But once our values and convictions are in place, then good comparative learning can *begin* to take place; nothing about uniqueness or difference suggests that Christians have nothing to learn from Hindus, or that we'd be better off thinking of Christ without ever thinking deeply about Krishna.

So here is a first suggestion: take a look at Kristin Johnston Largen's *Baby Krishna, Infant Christ: A Comparative Theology of Salvation* (Maryknoll, NY: Orbis, 2011). (She is a professor of theology at the Lutheran Theological Seminary in Gettysburg, Pennsylvania.) This very thoughtful and insightful book is also a fine introduction to Hinduism from a Christian perspective, Krishna for Christian reflection, and how best to do comparative study. If you know little about Hinduism, fear not, you can start here.

Part 1 focuses on the baby Krishna, part 2 on the infant Jesus.

Each part begins with an account of the scriptural sources on the baby, those around him, the dangers to which he was submitted in becoming human—evil kings and the like—and how each baby was also shown, sacramentally and dramatically, to be the savior, God in human, accessible form. If you've never read the Hindu stories of the birth of Krishna and his childhood, this is a fine place to start. We hear for instance the famous story of how Yashoda, mother of Krishna, wanted to scold her son for putting dirt in his mouth, only to find, upon making the child open it, that he, the lord, held all the world, and her too, within himself: God hidden in, as the child. But Largen's chapters on Jesus are also instructive for the Christian reader, providing excellent insights into what we learn of the birth of Jesus in the Gospels of Luke and Matthew, carefully complemented by the famed infancy gospels of James and Thomas. (Check the web on these.)

In each major part of the book, we find also a reflection on the grownup divine figure, how the indications given in the stories of the divine infant remain pertinent and become all the more evident in the subsequent accounts of their lives and works thereafter. Key to her account of Krishna's infancy, for instance, are insights into the charms and loveliness of the child, the playfulness that enchants his mother and the village women, the ways in which profound theological teachings on the sovereignty and freedom of God are at evidence in the whims and fancies of the child—and how, in all of this, the theme is affirmed over and again: here, in this child, God is accessible, the arduous journey to God made simple and direct. One need not climb to heaven; God is here. Similarly—in a way that cannot be summarized here—Largen also draws forth and summarizes how the canonical and extratestamental accounts of the young Jesus are underutilized resources for imagining love of God in the midst of our basic, human reality.

In Part 3, Largen draws together what her primarily Christian audience might learn from this extended reflection. Once we've excluded careless and overly general claims of similarity or difference, we are helped better to "think about salvation today . . . and to understand Jesus' particular identity as savior." The vivid accounts of the baby Krishna give a very human feel to the divine birth stories and human responses to infants and children—noticed carefully in light of traditional Hindu materials—illumined as guides to how we can relate to God: the vivid and embodied nature of divine love; God's love for us deeply engaged in the totality of who we are; the divine-human love as passionate and deeply enjoyed; opening up the mystery of God's action among us with a more vivid sense of divine play and playfulness. Her headings on how we can learn anew from Jesus, infant and grown up, are illustrative: "Expecting the Unexpected," "The Life of Jesus Is Salvific," "Relationships Matter for Salvation," "Salvation Happens 'in the Flesh,'" "Salvation Is in the Mundane."

It is hard to summarize what Largen does with the Hindu material, since she is not nearly so abstract and dry as I've been in the preceding paragraphs. A scholar of Hinduism with special attention to the literary traditions, she is doing more than simply summarizing stories of Krishna in a loose fashion. She is, rather, looking into some lovely, moving poetry of the baby Krishna and drawing forth the themes she enunciates. Just one example must suffice, a passage quoted from Barbara Powell's anthology of Hinduism, *Windows into the Infinite*:

> Naughty Krishna, though exasperating, brings supreme joy to His elders. Their anger never lasts long. He bats His lotus-like eyes, pouts His pretty lips, sheds a few counterfeit tears and before you know it the adult is overcome with love and sweeps the child up in her arms. The naughtiness is also partly a guise designed to obscure His Godhead from them. Were His contemporaries aware of His true identity, they would be too over-awed to exchange the natural loving intimacies for which he incarnated Himself. They must mistake Him for an ordinary boy and so, like a regular boy, Krishna is sometimes a pest.

(Largen, 57; Powell, 307)

This passage will seem odd and out of place next to the simple and austere Gospel accounts so familiar to us, though the extracanonical gospels reach some of the same imaginative range. Again, there is room for just one example. In the infancy gospel of Thomas, after some of the boy Jesus's more amazing and confounding exploits—he had not yet learned to discipline his divinity—Zacchaeus confesses:

> Poor me, I'm utterly bewildered [at what turn out to be the wise deeds of the boy], wretch that I am. I've heaped shame upon myself because I took on this child. . . . I can't endure the severity of his look or his lucid speech. This child is no ordinary mortal; he can tame fire! Perhaps he was born before the creation of the world. What sort of womb bore him, what sort of mother nourished him?—I don't know."

(Largen, 99; trans. Ronald Hock)

I therefore recommend to you *Baby Krishna, Infant Christ*, and I am sure that if you order it right away, you could have it in hand before Christmas. But in the meantime, I suggest two simpler meditations. First, attend carefully to your own varied responses to babies and small children, and meditatively bring those into play in a contemplation of the newborn and baby Jesus. Second, find some way to shift your reflection on some other religion away from the large and difficult questions of doctrine—for a moment at least—to imagine, enjoy, learn from the stories and poetry and images of that religion. Trust your imagination. And, as Largen shows us, these ancient traditions of Krishna are a fine place to start.

Singing the Baby Jesus in South India

December 20, 2011

Cambridge, MA. South India is blessed with an abundance of lovely poetry in the Tamil language. Tamil, though unfamiliar to many, is a language with a two-thousand-plus-year history that is spoken even today by over sixty million people in South India and by over sixty-six million worldwide. (Malayalam, Kannada, and Telugu are related to Tamil.) The poetry we find in Tamil is exquisite. In my 2005 book, *Divine Mother, Blessed Mother* (Oxford University Press), I translated some nineteenth-century verses from a Christian hymn, the *Matararacamman Antati* (Linked Verses in Praise of the Queen of all Women), in praise of the Virgin Mary as the queen of Mylapore, the old city within current day Chennai (Madras). The verses are in the style of old Tamil religious poetry, set in four lines, each verse ending with a word that in meaning or sound is linked to the first word of the next verse. It is hard to see a progression in such verses, which seem rather to offer a series of meditations around and about a single theme.

For example, these verses from this old Tamil text praise both Mary and her child:

O mother, virgin in Mylapore where swans flock,
you remember fondly how the child in the womb of that other gracious lady [Elizabeth]
looked with love on the creator in your womb and worshipped him;
the greatness of such devotees can hardly be understood even by the host of those above. (41)

She is the throne of the infinite threefold reality, a fine garden, and
she once gave milk to this incomparable lovely child who was crying;

she is the virgin in good Mylapore:
we don't think clearly but still she is gracious toward us,
she ends the dullness of our minds. (60)

With her foot she defeated and destroyed the snake, and then
on the bright mountain she bore as human one of the highest, radiant
Three;
when the immortals, shepherds, and everyone else worshipped,
she rejoiced;
now she dwells in Mylapore,
so write her in the cave of your heart, worship her. (67)

In my confusion
I did not submit myself to the mind of our guides,
I did not think of approaching your son
right here in your lovely arms,
I did not realize I would burn head to foot in hell fires—
so now rule me,
here in Mylapore surrounded by ocean waves where flowering trees
sway in the wind,
O sweet word, O Mary. (77)

For a second example of the use of the poetic styles of Tamil in South
India, I draw on a book entitled *Extraordinary Child: Poems from a
South Indian Devotional Genre* (Honolulu: University of Hawaii Press,
1997) by Paula Richman, professor at Oberlin College. Drawing on
the very human tendency to delight in babies and small children,
the genre of *pillai-tamil* (Tamil verses on the child) praises in stylized ways the divine child, one or another deity praised in his or her
childhood. Here, for instance, is part of a poem praising the Goddess
Minakshi with her child the divine Murukan:

From the corners of your black oceanlike eyes,
whose shapeliness surpasses your fish-shaped earrings,
you pour ambrosia,
casting clear waves of compassion.
You lay the divine child,
who set fire to the white waves,
on your small, fair, round, swaying ankles.
You bathe him,
kiss the top of his head,
apply fragrant oils to his hair
and put on holy ash. (105)

A chapter entitled "One Poet's Baby Jesus" offers a study and translation of the *Iyesupiran Pillaitamil* (the Tamil verses on the Lord Jesus
as a Child), published in the 1980s by Arul Cellatturai (a Hindu, I
think). He sought to use this beautiful Tamil style to speak of Jesus
in a way that all—Hindu, Christian, and Muslim—could appreciate.
He saw, Richman tells us, that these child poems would also be easily acceptable in the Christian context, where other Hindu images
of God would not be easily accepted. And he saw that everyone can
relate to a baby. I cannot reproduce much of his poetry (in Richman's
wonderful translation) here, but a sample will give you a feel for it:

> Source of knowledge,
> who encompasses all these things,
> making people look to the sky in wonder,
> to my rejoicing heart, come.
> practice balancing on your toddling feet,
> like honey-dripping lotus petals.
> Son of the loving God, come. (164)

In another section, the baby Jesus is like the moon that waxes and
wanes, comes and goes, illumined with the higher light (of the
Father), and so the poet addresses the moon:

> Since you receive light from another source,
> since you rise high in the sky
> while many people watch,
> since you receive life again
> even though your body dies,
> since you remove the darkness of the world
> with your light . . .
> and since the hero of my poem,
> the Lord born of a virgin
> who is conceived through the Holy Spirit,
> is like you,
> Moon in the beautiful sky,
> you should quickly agree
> to play joyously and happily
> with the one who is entwined with Tamil poetry,
> flowing like a waterfall. (168)

And in another poem, to the moon:

Is there any relish equal to the pleasure
of touching his radiant, shining body
treasured in the minds of the pure ones?
With the child of the Lord who gives eternal life,
come to play.
With the son of God,
seated at the right side of gracious God,
Moon, come to play. (176)

Reasons of space—and copyright—prevent me from quoting any more here from either source, but I think you get the idea: in the South Indian context, the reality and affective presence of the child, linked with the beauties of the Tamil language, opened the way to meditations on the baby Jesus and his mother that are both devout and tender. On one level, the feelings of Christmas may seem off-putting, the child too cute, the sentiments too sweet; but the idea is a good one: to find a way into devotion through a deep human feeling, love and delight in a child.

Yoga and Lent I

February 12, 2013
Cambridge, MA. It is Lent once more, and as I've often done in the past, I will take up a theme that I will return to every now and then until Easter. Since I am once again teaching my course on the *Yoga Sutras* of Patanjali—the classic synthesis of yoga theory and practice as understood some 1,500 or more years ago—I thought I would return to the sutras, on which I've blogged before.

This time I will focus on what the *Yoga Sutras* ask us to do, and for this, I focus on the Second Book (*Pada*), which begins this way:

> Austerity, appropriate study, and dedication to the master comprise the yoga of action,

> which is for the purpose of cultivating absorption and for the purpose of diminishing the afflictions.

> Ignorance, ego-centeredness, desire, aversion, and longing for continuity are the five afflictions.

(2.1–3)

(Lest these blogs become too long, I modify/simplify my own translations in places. You are advised to check other translations too.)

Before I go any further, full disclosure: I am not a particularly adept practitioner of yoga, nor have I ever taught yoga. I teach the *Yoga Sutras* as a brilliant intellectual system, and the sutras themselves are not a manual of how to do yoga. Any practitioner who knows the sutras will agree, I think: Patanjali clarifies what yoga is for and about, and synthesizes much older wisdom, but for the practice, even in ancient times one might go to other texts.

However Patanjali, in his sutras, gives much wisdom on what counts as yogic practice, what the practice is for, and how the whole of a yogic practice fits together. My suggestion is that this will help us who are Christian and thinking not simply about what we do to observe Lent but also why we do what we do. Even observing church and community practices, such as fast on Ash Wednesday or some acts of piety or self-denial in Lent, merit some thinking: okay, I am doing this—why?

The first three sutras (small verses) of *Yoga Sutras* book 2, as cited above, get us off to a clear start. The yoga of action involves austerity, study of one's appropriate and assigned texts, and turning to the master (the lord). Vyasa and other early commentators do not give a list of ascetical practices but do point out that "austerity" (*tapas*) is a matter of intensifying inner "heat," and this is different from doing more and more exotic and painful things to one's body and mind. Indeed, they stress that they must, as it were, follow a middle path, hard enough to make a difference but not so hard as to upset the delicate balance of the body and mind. Study, Vyasa says, might be a simple practice of reciting sacred texts assigned for this purpose, perhaps a mantra, or the reading of texts that lead to lasting freedom. Turning to the master—most often taken to mean a turning to God, one's chosen deity—is mentioned here, and in book 1, as a salutary practice that can change one's life. It does not mean that Patanjali's yoga is theistic, much less Christian, but it does mean that he recognizes this "turning to" the lord as beneficial.

Why do this? It is here that Patanjali starts to get more technical, and we begin to exercise our minds in thinking about whether yoga works for a Christian in Lent. The second sutra gives two reasons: "the purpose of cultivating absorption and for the purpose of diminishing the afflictions." Absorption (*samadhi*) is, in the first book of the sutras, conceived of as an ultimate, utterly simple state of consciousness, in which all the fluctuations of the mind and brain come to a halt, so that there is no more observing and knowing the world around us, no more errors and fancies about that world, and not even any more of those images that float in our minds in sleep or even in memory. (See the beginning of book 1 of the sutras). This is indeed a high state, the clear and luminous mind at rest. In book 1, Patanjali says that for this state, one might practice repeatedly and/or become detached and/or turn to the master (lord).

Clearing the mind for this state of simple absorption requires that we turn to the other side of this, the "diminishing of the afflictions." This is not about inventing a life without pain but about lessening, to the point of disappearance, those distractions and upsets of mind that make it turbulent, complicated, and unable to rest quietly in itself.

What those afflictions are is given in the third sutra: "Ignorance, ego-centeredness, desire, aversion, and longing for continuity are the five afflictions." These might serve as the material for an examination of conscience early in Lent, even if we tend to give them a moral tone. *Ignorance*: what are we ignorant of that causes suffering for ourselves and others? *Ego-centeredness*: how destructive is my ego, my insistence on seeing the world in light of myself? *Desire*: what do I crave, insatiably, so as to distort my view of reality? *Aversion*: what do I run away from as I divide the world into the parts I can accept and like and the parts I will not tolerate? Both desire and aversion are the basis of indifference, that great Ignatian virtue. The last in the list requires us to look to the commentaries, since *longing for continuity*, which Patanjali notes in a subsequent sutra to be an affliction even of the spiritually advanced, turns out to be a deep-down and very stubborn desire to keep on living, no matter what: a fear of dying, a fear of letting go. The yogic and Lenten virtue, dying that one might live, is very hard to actually do, even for the saints.

We can see that there is much here to think about. There is common ground, things we too might be doing in Lent and for not dissimilar reasons. But just as there is no wholesale rejection of any particular aspect of this yoga of action as we have thus far seen it, neither need we insist that all of this is "the same as what Christians do in Lent." Turning to God is not just an option, one of several, it is also something we *do*. Metaphorically, we can speak of a deep, quiet clearing of the mind, an utter calmness in God's presence, and all the purifying supports that go with that. As the psalm says: "Be still and know that I am God" (Ps 46:10). Or think of Jesus: we need not imagine that his mind was very busy and his mouth very talkative during those weeks in the desert—a mind entirely empty of everything but God.

Or, if absorption and this serenity is not our goal in Lent, how would we characterize what we are up to, when we pray or study or fast in this season? Why vex the body, do less of this and more of that?

Yoga and Lent II: *Sede Vacante*

February 17, 2013

Cambridge, MA. In the first of this Lenten series, I took up the opening of the second chapter of the *Yoga Sutras*, where the "yoga of action" is comprised of ascetical practice, study, and a turning to the lord. Such yoga serves to quiet the mind, leading it away from attachments, from the "afflictions"—including ignorance and ego and craving—and toward a state of absorption, a turning within. While this program cannot be thought to be identical to what a Christian might do in Lent, the idea that these forty days should foster this quest for inner tranquility and detachment should surprise no one, even those more inclined to acts of charity and service. There are other, similarly straightforward parts of the second chapter of the sutras to which we will turn soon, but it would be disingenuous to skip over some difficult intervening verses that have to do with karma—deeds and their residues that burden ordinary and spiritual being in a particularly deep and stubborn way; the world as a mass of activities and their results, often violent and for the worse. So bear with me as I summarize the rather dense verses that follow. (Again, there are many, many commentaries one can consult for fuller explanation.)

Like many a Hindu text, the *Yoga Sutras* see karma—analogous to a sweeping mix of original and actual sin, cosmic and personal—as causing pain and disorder such as pervade every aspect of life, seeping even into the very fact of living:

> Rooted in the afflictions (ignorance, ego-centeredness, desire, aversion, and longing for continuity), the residue of karma is felt in the arising of effects that we see and effects invisible to us. While that root of karma is still there, its ripening too is there: birth, the span of life, and experience.

All three of these have fruits that are delightful or very painful, because of merit and de-merit.

(2.12–14)

The reader may recall at this point the opening of the book of Ecclesiastes:

> Vanity of vanities, says the Teacher, vanity of vanities! All is vanity. What do people gain from all the toil at which they toil under the sun? A generation goes, and a generation comes, but the earth remains forever. The sun rises and the sun goes down, and hurries to the place where it rises. The wind blows to the south, and goes round to the north; round and round goes the wind, and on its circuits the wind returns. All streams run to the sea, but the sea is not full; to the place where the streams flow, there they continue to flow. All things are wearisome; more than one can express; the eye is not satisfied with seeing, or the ear filled with hearing. What has been is what will be, and what has been done is what will be done; there is nothing new under the sun.

(1.2–9)

Similarly, the *Yoga Sutras* contemplate life as momentarily joyful and pleasurable, sad and painful: "Due to change, pain, persisting impressions, and suffering, and because of obstacles that arise due to the movements of nature's constituents, the discriminating person sees that all is nothing but suffering" (2.15). The constituents (*gunas*) mark "nature" as a bundle of energies and possibilities, arising and decaying; even when the world is at peace, it is changing, devouring itself as its fuel, coming to be and passing away.

This manner of contemplation of good and evil—without and within—as momentary states may be overwhelming, for nothing is left out or to be taken for granted. But the sutras advise not passivity but a determination to change what can be changed: "It is future suffering that can be ended" (2.16). A sober, unromantic attitude toward life enables one to see the future in a cold and clear light—with a cleareyed freedom that changes one's relation to it.

The sutras will soon enough turn again to practices, things to do and not do. So why this very philosophical interlude? It seems clear that Patanjali, author of the sutras, is skeptical about unreflective actions, no matter how energetic or sincere. Action—as karma—may be intended to do good but just as easily, or more so, makes us part of the problem, not somehow a counterforce to it. One cannot say that the goal is to turn away entirely from the world, since the free person is, simply, the one who sees, and there is no reason, here at least, to think that one closes one's eyes to the world about one. The goal rather is to see with calmness, neither lust nor repulsion, neither comfort nor anger.

And so, although yoga is often thought of as very physical, the sutras primarily encourage exercises that are intellectual and spiritual. Even here, in the chapter that is about the "yoga of action," the sutras do not turn quickly to postures, breathing, and the like. The core solution to life's problem is a changed attitude to our very experience: "The very contact of seer and the seen is the root cause for what should be ended" (2.17). It is hard to be an observer without becoming entangled in what we see, even identifying with it as who we are. Freedom and the ending of suffering lie in a simple yet elusive insight: "The seer is simply the seeing; though pure, seeing in accord with ideas" (2.20). When we are ignorant, we have no sense of ourselves that is not determined by the things we have and do (2.25); insight into who we are—and are not—sets us free (2.26), and then our wisdom is complete with respect to what is wrong and right in life, the steadying of the self in its own self (2.27).

Only when this tranquility is in place can there be action that does not merely add to the hyperactivity of the world. This section of the sutras may beneficially remind us that what may be required is a sober, steady gaze at the mass of afflictions that beset the church today—the problem of our loud words and clumsy deeds, particularly at the top.

It was for this that, by a yogic insight of sorts, Jesus spoke so directly of the inner source of our problems: "Then do you also fail to understand? Do you not see that whatever goes into a person from outside cannot defile, since it enters not the heart but the stomach, and goes out into the sewer?" Rather, "it is what comes out of a person that defiles. For it is from within, from the human heart, that evil intentions come: fornication, theft, murder, adultery, avarice, wickedness, deceit, licentiousness, envy, slander, pride, and folly. All these evil things come from within, and they defile a person" (Mark 7:18–23).

I cannot help but add: It is early enough in Lent for us to consider the possibility that all we really need to do this Lent is to learn to see the world, ourselves included, as if for the first time, sober and cleareyed, without words and actions for a time. Right now, when the church is on edge, awaiting a new pope, it is easy to be overwhelmed by the complexity of what lies before anyone taking up that office, and it is tempting to spend our time thinking about who should do what, or stop doing what. So here's a real Lenten discipline: it might be good for the church to live *sede vacante* for a full year—contemplating an empty seat of power—before electing a new pope. We might think of it as a long Lent, to get down into the more stubborn roots of our bad and good deeds.

Yoga and Lent III: Empty Wisdom

February 23, 2013

Cambridge, MA. This Lenten series is dedicated to reflections on the second chapter of the *Yoga Sutras*, a chapter dedicated to the "yoga of action." As I explained in the first and second entries, however, "action" here is more of a spiritual and intellectual doing and undoing aimed at unclogging the deeper layers of the self that have been stifled and strangled, as we might say, by sin, the busy deeds and endless talking and thinking we have relied on for so long that we imagine them to be the solution when they are really the problem.

Thus my suggestion at the end of the second blog, that the church might practice some yoga by leaving the papal throne empty for a full year while we ponder the absence and presence of power in the church. I've seen no sign that anyone else thinks this is a good idea, but an empty throne seems a better idea than immediately settling another cardinal, any cardinal, into the chair of Peter. Let the roots of the problem wither for a good long while. And so, even on this second Sunday of Lent, a sutra we ended with last time bears repetition: "Unfaltering discriminative discernment is the means to ending (this confusion between the self and the world)" (2.26).

This is about a discernment that discerns the difference between the lasting and what passes away, between the spiritual and what is crass and selfish and violent in its ignorance. This is an ongoing, "unfaltering" seeing of things as they are, a letting go of our obsessive clutching at power, wealth, pleasure, even life itself.

Sound too negative? Not incarnational enough? Actually, it sounds a lot like Saint Paul in the second reading for this second Sunday of Lent: "Brothers and sisters, join in imitating me, and observe those who live according to the example you have in us. For many live as enemies of the cross of Christ; I have often told you of them, and now I tell you even with tears. Their end is destruction; their god is the belly; and their glory is in their shame; their minds are set on earthly things." By contrast, "our citizenship is in heaven, and it is from there that we are expecting a Savior, the Lord Jesus Christ" (Phil 3:17–20).

For Paul, and in this second chapter of the sutras, the solution is not merely more effort or a firmer expression of sincerity and willpower; for it is a deeper transformation that must take place. And so, as Paul sees it, Christ will effect a deeper and more powerful change that we can hardly have anticipated as he transforms "the body of our humiliation so that it may be conformed to the body of his glory, by the power that also enables him to make all things subject to himself" (Phil 3:21). It is not just the Christ of today's gospel who is transfigured: such is the destiny of us all.

Even if the work of Christ is never the same as the practice of yoga, the deep change Paul envisions—something no amount of activity can add up to—is not entirely different from what the next sutra hints at: "His wisdom is sevenfold, up to its very highest level" (2.27). Vyasa, the first commentator on the sutras, explains the sevenfold nature of this wisdom, beginning with these four new conditions: (1) the evils that have caused suffering—ego, lust, the craving for power, violence, the busy, everyday mind—are now gone; (2) their roots have been torn out and will not grow again; (3) this radical change in life is manifest for all to see, like a light in darkness; and (4) discerning wisdom is recognized as the sole sufficient cause for this deep change. The other three conditions of wisdom are found still deeper in this liberated person, Vyasa says: (5) the mind has done all it can, and rests; (6) the world, no longer tormented by human craving, is restored to its own equilibrium; and so (7) this person remains pure, illumined with her own inner light, and free. This is the end point of the yoga of action that begins, as we saw, in some fundamental, simple work: "Austerity, appropriate study, and dedication to the master comprise the yoga of action, which is for the purpose of cultivating absorption and for the purpose of diminishing the afflictions" (2.1–2).

We may be tempted to worry about this yogi—what will he do after all this? Will she be sufficiently engaged in the world? Will she improve the church and world? Is this not a merely quiet state? Again, I suggest that we put aside the competitive angle in all this and presuppose for now that Christ and yoga are not at odds. Yoga need not threaten or diminish what Christ does in us. If we consider all this with a certain tranquility, we will learn to be patient with this ideal too, the quiet that arrives after our sin has been rooted out, along with all its desires and impulsions to activity.

Do we not see this elemental, divine quiet in today's Lenten readings as well? Think of Abram in the first reading, who had refused to settle for what God said to him and showed to him: "As the sun was going down, a deep sleep fell upon Abram, and a deep and terrifying darkness descended upon him" (Gen 15:12). Or be there with Peter, James, and John in the Gospel, when they struggle between lethargy and wakefulness: "Now Peter and his companions were weighed down with sleep; but since they had stayed awake, they saw his glory and the two men who stood with him" (Luke 9:32). Both the intense darkness and the blinding light short-circuit the ordinary mind, ending the confusion of ordinary ways of seeing things.

Next time I will introduce the famous "eight limbs" (astanga) of yoga: "Restraint, observance, posture, control of breath, withdrawal, concentration, meditation, and deep absorption" (2.29), and those practices and states of mind will seem more Lent-like, things we can do and concentrate on. But in a too-busy world and a too-busy and talkative church where we keep thinking that more of the same will somehow solve our problems, it is important to honor the promise of deep discernment, the richer wisdom, the deeper transformation we cannot make happen.

The yoga of not doing, undoing: further advice to the elector cardinals about to meet in Rome to choose a successor to Benedict XVI.

Yoga and Lent IV: To See as Wisdom Sees

March 2, 2013

Cambridge, MA. The next section of the second chapter of the *Yoga Sutras* is the famous account of the eight limbs (*astanga*) of yoga, a famed list that is most often used to structure any account of yoga.

Contrasted with some of the subtler points I had to deal with in my previous entries in this series, this is a list that seems rather more easily useful in Lent, particularly if we think of Lent as a time when we are to do things that inculcate focus and discipline.

Patanjali introduces the list with a great promise:

> When, due to practicing the limbs of yoga, there is the destruction of impurity, then there dawns the splendor of knowledge, unto discriminative discernment. (2.28)

From the practice of the eight limbs arises the ending of all obscuration, the dawning of knowledge, and a final wisdom rooted in discrimination, that is, in seeing things just as they are. It seems fairly easy to affirm such goals as a Christian in Lent, as long as we stay on a general level: impurity is to be removed, knowledge illumines our situation so that nothing is obscured or shadowed, and this eventuates in a totally truthful encounter with reality, just as it is. There is nothing to this that a Christian need balk at, even if one might be concerned at first lest the final state seem to be merely self-produced.

So what are the limbs? Here is a pared-down list, omitting for now the many explanatory verses that accompany the basic enumeration (as always, in an approximate translation, largely of my own, though indebted to many good translators):

The eight limbs are: restraint, observance, sitting, control of breath, withdrawal, concentration, meditation, and the unitive state. (2.29)

The restraints are non-intention to harm, truthfulness, non-stealing, sexual restraint, and nongrasping. (2.30)

The observances are purity, contentment, austerity, one's own study, and dedication to the master. (2.32)

Sitting is steady and with contentment. (2.46)

When that is in place, a cutting off of the motions of in-breath and out-breath is control of breath. (2.49)

When there is no longer a close connection of the mind to its own contents, then there is withdrawal of the senses, as if in imitation of that mind's own form. (2.54)

Concentration is the fixing of the mind to a place. Meditation is the practice of extending a single idea there. When it shines forth simply as the object, as if devoid of its own form, there is the unitive state. (3.1–3)

For now, I offer three comments. First, this is an extraordinarily comprehensive set of considerations. An entire moral life is encompassed by the restraints and observances, whereas posture and control of breath take up in a very simple fashion two of the things we all do, all the time: sit and breathe. Withdrawing the senses, a rather obscure practice if we depend on the verse defining it (54), has to do with inverting the mind, turning it away from the endless array of external things it focuses on, to dwell simply in itself. All of this moral, physical, and mental work—or non-work—clears the way for the threefold meditative practice, concentrating (on the self, perhaps the light within), holding one's attention there for longer and longer periods of time, until one is, in a sense, nothing but that holding of attention, a single, long, unwavering glance.

Second, this impressive movement is of a piece, the mundane and the lofty interconnected. This is why the somewhat awkward word "limb" is preferable to "steps," since the latter gives the impression that the "lower" practices are finished and done with, as one moves on to the more important practices of meditation. But just as the limbs of the body or the movements integral to a dance or a ritual must occur all in coordination, not merely one at a time, Patanjali is suggesting that all eight practices belong together, all the way from the start to the finish. Not doing evil is not a onetime achievement, just as one does not get beyond learning to sit at rest or breathe mindfully. Meditation and the unitive state require, beginning to end, the moral, physical, and intellectual grounding that the limbs together provide.

Third, the remarkable end point, the *unitive state* to which the eight limbs cooperate seems to be a very simple abiding within one-self—staying there, alive and not caught up in the busyness of mind and body. That all ends in a simple gaze, like a flame that does not waver, a stream of oil never interrupted. If you are tempted to worry about this, as if it is too quiet or empty for a Christian—quietism in our busy church!—think for a moment of what Paul promises in 1 Corinthians 15:28: "When all things are subjected to him, then the Son himself will also be subjected to the one who put all things in subjection under him, so that God may be all in all," in the end, as it were, nothing but God. Or recall what Meister Eckhart wrote in one of his sermons: "The eye through which I see God is the same eye through which God sees me; my eye and God's eye are one eye, one seeing, one knowing, one love." The fruits of Lent can be simple too, if we manage to weave all our practices, of mind and body and heart, into a single, steady whole and learn just to wait there.

I realize that for some readers much of the preceding may seem rather abstract and not very helpful for Lent, too heady to be useful. True, yoga is a doing, not a blog writing. But all of this really is about how we do and learn not to do, especially in Lent. As we near the middle of this holy season, we do well to consider the eight limbs—or six or three or twelve—of our own Lenten observance: what are all the things we as individuals and church are doing in Lent, and how does it all cohere, for some final, simpler goal that cannot be sur-passed? Think, in the end, of what Paul indicates in Galatians 2:20: "I have been crucified with Christ; and it is no longer I who live, but it is Christ who lives in me." What if Lent ends there, and there is no longer anything else? At least some yogis would be content, an eye on the world.

Yoga and Lent V: Ten Lenten Commandments

March 9, 2013

Cambridge, MA. The world around me is uneasy and in dire straits: the pope resigns, Congress remains dysfunctional, the environment is increasingly out of balance, and so many people live in situations of terrible deprivation. And still I persist in blogging through Lent not on these timely issues but on the second book of the *Yoga Sutras*, the "Yoga of Action." My conviction, manifest in the previous entries, is that we are far too preoccupied with things that are important and compelling. Lent is in part about stepping away from those ordinary concerns. Jesus said, "There is need of only one thing" (Luke 10:42), and these Lenten reflections are dedicated to that proposition. Even if it takes a year or two to elect a new pope—emptiness can be good—we can progress spiritually and, in doing so, change ourselves and change the church. And for this, yoga is a needed friend. This is the fifth in a series of about eight.

My admission of stubborn uselessness aside, today's section of the sutras of Patanjali is actually useful. One might say that we have before us, finally, the "ten commandments" or (better) "ten recommendations" that lie at the heart of Patanjali's sutras, at the start of the famous "eight limbs (components) of yoga." It is as if he wanted to put these recommendations in context since, as we should know too, it is a wonderful thing to be truthful, nonviolent, and so forth, but it is not enough to stop with these virtues and practices, if we are seeking that "one needed thing."

"The limbs of yoga"—its integral components—are eight: "restraint, observance, posture, control of breath, withdrawal, concentration, meditation, and indrawing" (2.29). When we get to the last three in the list, we are at the heart of yoga, but Patanjali wants us first to build our base, with the five "restraints" (*yama*): "non-intention to harm, truthfulness, non-stealing, sexual restraint, and nongrasping" (30), and five "observances" (*niyama*): "purity, contentment, austerity, personal study, and dedication to the master" (2.32).

Patanjali notes, with respect to both sets of five, *agendo contra* (as we Jesuits used to say): go against the grain, strive to deflect those fixed activities of the mind that distract from the goal, cultivate what leads us to our goal (33). How do we reorient our lives so that we can actually pray, with intensity?

The restraints are five:

> When there is establishment in *non-intention to harm*, in proximity to such a one, there will be an abandonment of hostility. (35)

That is, when you are truly dedicated to nonviolence and no longer intend harm to any being, the level of hostility around you decreases exponentially. Be the peace you talk about.

> When there is establishment in *truthfulness*, there is a base for the fruits of action. (36)

For if we speak the truth, and mean what we say, we are free to do exactly as we know and speak. Gandhi made a life of this.

> When there is establishment in *non-stealing*, there is the arrival of all treasures. (37)

Perhaps this is the message of the Sermon on the Mount: "But strive first for the kingdom of God and his righteousness, and all these things will be given to you as well" (Matt 6.33).

> When there is establishment in *sexual restraint*, an obtaining of vigor. (38)

Brahmacarya (sexual restraint) amounts, most of the time, to celibacy, though the yogis are reputed to go very deeply into internalizing sexuality potency, not merely stopping sexual practices but turning the desire into a spiritual power. The world needs a few more celibates, not fewer, if they are of this yogic type, not compelled, not in disguise, not angling for power.

> When there is stability in *non-possession*, realization of how things are born. (39)

This somewhat obscure sutra is a plea that we let go, stop clinging. How "things are born" might refer to matters as large as birth and rebirth, or as small as how it is that holding onto even one thing leads to a whole series of greater attachments. The point of radical poverty—says this professor surrounded by his books—is that if we do not let go of possessions in some fundamental, radical way, we will start of accumulate lots of things, over and over. Owning one thing leads to owning many.

The observances too are five:

> From *purity* arise disgust for one's own limbs and noncontact with others. (40)

I would like this sutra to have been phrased otherwise, more positively. But before we rush to a hymn in praise of the special Christian affirmation of the world, think for a moment of the value of this closeup look at how dangerous and dirty our bodies and world are—after all, we all die in the end—and how paying attention entirely will deromanticize what we see when we look in the mirror. Other days, sure, we can praise the beauty of the world around us and love what the incarnation says about this world, but today this observance invites us to see the dirty and dark side of life.

> From *contentment*, the unsurpassed obtaining of satisfaction. (42)

Enough is enough, after all, and craving is never satisfied. Again, that yogi Jesus seems to have gotten the point: "So do not worry about tomorrow, for tomorrow will bring worries of its own. Today's trouble is enough for today" (Matt 6:34).

The last three observances we saw at the start of the second book of the sutras and in my first blog in this series, and so we can abbreviate here:

> From *austerity*, from the destruction of impurity, there is perfection of body and senses. (43)

This is oddly out of place it would seem—didn't we handle purity above?—but perhaps that is the point: if we learn to see ourselves with a terrible honesty and then a courageous contentment, we can afford to be austere. Not because we think that grim asceticism will make us better, but because "less is more," "small is beautiful," and what I've already received is enough for a lifetime; austerity not as "giving up" but as intensifying, focusing, making *best* out of the opportunities and bodies we happen to have right now.

From *personal study*, close connection with one's chosen deity. (44)

This may have various meanings in Patanjali's world, but the easiest meaning seems so very helpful to us: study the scriptures, devote yourself to the *lectio divina*, allow the words to come alive in your imaginations, and you will find God as you seek God. (For Lent: study the Song of Songs.)

From *dedication to the lord*, perfection in deep inwardness. (45)

It should surprise no Christian that in turning to God we find what we seek; is not Lent simply about that return to the Lord so movingly exemplified in the Gospel for the fourth Sunday of Lent, the Prodigal Son? Yes, Lent is the time to return to God.

But Patanjali is advising us, by putting this tenth and not first, that there is a lot of pious rhetoric (in the church too, I would add) that makes it seem that talking a lot—about God and feeling superior because our God is the best God—is somehow the same as receiving a spiritual identity. Patanjali in a sense urges us to delay turning to God, talking to God: rebalance your life, put it back in order, and later on, when you've cleaned up and cooled down, talk about God again. Again, the master speaks: "Why do you call me 'Lord, Lord,' and do not do what I tell you? I will show you what someone is like who comes to me, hears my words, and acts on them" (Luke 6:46–47) and "'Not everyone who says to me, 'Lord, Lord,' will enter the kingdom of heaven, but only one who does the will of my Father in heaven" (Matt 7:21).

Lent is more than half over. But it takes no time to get started on our Lenten yoga, seeking first God's kingdom—and knowing with detachment what that means.

Yoga and Lent VI: Sit, Breathe, Let Go

March 16, 2013

Cambridge, MA. Lent is rolling along, but we are also nearing the end of the second chapter of the *Yoga Sutras*, the chapter I am proposing for our Lenten reflection. Right now we are halfway through the "eight limbs" of yoga practice we introduced last week in our fifth Lenten blog on yoga: restraint, observance, posture, control of breath, letting go, attention, meditation, and indrawal. Now we handle posture, the control of breath, and the indrawal of the senses.

As a yogic, Lenten practice: sit at ease. Most people, asked about yoga, will immediately think of those very impressive and seemingly impossible positions that extraordinarily agile practitioners, mostly young, undertake. Yet, it is striking how little Patanjali says about posture (*asana*), the third limb of yoga: "Posture should be steady and with satisfaction, achieved by the relaxation of exertion and by a state of balance without end" (2.46–47). That is, sit comfortably in a manner you find pleasing, one that does not require great effort and that can be maintained for a long time, "without end." Lent, I have suggested, might be seen in this same light: as a time to lighten up, loosen one's burden, let things go, thus reaching a quieter and steady state that one can maintain over time.

The immediate fruits are two: first, "after this, there are no assaults by the opposites" (48)—that is, it seems, one reaches a certain physical and mental steadiness, undisturbed by oppositions such as heat and cold, the pleasant and painful, wealth and poverty, and so on. It may seem like a great deal to think that sitting with ease can accomplish this balance, but there is surely more to be said for just sitting quietly than we realize.

The second fruit of easy posture is that one can attend with a certain care and calm to one of those things that we will continue to do—breathing—and this is the fourth limb of yoga. First, we can notice how we actually breathe (rather than thinking about how we should breathe): "Breath's movement is external, internal, or stopped; closely measured according to time, place, and number; long or subtle" (50). With this attention, noticing our breathing patterns, we learn simply to sit and breathe: "After one's posture is settled, control of breath is cutting back on the motions of in-breath and out-breath" (49). The result is quite important, since by this breathing, "the covering of light is destroyed, and the mind becomes fit for acts of concentration" (52–53). We might consider that an excellent Lenten practice, even for its last weeks, would be to sit and breathe, and let that breathing dispel illusions about what and who we are. This removal of the coverings over the light is the removal of the bushel basket Jesus warns us again in the Sermon on the Mount: "No one after lighting a lamp puts it under the bushel basket, but on the lampstand, and it gives light to all in the house" (Matt 5:15). To sit at ease and attend to our breathing, hiding no longer, will prepare us for the quieter, vulnerable meditations asked of us in Holy Week. As always, less is more.

There is nothing in Patanjali's rule on breathing that would prevent us from following the third method of prayer recommended by Ignatius in the *Exercises*:

> The Third Method of Prayer is that with each breath in or out, one has to pray mentally, saying one word of the Our Father, or of another prayer which is being recited: so that only one word be said between one breath and another, and while the time from one breath to another lasts, let attention be given chiefly to the meaning of such word, or to the person to whom he recites it, or to his own baseness, or to the difference from such great height to his own so great lowness.

Yet, Patanjali might find the words and the pairing of breaths and thoughts unnecessary; just breathe, that is God's spirit.

As for the fifth limb of yoga, "letting go," it seems that Patanjali had in mind that if we have reformed our lives (by the first two limbs of yoga), and if we sit quietly and with pleasure and attend to our breathing (in the third and fourth limbs), then the mind naturally lets its thoughts and the senses of their objects come and go, no longer clinging to what we think or see or hear or taste: "When there is no close connection between the mind and its own contents, there is an in-turning of the senses, now as if conformed to that mind's own inner form" (54). Again, we may be surprised by how little is asked of us in order to accomplish so much: the quieted, contented mind, a comfortable seated position, and calmed breathing together allow us a certain indifference even to our own thoughts—most of which, truth be told, turn out to be not all that urgent. It is this, not the asceticism of the rigorist or romantic, that allows us finally to control the experiences and pulls of our five senses: "Thence arises the highest control of the senses" (55).

Yoga and Lent VII: The Contemplative Gaze

March 24, 2013

Cambridge, MA. I have already introduced the first two segments of the "eight limbs" (*astanga*) of yoga, such as emphasize respectively moral and bodily discipline. Now I take up the sixth and seventh of these limbs, those dealing most directly with meditation: holding (*dharana*) and meditation (*dhyana*):

> The holding is the tying of the mind to a place.

> Extending this single thread of attention is meditation.

(*Yoga Sutras* 3.1–2)

The images in these verses are rather simple: as if with a thread, the mind is tied to some particular place; as if by a rolling out of that thread, it stays there, over a longer time, possibly indefinitely. The idea, to put it very simply, is that the detached and free mind, calmed by moral practice and rhythmic, mindful breathing, can simply "hold" itself in some given place for a long time. This turn to meditation—perhaps contemplation is the better term—follows upon the entirety of the second book of the sutras, such as I have covered in past weeks: the philosophical reflection on action and its implications, the problem of the mind's entanglement in things, the moral foundations of indifference and freedom, and the triple practices of sitting, breathing, and letting go that we considered last time. It is only with all of that in place that Patanjali turns to the interior holding of the mind in some place (*what* is in that place matters less) and resting in that holding for a long time. For how long? The great commentator Vijnana Bhiksu indicates that the holding takes up the time of twelve practices of mindful breathing (inhalation, holding, exhalation), and that one meditation is comprised of twelve instances of holding.

We cannot fail to note that here too Patanjali leaves it up to the person meditating to decide on where she or he should hold the mind. He does not say, but the first commentator, Vyasa, suggests that it is best to stay local: in the navel, on the tip of the tongue or of the nose, in the lotus in the heart, or within the light shimmering in the center of the brain. Patanjali does not insist that meditation be theistic or devotional; neither does he say a word against this possibility. His insistence, though, is that whatever the focus, it come after a mindfulness that is first of all moral and bodily. The place where one holds one's attention could therefore be entirely neutral with respect to our relationship to God, or Christ, or it could be a simple, long gaze upon what is local for the Christian in Lent, in Holy Week, the Christ with whom we sit at table, or with whom we pray in the garden, or at whose cross we stand.

None of us reads or writes neutrally, and it should not be surprising to anyone that my reading of Patanjali—one of the many available, many of which are more expert than mine—is deeply influenced by the *Spiritual Exercises*. The *Exercises* are not the same as yoga, of course, but the comparisons can be endless and not merely of notional value. Attention to yoga—as holding, meditating—can help us to open up the contemplative depths of the *Exercises*.

Ignatius the yogi: here I must defer to the experts on Ignatian spirituality, but I have found most helpful in this regard the insights of W. H. Longridge, a monk in the Anglican Society of St. John the Evangelist, in his book *The Spiritual Exercises of Saint Ignatius Loyola, translated from the Spanish with a commentary and a translation of the Directorium in Exercitia* (Mowbray, 1919; a volume hard to find). In an "additional note" near the end of the volume "on 'contemplation' as used in the *Exercises*, and its relation to contemplation as understood in mystical theology," Longridge admits that the *Exercises* may seem rather busy, active, mental compared with the contemplative goal of "a simple regard, accompanied by love," a long, sustained, loving glance at what one loves. But in an analysis too rich to summarize here, Longridge shows how the *Exercises*, as its traditional readers understood it, eventuates in simpler and simpler affective, quiet attention. He quotes (pp. 258–59) Francisco Suarez, the great seventeenth-century Jesuit writer, on the movement of the

Exercises, from the disciplined activities Ignatius prescribes in detail, to the awakening of the "spiritual senses," "applied in such a way that the mind by means of them gazes upon some object with admiration and love, or hears words so as to be deeply moved by their meaning, or inhales the fragrance of the virtues or gifts of some soul, and so with the other senses." For Suarez, the higher states of contemplation are barely mentioned by Ignatius, for the simple reason that while the beginnings of prayer can be mapped in many words, "the end of it lies in the Spirit"; accordingly, "Ignatius says little about the actual union of the soul with God, and the act of simple contemplation in which it is realized" (p. 262).

Patanjali too says little, but it all counts, for us as well. When Patanjali writes of "holding" and "meditating," he turns out to be offering us a gift, first regarding the practice—we learn to be moral, detached, to sit, breathe, let go, attend, hold our gaze, just there—and then regarding the inner states of contemplation to which we aspire as Christians, including those of us versed in the *Exercises*. We are far here, I think, from extrinsic worries about pluralism or diversity, from fears about syncretism, and even from the well-intentioned efforts to put together dialogues among people of different faiths. This simpler, deeper meeting in contemplative practices—and yoga is just an example—has to do with the inner depths of Christian faith; there too, we may pray better if we humbly learn from those who practice yoga. Other dialogues, and then too theologies of religions, can come from here after this.

Yoga and Lent VIII: The Samadhi of Jesus

March 30, 2013

Cambridge, MA. This is the last of my Lenten reflections on the second chapter of the *Yoga Sutras*, the "Yoga of Action," yoga in action.

We have up to now been looking at the last part of the chapter, the eight "limbs"—integral but subordinate parts of yoga—and most recently, the sixth and seventh limbs, holding (*dharana*) one's attention on a chosen object and meditating (*dhyana*), wherein one abides for increasingly longer periods of time in attentive presence to and with some object of meditation. I suggested that this was a perfectly fine practice for Holy Week.

The last of the limbs is *samadhi*, a state of concentration, "enstasy" (a turning within, rather the opposite dynamic to the also familiar religious state of "ecstasy") or, as I prefer at the moment, "indrawing" or "indrawal." Even if in the first chapter of the sutras, Patanjali carefully traces a gradual quieting of the mind, the several ever-simpler modes of intellectual work that take place, here he speaks rather concisely of this state:

> When meditation shines forth simply as the object, as if empty of proper form, that is indrawal.

(*Yoga Sutras* 3.3)

The meditating person is given over entirely to the object, as if the object alone, radiant and present, was the entirety of the contemplation. If one is open to the connections and not worried about keeping yoga away from the deepest reaches of Christian prayer, then this is perhaps something of what Saint Paul meant in saying, in words perfect for Holy Week,

> I have been crucified with Christ; and it is no longer I who live, but it is Christ who lives in me. And the life I now live in the flesh I live by faith in the Son of God, who loved me and gave himself for me.

(Gal 2:19b–20)

That is, it seems, one no longer stands apart from that upon which one meditates, but simply gives way entirely before its luminous presence, becoming (as it were) that upon which one looks. This is perhaps a kind of farthest reach of the biblical exhortation, "Be still and know that I am God" (Ps 46:10). In this state, where holding and meditating have become a serene indrawing that gives itself over to that upon which one meditates, there is, Patanjali adds, "the shining forth of wisdom" (3.5).

This last moment in yogic practice (as meditation, though Patanjali has much to say in the rest of the third chapter on the fruits of specific focused meditations; the post-Easter topic for another year) is not necessarily a permanent state, since as with the movements of the body in yoga and the quieting of breathing, one must learn to extend this long moment, holding it in place before returning to our ordinary, more fragmentary consciousness. But luckily, one can keep practicing without any urgent deadline to meet. For the sake of yoga in Lent, it is good that Lent comes back year after year.

But to conclude on another note: *samadhi* refers not only to this yogic state of advancing meditative practice but also to the state of the yogi at "death," when the fluctuations and changes of this life give way permanently and irreversibly to full, quiet, luminous, wise attentiveness. By extension, *samadhi* refers also to the place where this yogi, who is not cremated, is buried. His or her *samadhi* is a deep state that is like sleep, like death, and yet too a final extending of the meditation.

I write these words on Holy Saturday, just a few hours before the Vigil. Jesus is still in the tomb, dead, descended, not yet risen. It would seem that for the sake of understanding, a deeper understanding, we might consider too that Jesus is asleep, in yogic *samadhi*, as he lies there in what we call the Holy Sepulchre.

Now one might immediately worry that this makes it seem that Jesus did not really die on the cross, it was all a show; we do not want to move in that direction, to be sure, even if the Eastern Churches were not afraid to speak of the Dormition of the Virgin. Perhaps we do not yet understand the real death of the person who is truly alive.

Attention to the stillness of *samadhi*, a complete giving over of the self to that which is one's object of meditation, may help us to rethink what death is for the person entirely given over to God: it is not an evil thing (even if one had suffered terribly beforehand), nor a plunge into oblivion (even if there is, as tradition puts it, a descent into hell), or an entirely passive experience, but rather, as Jesus puts it, a putting down and taking up. "For this reason the Father loves me, because I lay down my life in order to take it up again" (John 10:17).

The *samadhi* of Jesus in the tomb, awaiting the utterly simple awakening that comes next: resurrection.

The *Gita* in Lent I

February 24, 2015

Cambridge, MA. I doubt if you are holding your breath, but at the end of my last posting, on Jesus's transformative encounter with a leper in Mark 1, I mentioned that I would be blogging on the *Bhagavad Gita* during Lent. The idea came to me while reflecting on Mark 1, since the *Gita* too tells the story of a man in trouble who rises up renewed to his mission. The warrior Arjuna is led from despondency and spiritual paralysis to action, as the leper, cured, rose up and on his own started to preach boldly of what Jesus had done for him. Krishna, Arjuna's divine chariot driver, teaches Arjuna of detachment, self-knowledge, duty according to tradition, doing what is right without care for the fruits of one's actions, participation in God's selfless and detached action in the world, utter devotion to that Lord in one's actions. The words sink into Arjuna; he sees Krishna in his divine totality.

So, I will try to figure out with you how the *Gita* is relevant to Christians during Lent. If you are not familiar with the *Gita*, there are innumerable translations available; two old but reliable ones are free online: Edwin Arnold's (much appreciated by Gandhi early in his study), and that of Kashinath Trimbak Telang, in the Sacred Books of the East series. You can also find online, from Peter Brook's stage play and movie version of the *Mahabharata*, a brilliant visual summary of the *Gita*, about ten minutes long.

The easiest point of entry, perhaps, is another Gospel text, for the first Sunday of Lent this year, Mark 1:12–14. Jesus has already been baptized by John, but just then, as he seems ready to take up his mission, he is pulled away, driven into the desert by the Spirit.

> And the Spirit immediately drove him out into the wilderness. He was in the wilderness for forty days, tempted by Satan; and he was with the wild beasts; and the angels waited on him.

After some kind of spiritual contest amid nature's raw realities, he is able to take up his mission with energy and intensity:

> Now after John was arrested, Jesus came to Galilee, proclaiming the good news of God, saying, "The time is fulfilled, and the kingdom of God has come near; repent, and believe in the good news."

Jesus thus moves quickly from his private life to the Jordan, to the desert, to a very public ministry from which there is no turning back. Was he strengthened by his penances, toughened in resisting Satan—or had his moment simply come? The mystery of the desert, of course, is that somehow it was there, even more than at the baptism, that Jesus found his moment and rose up.

Transformation, mission, duty—at the start of chapter 2 of the *Gita*, Arjuna is slumped in his chariot, without a mission, refusing to act. He is overcome, we are told, by confusion about the purpose of the war about to begin—despite many, many pages of debate earlier in the epic about the ethics of war—and dismay at the prospect of killing relatives and his esteemed gurus. Commentators ancient and modern (in class, we are using Madhusudana Sarasvati [sixteenth century] and Mohandas K. Gandhi) explain that Arjuna's real problem is confusion about his own self, what it means to be a human being of a certain age and in a certain body, and why one would get up and act. This may be why Krishna starts his teaching of Arjuna, the reluctant warrior, in this way:

> You have grieved for people not to be grieved for; you speak the words of the wise; yet the learned grieve for neither those whose life's breath is gone, or not gone.

> Never indeed did I not exist, nor you, nor these rulers of humans; nor will any of us ever hereafter cease to be. (2.11–12)

Several times in the *Gita*, Krishna commands Arjuna to get up:

> Killed, you will reach heaven; having conquered, you will enjoy the earth. Therefore, Kunti's son, rise up, determined to fight. (2.37)

Therefore, rise up, gain glory; having conquered the enemy, enjoy a prosperous rule. These have already been slain by me; be simply my instrument, skilled with your left hand. (11.33)

And like the leper, like Jesus himself coming in from the desert, Arjuna does get up, returns to his duty, as the terrible war ensues. (Recall: most commentators on the *Gita* see it as a teaching so powerful and transformative that Arjuna would not return to battle.)

Why does someone get up, put aside their confusions and divided loyalties, and do her duty in detachment and love? Why do we change spiritually and then act? This transformation, this conversion of life, will be the subject of this Lenten series as we look deeper into the *Gita* and the mystery of human transformation.

The *Gita* in Lent II

February 28, 2015

Cambridge, MA. While even short passages of the *Gita* merit long reflection, it is also valuable to stay close to the rhythms of Lent and, more particularly, to the Sunday readings (Year B). How can we read the *Gita* on Sundays? Consider the second Sunday of Lent, with its two fearsome mountains: Abraham goes to the mountain with Isaac, ready to sacrifice his son at God's frightening command:

> After these things God tested Abraham. He said to him, "Abraham!" And he said, "Here I am." He said, "Take your son, your only son Isaac, whom you love, and go to the land of Moriah, and offer him there as a burnt offering on one of the mountains that I shall show you." So Abraham rose early in the morning, saddled his donkey, and took two of his young men with him, and his son Isaac; he cut the wood for the burnt offering, and set out and went to the place in the distance that God had shown him. On the third day Abraham looked up and saw the place far away. Then Abraham said to his young men, "Stay here with the donkey; the boy and I will go over there; we will worship, and then we will come back to you." Abraham took the wood of the burnt offering and laid it on his son Isaac, and he himself carried the fire and the knife. So the two of them walked on together.

(Gen 22:1–6 NRSV)

In the Gospel, Jesus goes up the mountain with Peter, James, and John and is transfigured before them:

> Six days later, Jesus took with him Peter and James and John, and led them up a high mountain apart, by themselves. And he was transfigured before them, and his clothes became dazzling white, such as no one

on earth could bleach them. And there appeared to them Elijah with Moses, who were talking with Jesus. Then Peter said to Jesus, "Rabbi, it is good for us to be here; let us make three dwellings, one for you, one for Moses, and one for Elijah." He did not know what to say, for they were terrified. Then a cloud overshadowed them, and from the cloud there came a voice, "This is my Son, the Beloved; listen to him!" Suddenly when they looked around, they saw no one with them anymore, but only Jesus.

(Mark 9:2–8 NRSV)

We are given then an ascent into a blinding darkness and an ascent into a blinding light—both ascents fall into the mystery of God, at the fragile borderline between earth and heaven, life and death, death and what we do not know, beyond death. Abraham, already shown to be a man of faith, is tested further, even to a scandalous level. The three apostles, still early in learning the ways of the Master, have no idea what is going on, either on the mountain or in coming down from it; yet they will remember this moment, a manifestation of who Jesus is, suddenly and in the midst of the "ordinary flow" of his ministry, and Jesus himself hears and sees too clearly, in that light, his own coming death. We, in Lent, are asked to be ready to at least climb these same mountains—remembering, recollecting our darkest and brightest encounters with God, and readying our souls, should we be called to such encounters once again. Yet, how can we relate to such rare and overwhelming scenes?

This is where the *Gita* comes in, to help us rethink what such scenes are telling us. Of course, there is no mountain here: Krishna's teaching takes place on what is presumably a level field, ideal for a staged battle. Yet Arjuna, the warrior who faces a spiritual crisis just as the battle is to begin is entering deeper and deeper into the mystery of his own self, the changing, unreliable, and violent world of ours, and what Krishna, whom he thought he knew, is really like. At every level, the mystery of living and dying and living across the abyss of death is impressed upon Arjuna. Twice in the *Gita*, the drama diverges from instructive words, Krishna's teaching, to existential scenes closer in feel to those of Genesis and Mark.

In chapter 1, Arjuna is horrified by where his duty might lead him, the slaughter of his teachers and kin, his triumph by way of a bloody war, or death in that same war—he faces the horror at the core of the

warrior's destiny, his duty as a warrior. Using here for copyright reasons the old Kashinath Trimbak Telang translation, free online:

> Seeing these kinsmen, O Krishna! standing (here) desirous to engage
> in battle, my limbs droop down; my mouth is quite dried up; a tremor
> comes on my body; and my hairs stand on end; the *Gandiva* (bow) slips
> from my hand; my skin burns intensely. I am unable, too, to stand up;
> my mind whirls round, as it were; O Keshava! I see adverse omens; and
> I do not perceive any good (to accrue) after killing (my) kinsmen in the
> battle. I do not wish for victory, O Krishna! nor sovereignty, nor plea-
> sures: what is sovereignty to us, O Govinda! what enjoyments, and even
> life? Even those, for whose sake we desire sovereignty, enjoyments, and
> pleasures, are standing here for battle, abandoning life and wealth-
> preceptors, fathers, sons as well as grandfathers, maternal uncles, fathers-
> in-law, grandsons, brothers-in-law, as also (other) relatives. These I do
> not wish to kill, though they kill (me), O destroyer of Madhu! even for
> the sake of sovereignty over the three worlds, how much less then for
> this earth (alone)?

(*Gita* 1.28– 35)

Everything in the *Gita* follows from his vulnerability at this opening
moment.

In chapter 11, Arjuna is shocked again, but only after asking to see
Krishna as he truly is:

> O highest lord! what you have said about yourself is so. I wish, O best of
> beings! to see your divine form. If, O lord! you think that it is possible
> for me to look upon it, then, O lord of the possessors of mystic power!
> show your inexhaustible form to me.

(*Gita* 11.3–4)

The vision begins mildly enough but soon overwhelms Arjuna, who
cannot bear to see his lord face to face. He prays:

> Seeing your mighty form, with many mouths and eyes, with many
> arms, thighs, and feet, with many stomachs, and fearful with many jaws,
> all people, and I likewise, are much alarmed, O you of mighty arms!
> Seeing you, O Vishnu! touching the skies, radiant, possessed of many
> hues, with a gaping mouth, and with large blazing eyes, I am much
> alarmed in my inmost self, and feel no courage, no tranquility. And see-
> ing your mouths terrible by the jaws, and resembling the fire of destruc-
> tion, I cannot recognise the (various) directions, I feel no comfort. Be

gracious, O lord of gods! who pervadest the universe. And all these sons of Dhritarashtra, together with all the bands of kings, and Bhishma and Drona, and this charioteer's son likewise, together with our principal warriors also, are rapidly entering your mouths, fearful and horrific by (reason of your) jaws. And some with their heads smashed are seen (to be) stuck in the spaces between the teeth. As the many rapid currents of a river's waters run towards the sea alone, so do these heroes of the human world enter your mouths blazing all round. As butterflies, with increased velocity, enter a blazing fire to their destruction, so too do these people enter your mouths with increased velocity (only) to their destruction. Swallowing all these people, you are licking them over and over again from all sides, with your blazing mouths. Your fierce splendors, O Vishnu! filling the whole universe with (their) effulgence, are heating it. Tell me who you are in this fierce form. Salutations be to thee, O chief of the gods! Be gracious. I wish to know you, the primeval, one, for I do not understand your actions.

(*Gita* 11.23–31)

Krishna responds by a still starker revelation of his divine identity, all contained within him:

I am death, the destroyer of the worlds, fully developed, and I am now active about the overthrow of the worlds. Even without you, the warriors standing in the adverse hosts, shall all cease to be. Therefore, be up, obtain glory, and vanquishing (your) foes, enjoy a prosperous kingdom. All these have been already killed by me. Be only the instrument, O Savyasacin! Drona, and Bhishma, and Jayadratha, and Karna, and likewise other valiant warriors also, whom I have killed, do you kill. Be not alarmed. Do fight. And in the battle you will conquer your foes.

(*Gita* 11.32–34)

Of course, much more needs to be said about these scenes, how life and death, killing and being killed are presented and interpreted in Genesis, in Mark, in the *Gita*. If you've never read the *Gita*, you need to read more of it than is given here! Throughout these readings ethical issues abound, and the images of God in all three readings are puzzling. We must ask: what do the rawest and most frightening experiences have to do with growing spiritually, as we are called to do in Lent?

Certainly, we learn that such growth is not necessarily tame and reassuring: the word, vision, call of God can ask of us more than we can possibly give or even comprehend: we fail, faint, collapse, seem to die in the dark and the light, that God might lead us beyond our capacities. Or at least we need to be ready to be an Abraham or a Peter—or an Arjuna.

And so there is a wilder kind of piety put before us in Genesis and Mark, the risk of a very dangerous Lent indeed. Holiness is not for the timid. If the *Gita*—chapter 11 in particular—helps us to feel anew the unsettling power of these Sunday readings, our Lent with the *Gita* will be progressing nicely.

The *Gita* in Lent III: You Are the Temple

March 8, 2015

Cambridge, MA. I have been puzzling over the Gospel for this third Sunday of Lent, the scene in John 2 where Jesus drives the merchants and money changers out of the temple:

> The Passover of the Jews was near, and Jesus went up to Jerusalem. In the temple he found people selling cattle, sheep, and doves, and the moneychangers seated at their tables. Making a whip of cords, he drove all of them out of the temple, both the sheep and the cattle. He also poured out the coins of the moneychangers and overturned their tables. He told those who were selling the doves, "Take these things out of here! Stop making my Father's house a marketplace!" His disciples remembered that it was written, "Zeal for your house will consume me" [Psalm 69].

(John 2:13–17)

The first puzzle: why this Gospel on the third Sunday of Lent (B)? This is resolved, I think, by noticing the two things John does here.

First, he takes the account from where we find it in Mark, Matthew, and Luke—just after the triumphal arrival in Jerusalem, such that in going to the temple Jesus is with authority taking possession of his Father's house—and places it near the beginning of his Gospel. Most tellingly, it now follows upon the scene in Cana where in his first sign Jesus turns water into wine so that they may enjoy the wedding feast to the full. It may seem a harsh and clumsy transition from the wedding to the cleaning out of the temple. But it is not so in

John's mind: both are scenes of transformation: water becomes wine, a good human event becomes the manifestation of divine presence. His sign is in the transformation that takes place, first in the water-made-wine, and then in the temple-made-house-of-God.

In the temple, Jesus is striving to change the material, piecemeal transactions of exchange, the buying and selling on the border between the profane and sacred precincts, into a purer, simpler realization: this is God's house.

Second, John drives this point home by the argument that ensues:

> The Jews then said to him, "What sign can you show us for doing this?" Jesus answered them, "Destroy this temple, and in three days I will raise it up." The Jews then said, "This temple has been under construction for forty-six years, and will you raise it up in three days?" But he was speaking of the temple of his body. After he was raised from the dead, his disciples remembered that he had said this; and they believed the scripture and the word that Jesus had spoken.

(John 2:18–22)

What happened, Jesus is saying, is really not even about the temple structure and its economy at all. Rather, it is about the person in whom the human and divine meet, a very different person, almost bound to clash with those who do not know themselves: "Jesus on his part would not entrust himself to them, because he knew all people and needed no one to testify about anyone; for he himself knew what was in everyone" (John 2:24–25). To purify the temple, turn religion back to the spiritual; to center it in the self, water becomes wine. This is not cost free, and so another transformation has to take place, life into death, death into life. It begins here.

It is here that the *Gita* comes in—I haven't forgotten the "*Gita* in Lent." I am thinking of this famous passage from chapter 2:

> The awakened mind subsists in focus, it is one, Arjuna. Those lacking in focus have minds branching out in many directions, endlessly. Flowery speech they speak forth, uninspired, pleased with what the Veda says,—O Arjuna—saying, "There is nothing else," pleasure their very self, intent on heaven. Speaking that way, these people are addicted to enjoyment and power and the ways to enjoyment and power. By all those many specific rites giving the fruits of action in births, their minds are held captive. They have no intelligence comprised of certitude, settled in deep unity. The Veda is caught up in the threefold way of this

life. Be free of all that, Arjuna. Entertain no polarities, be settled firmly in what is best in life, free from gaining and preserving possessions. Be yourself.

(*Gita* 2.41–45)

What is at stake here is not a total rejection of the Vedic ritual world any more than Jesus's cleansing of the temple could be considered a total rejection of the Jewish ritual tradition. Rather, the *Gita* here is concerned with the scattered, transaction-addicted mind that reduces religion to a series of activities, measured in terms of the payoff, benefits and losses, good and bad, success and failure. The way to true freedom is to step away from the endless busyness of life, including the life of religion, and catch onto one true inner focus. So a change of mind is needed, a shift in direction.

Jesus knew this and marked this ground when he took up that whip of cords, when he argued back, that the true temple was his self. In the temple that Passover day, he was turning the water of ordinary life, spread everywhere, into the special, richer wine of a spiritual life, awakened to the signs of God.

And so too ourselves: what is the one thing that matters, deep inside us, below the surface of the busy Christian's life? Finding our way there is what purifying our temple is all about.

The *Gita* in Lent IV: Waking Up, Slowly

March 17, 2015

Cambridge, MA. With the Gospel for the fourth Sunday of Lent (B), we've reached a very obvious and yet very subtle moment in Lent: everything is simple, and everything is at stake. In the select section of John 3 we heard at Mass on March 15, the evangelist gives the teaching of Jesus in a very succinct form, of which the famous 3:16 is only a small part: "For God so loved the world that he gave his only Son, so that everyone who believes in him may not perish but may have eternal life. Indeed, God did not send the Son into the world to condemn the world, but in order that the world might be saved through him" (John 3:16–17 NRSV). The news is good news: God is intent on the salvation of all. It is as simple as that.

But in the simplicity, there is a stark, take-it-or-leave-it choice:

> Those who believe in him are not condemned; but those who do not believe are condemned already, because they have not believed in the name of the only Son of God. And this is the judgment, that the light has come into the world, and people loved darkness rather than light because their deeds were evil. For all who do evil hate the light and do not come to the light, so that their deeds may not be exposed. But those who do what is true come to the light, so that it may be clearly seen that their deeds have been done in God.

Choose the light not the dark, choose the salvation God wants for us or suffer condemnation. Take your pick, and the work of Lent will be over.

But the evangelist knows that the reception of this simple good news is complicated, because we are usually not ready for anything so simple. It is here that the *Gita* can shed some light on the Gospel.

Given that the frame story for this teaching is Nicodemus's night visit to Jesus, it is impossible not to think of *Gita* 2.69, "The self-restrained man is awake, when it is night for all beings; and when all beings are awake, that is the night of the right-seeing sage." And so it is that the verse usefully points us to three kinds of respondents: the asleep, the awake, and the awakening.

Who is asleep? Here, the leaders of the people, who see but do not understand the signs of Jesus, who have no place in their system for something so startling, new, immediate. They sleep right through the great drama of the Word made flesh—or perhaps see Jesus only in their nightmares.

And who is awake? In the scene immediately following, we meet again John the Baptist, that awakened soul who seems always to have known who Jesus is. He is the one who picks Jesus out in a crowd and recognizes him, and here he appreciates both the wedding feast already begun and the cost for himself, his imminent departure from center stage: "No one can receive anything except what has been given from heaven. You yourselves are my witnesses that I said, 'I am not the Messiah, but I have been sent ahead of him.' He who has the bride is the bridegroom. The friend of the bridegroom, who stands and hears him, rejoices greatly at the bridegroom's voice. For this reason, my joy has been fulfilled. He must increase, but I must decrease." John needs no more information. He knows.

And then there is Nicodemus, the awakening person. He is the one religious leader who is hesitant but curious enough about Jesus to get up in the middle of the night and come to see him in the dark. He is baffled by Jesus's words: "Very truly, I tell you, no one can see the kingdom of God without being born from above." He responds, "How can anyone be born after having grown old? Can one enter a second time into the mother's womb and be born?" Nor does any easy transformation of Nicodemus ensue. Chapter 3 says nothing more about him. He appears for a moment in chapter 7, tentatively sticking his neck out to urge caution in judging Jesus. After that, he steps forward only at the crucifixion, daring to claim the body of Jesus precisely at the worst moment, when all seems night again, entirely lost. By chapter 19, the words given him in chapter 3 have done their work: he is awake, he has made his irrevocable choice, for life, for Jesus.

But it took him a while. It is here that another *Gita* passage comes to mind. In chapter 6, Arjuna asks Krishna whether the small efforts we make to find our way aren't often wasted, coming to nothing: "What is the end of him, O Krishna, who does not attain the consummation of his devotion, being not assiduous, and having a mind shaken off from devotion, though full of faith? Does he, fallen from both paths, go to ruin like a broken cloud?" (6.37–39; trans. Telang).

Krishna responds to Arjuna that no right effort—or lucid thought in the night—is wasted:

> O son of Pritha, neither in this world nor the next, is ruin for him; for, O dear friend, none who performs good deeds comes to an evil end. He who is fallen from devotion attains the worlds of those who perform meritorious acts, dwells there for many a year, and is afterwards born into a family of holy and illustrious men. Or he is even born into a family of talented devotees; for such a birth as that in this world is more difficult to obtain. There he comes into contact with the knowledge which belonged to him in his former body, and then again, O descendant of Kuru, he works for perfection. . . . The devotee working with great efforts, and cleared of his sins, attains perfection after many births, and then reaches the supreme goal.

(6.40–45)

Even if we cannot simply embrace the teaching of *Gita* 6 on rebirth—even when reading of being born again/from above in John 3—we can appreciate the slow but sure process to which Krishna points, the seeds planted, change from old and fixed ways gradually taking place over what can seem to be a very long time.

Some don't get the point at all, some already see, and some, perhaps most of us, need a little more time. In other words, the *Gita* is reminding us that there is a point to hearing this Gospel in the middle of Lent. The word is sure and the choice is clear, but the rest of Lent is the time for it to sink in, for us to fully wake up.

The *Gita* in Lent V: Learning to Do Nothing

March 22, 2015

Cambridge, MA. In my seminar this week we are reading chapter 3 (yes, third chapter, and the semester is at least half over!) on detached action, action as a sacrifice and service for the sake of the world, and hardest of all, action as what happens by way of nature and time and providence, our selves not really the doers of "our" actions.

> The person who is attached to his self only, who is contented in his self, and is pleased with his self, has nothing to do. He has no interest at all in what is done, and none whatever in what is not done, in this world; nor is any interest of his dependent on any being.
>
> (*Gita* 3.17–18; trans. Telang, slightly adapted)

But this utter detachment—when the bond between self and action is severed—does not lead to inertia or flight from the world. Rather, it is a path of serene action for the sake of the world and leading directly to God:

> Therefore always perform action, which must be performed, without attachment. For the person who performs action without attachment attains the Supreme.
>
> (*Gita* 3.19)

Later in the chapter, Krishna says,

> Dedicating all actions to me with a mind knowing the relation of the supreme and individual self, engage in battle without desire, without (any sense of) "mine," and without any mental upset. Those who always

act on this opinion of mine, full of faith, and without carping, are released from all actions.

(*Gita* 3.30–31)

Such people, on whom the world depends if it is to run smoothly at all, are at rest, actionless, even in the busiest of moments. They are busy all the time, but always at rest: "The self-restrained person is awake, when it is night for all beings; and when all beings are awake, that is the night of the right-seeing sage" (*Gita* 2.69).

Perhaps oddly, I am reminded here of Jesus's utter detachment as he faces the growing conflict around his mission and yet with both equanimity and power contemplates laying down his life and picking it up again. Once again, it is in the Gospel according to John that we see the greatest resonance to this dimension of the *Gita*, since John's Jesus is ever serene, no matter what happens. In chapter 10, after conjuring the image of the good shepherd, Jesus says this:

For this reason the Father loves me, because I lay down my life in order to take it up again. No one takes it from me, but I lay it down of my own accord. I have power to lay it down, and I have power to take it up again. I have received this command from my Father.

(John 10:17–18)

Or in chapter 5:

I do nothing on my own. As I hear, I judge; and my judgment is just, because I seek to do not my own will but the will of him who sent me.

(John 5:30)

The work of Jesus happens; it is in accord with the will of God. Naturally and rightly, today we value the struggle of Jesus, his human fears and desires, how terrible a moment his passion and death must have been for him. But there is a power to this alternative insight, which John insists on putting before us: Jesus takes up his life, he lays it down. God's great plan is unfolding, and by his simple and clear attentiveness to the present moment, Jesus sees where everything is heading. There are no surprises, and even in his Passion—in his passion—Jesus stands detached, allowing his Father's plan to unfold. The end is clear in the beginning; all this will happen while I, Jesus, observe it happen.

We cannot simply make this happen for us. Both the *Gita* and John make clear that this is no light venture. The *Gita* warns against giving the wrong impression to people who *need* to keep busy:

> A wise person should not shake the convictions of the ignorant who are attached to action, but acting with devotion (himself) should make them apply themselves to all action.

(*Gita* 3.26)

Let us try, then, as we look all the more closely at Jesus in these last weeks of Lent, to be as quiet as he is. The greatest and tumultuous things in our lives can be, if we understand this, as simple as the rising and setting of the sun; we just need to be there, we don't have to do anything.

Or so it should seem, once in a while in Lent.

The *Gita* in Lent VI: The Worst in Us, in Holy Week

March 31, 2015

Cambridge, MA. As a comparative theologian, I can affirm that Holy Week is incomparable. The last days of Jesus, his last supper, and his passion and death can be revered as without any exact parallel in other religious traditions.

So it may seem that here finally we will need to leave behind the *Bhagavad Gita*, which we have visited over and again during Lent. But this is not the case, for even if the scene that Christians contemplate this week is beyond compare, we ourselves still struggle to make sense of what we see; and to see and make sense, we must know who we are, seeing ourselves with a detached gaze. Jesus is, in a certain sense, incomparable; we are not. And so even this week the *Gita* still instructs us.

How? I will return to the issue several times in the days to come, but let's begin with the famous analysis, in *Gita* 3, of the downfall people suffer due to desire, a craving in the wrong direction for the wrong things that, when frustrated, flames up in anger and violence. Near the end of chapter 3, Arjuna asks Krishna,

> But by whom is a person impelled, even though unwilling, and, as it were, constrained by force, to commit sin?

(3.36; trans. Telang, adapted)

Krishna in turn traces the downward spiral, stating the root cause of our troubles is desire, "it is anger, born from the quality of passion; it

is very ravenous, very sinful. Know that this is your foe in this world"
(3.37).

Desire, it seems—as the first chapters of the *Gita* keep telling us—is
a craving that diverts our attention from the simpler, interior goods
that satisfy us spiritually. As a supplementary reading in the critical
edition of the epic adds, "This is the subtle supreme foe of embodied
beings caught in their senses. It persists, seated in what seems to
be a web of pleasure, deluding (everyone), Arjuna. Made of desire,
anger, this foe is terrible" (trans. Feuerstein [Shambala, 2011], slightly
adapted).

Desire shrouds us and blinds us so that we cannot see our way, nor
even see who we are ourselves:

As fire is enveloped by smoke, a mirror by dust, the fetus by the womb,
so is this enveloped by desire.

(3.38)

Krishna therefore appeals to Arjuna:

Arjuna, first restrain your senses, then cast off this sinful thing which
destroys knowledge and experience. It has been said, "Great are the
senses, greater than the senses is the mind, greater than the mind is the
understanding. What is greater than the understanding is this (foe)."

(3.41–42)

Strong, sharp action has to be taken, not striking out at others but
cutting through the enemy within:

Knowing this which is higher than the understanding, and restraining
yourself by yourself, Arjuna, destroy this unmanageable foe in the shape
of desire.

(3.43)

Why is desire anger? It seems that when we cannot get what we
want, desire turns into anger; when we *do* get what we want and see
how foolish we were, desire turns into anger.

Krishna is offering a strong and simple analysis (so simple, of
course, as to require further analysis in light of many other *Gita* passages) of what drives us off course into a downward spiral.

In turn, the *Gita* then offers a way—just one way, but a real way—to read the passion narratives, to discern what's wrong with the leaders, the soldiers, the rulers, the apostles, and the crowds, that they so suddenly and completely forget who Jesus is, so that all they want is his death. His goodness and truth expose and shame their desire; shamed, thwarted, their desire flares up in anger, erupting in ugly violence. The exultation and triumph of Palm Sunday are suddenly forgotten, and so too what it means to be God's people awaiting God's joyful arrival. They can no longer see who he is or who they themselves truly are. So they kill the one who showed them their better selves.

As I said at the start, the passion and death of Christ are incomparable events, at the heart of Christian faith. But I suggest that the *Gita*'s wise words—on our loss of self-knowledge, our stubborn lurching in the wrong direction, our anger—can shed light on how it was, and is, that people *just like us* can do terrible things, such as killing Christ.

The *Gita* in Lent VII: The Many Meanings of Sacrifice

April 2, 2015

Cambridge, MA. In the past weeks of Lent, I have used passages from the *Bhagavad Gita* to gloss, illumine, shadow, and enhance texts and themes familiar from the Lenten season. Underlying it all, however, is really an invitation to read the *Bhagavad Gita* during Lent: find a recent translation, read it, and hear it in the background as you travel the Lenten season.

I am just back from church on Holy Thursday and want to post a second to last entry (saving the last for Easter), to lead us into Good Friday. It is late, and for this occasion I will simply invite you to read the ancient Christian hymn the "*Crux Fidelis*" (related to the "*Pange Lingua*") by Venantius Fortunatus (sixth century), a meditation on the sacrificial death of Christ often used during the Veneration of the Cross on Good Friday, with a passage from the fourth chapter of the *Gita* (in the R. C. Zaehner translation), where sacrifice is understood in different ways by different people. To save words (and time) tonight, I simply interweave the texts here and invite you to read and study them, back and forth.

And here are the texts, interspersed for your meditation, the *Gita* verses indented. As you start, remember, then for a moment forget, everything you know about sacrifice and Good Friday:

> Sing, my tongue, in exultation of our banner and device! Make a solemn proclamation of a triumph and its price: how the Savior of creation Conquered by his sacrifice! (Roman Missal translation)

> The offering is Brahman, Brahman the sacrificial ghee offered by
> Brahman in Brahman's fire: who sinks himself in this sacrificial act
> which is Brahman, to Brahman must he thereby go. (24)

For, when Adam first offended, eating that forbidden fruit, not all hopes
of glory ended with the serpent at the root: broken nature would be
mended by a second tree and shoot.

> Some adepts offer sacrifice to the gods as their sole object; in the
> lire of Brahman others offer sacrifice as sacrifice which has merit in
> itself. (25)

Thus the tempter was outwitted by a wisdom deeper still: remedy and
ailment fitted, means to cure and means to kill; that the world might be
acquitted, Christ would do his Father's will.

> Yet others offer the senses—hearing and the rest—in the fires of
> self-restraint; others the senses' proper objects—sounds and the
> like—in the fires of the senses. (26)

So the Father, out of pity for our self-inflicted doom, sent him from
the heavenly city when the holy time had come: He, the Son and the
Almighty, took our flesh in Mary's womb.

> Others offer up all works of sense and works of vital breath in the
> fire of the spiritual exercise of self-control kindled by wisdom. (27)

Hear a tiny baby crying, founder of the seas and strands; see his virgin
Mother tying cloth around his feet and hands; find him in a manger
lying tightly wrapped in swaddling-bands!

> Some offer up their wealth, some their hard penances, some spiri-
> tual exercise, and some again make study and knowledge their sac-
> rifice—religious men whose vows arc strict. (28)

So he came, the long-expected, not in glory, not to reign; only born to
be rejected, choosing hunger, toil and pain, till the scaffold was erected
and the Paschal Lamb was slain.

> Some offer the in-breath in the out-breath, likewise: the outbreath
> in the in-breath, checking the flow of both, on breath control
> intent. (29)

No disgrace was too abhorrent: nailed and mocked and parched he died;
blood and water, double warrant, issue from his wounded side, washing
in a mighty torrent earth and stars and ocean tide.

Others restrict their food and offer up breaths in breaths. All these know the sacrifice, and by sacrifice their defilements are made away. (30)

Lofty timber, smooth your roughness, flex your boughs for blossoming; let your fibers lose their toughness, gently let your tendrils cling; lay aside your native gruffness, clasp the body of your King!

Eating of the leavings of the sacrifice, the food of immortality, they come to primeval Brahman. This world is not for him who performs no sacrifice—much less the other world. (31)

Noblest tree of all created, richly jeweled and embossed: post by Lamb's blood consecrated; spar that saves the tempest-tossed; scaffold-beam which, elevated, carries what the world has cost!

So, many and various are the sacrifices spread out athwart the mouth of Brahman. They spring from work, all of them; be sure of this; for once you know this, you will win release. (32)

Wisdom, power, and adoration to the blessed Trinity for redemption and salvation through the Paschal Mystery, now, in every generation, and for all eternity. Amen.

Better than the sacrifice of wealth is the sacrifice of wisdom. All works without exception in wisdom find their consummation. (33)

You can also find these texts online and listen to them one after the other.

Stopping on Holy Thursday: How a Hindu Sacred Text Helps

March 24, 2016

Cambridge, MA. It is Holy Thursday, and even today I have experienced the phenomenon—which I am sure many of you also suffer—of being too busy to really get into the flow of this holiest time of the church's year. The entirety of Lent is a long preparation for participation in these holy days—think of the readings on Sundays: the desert, the utter darkness shrouding Abram, the transfiguration, the burning bush, the prodigal son, the woman caught hold of by the religious leaders. One can meditate through Lent just by taking the readings to heart.

We are prepared by Lent to divest ourselves of ordinary life and enter into those last days with Jesus, his facing up to his destiny without turning away from it. To walk resolutely with Jesus to his/our fate would be hard, of course, in any case, but the busy schedule of Harvard does not make even contemplating the idea any easier. Yet, how can the flow of ordinary life show itself to be conducive to the spiritual values central to our lives? One can't easily do one's daily work and also be with Christ in Jerusalem! Or so it may seem.

Oddly, my quandary in Holy Week is intensified and illumined in the challenge I have had of making space in my daily routine for the seminar I am teaching on the Brihadaranyaka Upanishad. This sacred Hindu scripture from about the eighth century BCE is one of the greatest of ancient India's philosophical and mystical texts. It is a difficult text, surely, but also a wonderful mix of reflections on ritual and the deeper meaning of ritual and on death and creation. It is a record of a dozen dialogues on the self, some friendly, some fiercer intellectual contests. It contains teachings on the experiences of deep sleep, on death and world renunciation, and throughout it all, on the self that pervades all that is but that also seems invisible, inaccessible, within ordinary realities.

As read by the great Hindu commentator Shankara, the Brihadaranyaka Upanishad is understood to offer a concerted teaching on the overarching importance of realizing the self, and in a way that is transformative of one's life as a whole.

According to this understanding of the Upanishad, we ordinarily live a distorted and unreal life, with a distorted worldview that accommodates a distorted sense of self. We think ourselves small and finite, between birth and death, and in need of all kinds of things in order to survive in the short run and flourish in the long run. We think of ourselves as in need of material increments; we fear losses and so plan, strategize quantitatively, our journey through each day and our whole lives.

Shankara thinks that the Upanishad—and he glosses "upa-ni-sad" to indicate a shattering of ignorance and false ego—shows that we are not what we think ourselves to be, but much more. Once we realize our true self—which for Shankara is radically simple and pure, one for all—we can no longer live an ordinary life of planning, ambitioning, needing, fearing, desiring, growing and declining, and so on. As if waking from a dream, the drama of small self-existence falls away, and we stop. For Yajnavalkya, the great sage in the Upanishad, what follows next is clear: you leave your home, go forth, probably to the forest—an other, natural, simple, detached space—and live an entirely different kind of life. Easily said, hard to do.

The very idea is intrusive, sudden, powerful, and dramatic. It is very hard to run through the ordinary work of a busy day and at the same time prepare class, or actually sit down with students for two and half hours to read and discuss a section of the Upanishad. Speaking, evoking the true self, pondering death and birth, questioning how far your five senses will take you in understanding what reality really is, sorting out the states of consciousness that make up waking consciousness, dreaming, and deep sleep—all this is quite out of tune with the rhythms of the ordinary day or any ordinary schedule, wherein we move from one task to another all day (and night) long. So, aside from the busy and hectic nature of daily life, to read such a text, and read it with students, is against the flow of ordinary existence and not really supportive of all that busyness.

Similarly, going up to Jerusalem with Jesus is quite out of keeping with our ordinary rhythms of life, even at a university. To hear the passion narrative on Palm Sunday—and to be aware that the week to follow marks the final days of Jesus in Jerusalem, leading up to his death and burial—is an appeal to come to a halt, change course, take the less traveled path. And all this on a calendar where stopping is hardly possible. Even today, Holy Thursday, my Center for the Study of World Religions is hosting three events (though I am skipping all three, but not my office hours and some Sanskrit tutorials).

In a strange way, reading the Upanishad, and the hard practice in the past weeks of abrupt shifts in levels of concerns, has been a preparation for trying to be attentive in Holy Week. If you can stop and think and read in a meditative way, you can stop and contemplate in a thoughtful way. Ordinary ways of thinking and feeling are shaken up by Shankara's reading of the Upanishad's meditations on false and real consciousness, distracted and focused attention, all for the sake of acquiring the bold freedom to let go of everything we previously thought was important, for the sake of the self beyond our ordinary selves. In this Upanishadic light, attending suddenly to Christ in Jerusalem—when the world seems not to remember—can be seen to be a shift in consciousness that is always abrupt but for which we have to prepare ourselves little by little, day by day, if we dare.

A Hindu View of Holy Thursday:
Yogananda I

April 7, 2009

Cambridge, MA. In this Holy Week, we are of course invited to quiet ourselves down, pull back a bit, and reflect on the meaning of our lives in light of the death and resurrection of Jesus. We are fortunate to have an abundance of aids in this reflection, ranging from the Bible and the liturgies of the *Triduum* to myriad homilies, spiritual writings, works of music, and art. What we are not used to doing is listening to how people of other faith traditions think about the death and resurrection of Jesus. Hindus and Buddhists, Jews and Muslims have been listening for centuries to what we Christians think of them and their faiths; rarely do we take time in a week like this to listen to their insights. Even if they see things differently than we do and perhaps misunderstand parts of what we believe—as we have always tended, even with best intentions, to misunderstand the traditions of others—learning is still possible.

I would like to take a step in this direction with a small series of reflections for Holy Thursday, Good Friday, and Easter, based on the reflections on the Gospels by Paramahamsa Yogananda (1893–1952). Founder of the Self-Realization Fellowship and author of the famous *Autobiography of a Yogi*, Yogananda lived a good part of his life in the West. During these years, he studied the Gospels and wrote *The Second Coming of Christ: The Resurrection of the Christ within You* (Los Angeles: Self-Realization Fellowship, 2004), a nearly 1,600-page reflection on selected Gospel passages, published posthumously. For the three days, I will simply offer a summation of a few of his insights into the relevant texts.

Holy Thursday: In commenting on chapter 22 of the Gospel according to Luke in his sixty-ninth discourse, Yogananda reports on the Lukan basic account, making, as always, a number of small points along the way. For instance, he draws parallels with sacred meals hosted by Indian spiritual figures, and he also shows great discomfort with the idea that Jesus and his disciples drank wine, since this could diminish spiritual awareness. But two points stand out as I read the text.

First, when Jesus says that his blood is to be shed "for many for the remission of sins," Yogananda argues that this cannot mean that Jesus died for future sins, even thousands of years later. While he admits that Jesus could indeed absorb his disciples' bad karma, he thinks an overly literal expectation that Jesus takes away sins encourages laziness and irresponsibility on the part of people who would do better to grow in their divine awareness. Rather, Jesus was putting forward "the extraordinary example of his sacrifice on the cross, through which he attained complete liberation in Cosmic Consciousness—freedom from the willingly accepted bonds of his mortal incarnation" as an example for his followers too to forsake any attachments that would slow their path to God-consciousness.

Second, Yogananda is also uncomfortable with the idea that based on the Last Supper meal, Christians come to think of themselves of eating the body of Christ. He insists that even with Jesus, the body should not be allowed to block the Spirit within. The flesh of Jesus is his consciousness; his blood is his spiritual Cosmic Energy. To share this meal, then, is to learn to see Jesus "in his formless infinitude as one with the all-pervading Christ Consciousness and universal light of the Holy Ghost Cosmic Energy." To make sense of this claim—perhaps realizing that this is not the way Christians see Jesus at the Last Supper—he points to the teaching of Thomas Aquinas on the "formless Christ" (a footnote alludes to Aquinas's teaching on the infusion of God's essence into our minds at the Beatific Vision) and Teresa of Avila on her vision of the formless Christ.

Finally, in his seventieth discourse, commenting on John 13, Yogananda stresses the spirit of service as physical and spiritual and adds that what Jesus does reminds us of what the Father too had done: "Even the Heavenly Father serves impartially in silent humbleness: he has created the water in the well, and as the indwelling Spirit in the water and in every person, it is He who washes the feet of His children—even the egotistical and materialistic persons who never honor Him."

These brief comments just touch the surface of Yogananda's lengthy reflections, and I encourage readers to take a look for themselves. But what to make of all this? As I admitted above, Yogananda does not read the Last Supper accounts as most Christians do; he looks for other values, and some of his conclusions are quite apart from the traditional teachings on the meaning of Holy Thursday. We might tend to think of his reading as gnostic or alien to the integral spirituality of the Bible. But we need not judge Yogananda as if he were simply a reincarnation of some ancient heretic, nor need we worry about refuting his readings—which were, I think, meant as a gift to the Christian community, not as a threat. We do well, instead, to read him (and a host of others who have commented on Jesus from outside our tradition) and see if his insights into "his" Jesus as radiant of divine consciousness can illumine our own ways of seeing Jesus—and one another—in this Holy Week. Can we actually glimpse this Divine Consciousness at play in the Holy Thursday liturgy?

acceptance
not judgement

A Hindu View of Good Friday: Yogananda II

April 9, 2009

Cambridge, MA. I am offering three entries this Holy Week, in meditation on the mysteries of the Last Supper, the death of Jesus, and the resurrection. But not my own thoughts; rather, recognizing that we have so many resources within the Christian tradition for this meditation, I thought it wise to stop for a moment to hear how someone who is not a Christian understands these mysteries, and so I have turned to the great commentary on the Gospels by Paramahamsa Yogananda, whom I introduced in that first blog.

In discourse 74, Yogananda comments in some detail on the accounts of Jesus's passion and death, and it is impossible even to summarize his extensive reflections here. Small insights stand out along the way, such as the lovely meditation (borrowed by the editors from *Autobiography of a Yogi*) on what the silence of Jesus before Pilate meant. In essence, Jesus did not need to utter any words, since he expressed the truth fully, simply in his total conformity to reality: "Jesus, by every act and word of his life, proved that he knew the truth of his being—his source in God. Wholly identified with the omnipresent Christ Consciousness, he could say with simple finality: 'Everyone that is of the truth heareth my voice.'" So nothing needed to be said. Yogananda additionally points to the silence of the Buddha, and also cites Psalm 46:10, "Be still, and know that I am God." He explains Jesus's compassion toward the daughters of Jerusalem who had tried to comfort him: in saying "Weep for yourselves," he is urging them to change their lives while there is time. In another brief insight, Yogananda explains why the crucified Jesus calls his mother,

Mary, "woman": Jesus knew all the more clearly then that "God alone is Father, Mother, Beloved. Thus Jesus called his mother 'woman'—a God-created woman."

He likewise comments in lovely detail on Jesus's exchange with the good thief, to whom he promises paradise that very day. Paradise is the abode of bliss, which is real and which Jesus offers to whoever will be crucified with him. Even on the cross, he could summon "the astral body of the thief into the blissful presence, the realized perception, of the Father." Yogananda advises everyone who is "crucified by evil tendencies and miseries" to "pray to their Christ Consciousness within" for "the redemption of the soul from the physical world and its limitations into the greater freedom of consciousness of astral existence, and the eternal paradise of complete liberation in Spirit."

And as for Jesus's actual death on the cross, even he could feel forsaken for a moment, since by "satanic temptation" he found "God slipping from his consciousness; in exceedingly great sorrow, he cried out his experience of forsakenness." Yet even in this moment, he still addresses God as "my Father," as if he were torn between his personal knowledge of God and his sense that God was slipping away from him. It was only thereafter, when he again lifted his consciousness into Christ Consciousness and Cosmic Consciousness, that "his suffering on the cross dissolved in the bliss of Spirit," as he saw that his suffering would "awaken other souls in Spirit."

And then, when Jesus said, "It is finished," he was declaring that his work was complete, that he was ready again to "withdraw his soul from the body and plunge it in Spirit." By death, Jesus was withdrawing "not only his bodily consciousness and life force, but also his acquired Christ Consciousness, his omnipresence in creation, to merge in the Father's Cosmic Consciousness beyond."

Echoing an invitation extended by Krishna in the *Bhagavad Gita* 7.14 that all should approach him for refuge, Jesus died surrendering his spirit into the hands of God, into the "vibrationless transcendent realm where the Creator Himself abides." Concluding this section on the death of Jesus with some more complex reflection on the Cosmic Consciousness (the Father), the Christ Consciousness (Jesus), and the Cosmic Vibration (the Spirit), Yogananda suggests that by his ascent on the cross, Jesus was finding his way through all three stages of divine energy. His time in the tomb after death was simply a time of "ecstatic purification" that removed all remaining karma, so that Jesus would be able, at the resurrection, "to merge his Christ Consciousness with the Cosmic Consciousness, or God the Father, the Absolute beyond all delusory relativities of vibratory manifestation."

We are, indeed, in a realm somewhat removed from what we are likely to read or hear in church on Good Friday. Even if we become more familiar with Yogananda's exegetical vocabulary (explained over 1,500 pages, after all), it may well be that we will still not recognize or welcome all that he says about Jesus's passion and death. But the unfamiliarity and strangeness of his teaching are, I think, virtues: we can reflect on his words, bring them with us to Calvary, and then see Jesus again as we wish, but without the delusion that only we Christians have meditated on or found meaning in the crucified Jesus.

A Hindu View of Easter:
Yogananda III

April 11, 2009

Cambridge, MA. Here is the third installment in my *Triduum* exercise in listening to Paramahamsa Yogananda, whose reflections on the Gospel accounts of the Last Supper and crucifixion I sampled for you in the preceding days. Like many a preacher, I find Easter a rather daunting feast on which to preach: the resurrection is, in a way, the fulfillment of all our hopes in the face of death and yet too something strange and new, much harder to relate to and speak of than a birth, a last meal, or a death. Yet, it should by now be no surprise that Yogananda engages directly and forcefully in reflection on the resurrection of Jesus.

As we have seen, consciousness—God, world, Christ, Spirit—is a key theme for Yogananda in discourse 75 of *The Second Coming of Christ*. In the resurrection, Christ's Consciousness is perfectly manifest for those whose eyes have been opened. On Easter, Jesus's soul rose into "oneness with Spirit—the soul's ascension from delusory confinement of body consciousness into its native immortality and everlasting freedom." At his death, Jesus entered a highest unitive state (*mahasamadhi*), "a God-realized soul's conscious ascension from the physical body at the time of death," merging his consciousness "in the blissful presence of the Cosmic Consciousness of God the Father." As he rose from the dead, Jesus "began to unloose, with the supreme-soul science of liberation, the knots of life and consciousness that both enabled and resulted from his earthly incarnation." This is why, Yogananda says, Jesus instructed Mary at the tomb not to touch him: the disentanglement of the restrictions of his pre-resurrection body were not yet complete. Later, he could eat with his disciples, he could invite Thomas to touch him, because by then the process had come to fruition.

Yogananda devotes much of discourse 75 to describing the ascent of Jesus through the several astral realms, his liberation through and from the "physical, astral, and idea bodies." The details are arcane and beyond the reach of this blog, but the point seems clear: in his resurrection, Jesus encompassed and liberated all the realms of material and spiritual existence, and thus gained perfect freedom to ascend and descend into earthly bodies as needed.

Yogananda knew the stories of masters who were said to have gone into deep concentration, seeming even for a long period of time to be dead. It is interesting then that he takes the realm of the physical very seriously. He insists that Jesus did really die, since no one who was crucified as he was would be simply in meditation. Death and resurrection can be charted in, as well as beyond, the body. The resurrection itself was a regaining of the material realm, even after leaving it behind: "That Jesus was able to rebuild his body at will after death had claimed it was possible only when his soul was liberated from the three bodies. Having attained complete ascension in Spirit, he had the creative power of Spirit to bring specialized life back into his deceased body to regenerate its cells and resurrect that form to live and breathe again." He rose by drawing into oneness the "Cosmic Vibration of Holy Ghost" and the "Christ Consciousness Intelligence of God" and expressing this oneness "in every atom and creative principle of cosmic manifestation." As a result, his return to his physical body at the resurrection was its transformation by a kind of divine light; while God is always present in every cell of every body, it was at the resurrection that this light became concretely, vividly manifest.

It is clear that Yogananda has the highest respect for Jesus and what happened in his death and resurrection. Yet he makes clear near the end of discourse 75 that he does not think the resurrection is an entirely unique event. He mentions several masters from the Indian context: Kabir, the medieval poet-saint whose body was transformed at death, thus eluding both Hindus and Muslims who wanted it only for themselves; Yogavatar Lahiri Mahasaya, who, at death, was manifest in a number of North Indian cities; and, appealing to what he has seen with his own eyes, Yogananda mentions his guru Sri Yukteswarji, who "appeared to me in flesh and blood more than three months after his death in 1936." Indeed, Yogananda seems to agree that what happens in the resurrection is a promise for what will happen to all: "the resurrected Jesus . . . manifested his Jesus form not apart from Spirit but as the Infinite who has become Jesus, all individualized souls, and all manifestation." Rising, Jesus could "change the dream of his crucified body into a remodeled resurrected dream form in God's cosmic dream."

Even as I finish this third reflection, the teacher in me whispers that all of this may be too much for a simple blog for *America*. Even the most stalwart readers may agree! It should be no surprise; 1,500 pages of Yogananda's reflection on the Gospels, climaxing in the passages I have recounted, may not be easily digested in so brief a space, without footnotes, review, and rereading. But I hope the point is clear: if we are called to dialogue, it will be fruitless if we hear only what we already know; if we can actually learn, it will be pointless to restrict learning to things easy to understand; if we are open, it will be unwise to limit our learning to our reflections on their religions, as if we cannot learn anew of the mysteries of our own faith by listening to wise teachers like Yogananda. If all of this is hard, that is simply a fact of life—but even so, perhaps I have stretched a blog about as far as it can go.

More immediately, I am faced with the prospect of preaching twice tomorrow, on Easter morning. I am at this point planning to speak of the Colossians 3 text that occurs as our second reading:

So if you have been raised with Christ, seek the things that are above, where Christ is, seated at the right hand of God. Set your minds on things that are above, not on things that are on earth, for you have died, and your life is hidden with Christ in God. When Christ who is your life is revealed, then you also will be revealed with him in glory.

I doubt very much if I will mention Yogananda's teaching during my homily, but I will have his insights in the back of my mind. As far as I know, he did not comment on Colossians, but this passage seems ideally suited to his insights: with Christ we are raised, transformed, revealed in glory—so let us set our minds on "the things that are above." Yogananda helps us to understand what the uplifting of our minds in Christ can really mean.

From Darkness to Light: A Hindu Mantra during the Easter Vigil

March 26, 2016

Cambridge, MA. At the Vigil tonight in my neighborhood church (I go to my regular parish in the morning), I enjoyed as always the first hour in particular, the actual vigil: the lighting of the new fire, the lighting of the candle, the Exultet chant, and the meditative hearing of several of our great founding stories in Genesis and Exodus, Isaiah and Ezekiel. It is indeed a holy night, when Christ passed over, taking us with him from darkness unto light and death to immortality.

It is not surprising then—for me at least—that I would think of the Brihadaranyaka Upanishad, which I am teaching this semester and on which I posted a reflection just two days ago. How could I not think in particular of the famous mantra chant that occurs near its beginning:

asato ma sad gamaya tamaso ma jyotir gamaya mrtyor ma amrtam gamaya

From what is not, lead me to what is; from darkness, lead me to light; from death, lead me to what is undying.

(Brihadaranyaka Upanishad 1.3.28)

In the Upanishad, this is a mantra that the patron of the sacrifice—the lay person who causes it to be performed by his benefaction—is to chant softly to himself while the priests are singing aloud a set of seven purification chants. You can listen to the mantra in many places online.

The context is rather complex, but in brief: this chant comes at the end of the chapter (1.3) that is a meditation on life, the life's breath, and the transformative power of sacred utterance as an expression of the deep life force within us. The chant is termed an "ascent" (*abhyaroha*) that leads the person chanting from this world—what is not, what is dark, what is mortal—to the divine world—what is, what is light, what is immortal. Shankara, the great commentator, explains at some length the process of assimilation to the gods that occurs here, as the person chanting comes, for a moment at least, to share their higher way of being. It is a prayer for passing over to a new way of life.

So, I ended up repeating to myself the Sanskrit words (in this case, quite clear and easy) during the Exultet and during the readings in the still darkened church, as we all held our small candles in the dark.

Surely not what the Upanishadic authors could possibly have imagined, and yet something of a similar counterpoint, a soft inner chant by an individual amid the singing by the soloist and then the choir. (Everyone heard the choir; no one heard me.) And, of course, the prayer appears all the more appropriate if we think of what this holiest of nights is all about: in creation, what is not comes to be; from the darkness of sin, we enter the light of God's love; and as Christ is raised from the dead, we too pass over, Passover, from death to what is undying. Or, as the Exultet puts it,

> This is the night, when once you led our forebears, Israel's children, from slavery in Egypt and made them pass dry-shod through the Red Sea. This is the night that with a pillar of fire banished the darkness of sin. This is the night that even now throughout the world, sets Christian believers apart from worldly vices and from the gloom of sin, leading them to grace and joining them to his holy ones. This is the night when Christ broke the prison-bars of death and rose victorious from the underworld.

You can hear the Exultet too in many versions on the web.

Okay, you may say, one could imagine softly repeating the ancient mantra during the Vigil, during the Exultet. But don't many questions and objections arise? To whom is one addressing this chant for passage from what is not to what is, from darkness to light, from death to immortality? The Brihadaranyaka does not say. But if the mantra is respected as part of its own ancient religious culture, is it not at least a bit disrespectful to bring it to church? I suppose it could be disrespectful—but need not be; it is good and not an evil that we hear, learn from, and draw into our own prayer what we learn from another tradition. The mantra itself seems to have been placed in the Brihadaranyaka Upanishad, drawn from a still older source. To be religious is to borrow, with humility and gratitude.

Nor am I the first Catholic to take up this mantra. Most famously, Paul VI prayed with this mantra over fifty years ago, at a public gathering in India. On December 3, 1964, addressing an interfaith gathering, he said:

> This visit to India is the fulfillment of a long-cherished desire. Yours is a land of ancient culture, the cradle of great religions, the home of a nation that has sought God with a relentless desire, in deep meditation and silence, and in hymns of fervent prayer. Rarely has this longing for God been expressed with words so full of the spirit of Advent as in the words written in your sacred books many centuries before Christ: "From the unreal lead me to the real; from darkness lead me to light; from death lead me to immortality."

Pope Paul went on to make clear that he knew what he was doing. He says that in a time of historic change, both globally and in India, this is a prayer "which belongs also to our time." It is a prayer that "should rise from every human heart." Given the crises facing all human beings, "we must come closer together, not only through the modern means of communication, through press and radio, through steamships and jet planes—we must come together with our hearts, in mutual understanding, esteem and love. We must meet not merely as tourists, but as pilgrims who set out to find God—not in buildings of stone but in human hearts." This was surely a case when a pope is leading the way, even before "*Nostra Aetate*" was written. Pope Paul would be happy, I think, to see his words echoing down through the decades, even until tonight. Surprised, but also happy.

But what would happen if a Hindu softly sang the Exultet in a Hindu temple, let us say, on the holy night of Lord Shiva? Personally, I would think this a great step forward, a gift generously given and received across religious borders. We need borders, but borders that are open, not barred with high walls of hostility. In Advent of 2015, I encouraged my readers to study the Qur'an; I am delighted when I hear of Muslims who study the New Testament with care. In the past, I urged readers to learn from the practice of yoga in Lent; I would be happy to hear of Hindus adapting the *Spiritual Exercises* to their own spiritual needs. And so on.

I admit that theological questions remain about the finality of such prayers, or how there can be space at the Easter Vigil, on this most holy night, for a priest in the pews recollecting the words of a Hindu mantra. Most parishes do not anticipate this. But it is not a bad thing to leave aside the harder questions when in church. Pray, act, then later on inquire theologically. If the prayer takes place, and if there is some benefit to it—and I found it right and holy tonight—then, later on, we can find ways to face up to the difficult theological questions.

Moreover, it is terribly urgent in today's world that we take steps to bring our traditions together in deeper, more intimate, personal ways. Too many of our politicians, would-be political leaders, are rushing to ape Donald Trump and Ted Cruz in their calculated ignorance, fearmongering, and wall building and the militarization of our culture; and too many Americans—who should know better even in times of real economic hardship and amid fears of terrorism—are voting for Trump and Cruz. We must move in the other direction, crossing religious borders as witnesses to openness and peace, building sisterhood and brotherhood such as will be the real antidote to violence, fear, and ignorance. In a world of denial, the lie, and what is not, we must move toward what is and what is true; from our individual and cultural darknesses, we must move into a light that can only be shared; and from the shadow of death, we must move into a light that is no one's private possession.

At least try listening to the mantras alongside the Exultet. It really will not hurt to try this for a time: Christ our Light is risen; from what is not, lead me to what is; from darkness, lead me to light; from death, lead me to what is undying.

The *Gita* at Easter: Our Rising Up

April 5, 2015

Cambridge, MA. As you know by now, the *Bhagavad Gita* is a complex, multilevel text that explores the nature of self, the world, action, and God, and proposes as its ideal—or one of its ideals—detached action, playing one's role in the world, without care for personal benefit or fear of personal loss. For many, this works at the level of a robust, active devotion: do all for God, for Krishna, and all will work out. Thus, in the frame story of the *Gita*, the warrior Arjuna has been suddenly overwhelmed by the prospect of the civil war that looms—he is poised in the middle of the battlefield, in conversation with Krishna, his charioteer—and refuses to fight. The *Gita* is the teaching that helps him to find himself, to do his duty without hesitation or doubt. Krishna's teaching is punctuated with appeals to Arjuna to rise up:

Don't be a coward, Arjuna—this is not suitable for you! Get rid of this wretched weakness of heart and rise up! (2.3)

If you are killed, you will go to heaven; if you win, you will enjoy the earth. Therefore rise up, Arjuna, firmly committed to this battle. (2.37)

Therefore, with the sword of knowledge cut through this doubt arising in ignorance and standing in your heart. Become focused, and rise up, Arjuna! (4.42)

Therefore, rise up, choose glory, defeat your enemies, enjoy a prosperous kingdom. They have all already been slain by me, you are simply the instrument of my will. (11.33)

But the teaching can be just words on the page. The *Gita* has its real point less in what Krishna says than in how Arjuna finds himself again and rises up to return to life's battles, to do his duty in accord with the word spoken to him. At last, after the final and summary teaching of the eighteenth chapter, Arjuna replies:

> My confusion is banished, my wits restored, by your grace, unfailing lord. I am steady now, my doubts gone. I will act according to your word. (18.73)

Nice, but what, you may be asking, has this to do with Easter? The resurrection—like the crucifixion—is unique, not simply a perennial wisdom told in every tradition. But as I have pointed out before, even if the event is unique, we are not. We are lost, we struggle to find our way and overcome our doubts; we live in fear and either despair (and hide in our rooms, like the apostles) or want (like the women) to return to where we once had certainty, rather than facing what lies before us.

While the lovely stories of the resurrection appearances of Jesus rightly occupy much of our attention, it is perfectly appropriate that this year's Gospel for Easter is the very end of Mark, unadorned by all the additions accruing to it in the early church:

> When the Sabbath was over, Mary Magdalene, and Mary the mother of James, and Salome bought spices, so that they might go and anoint him. And very early on the first day of the week, when the sun had risen, they went to the tomb. They had been saying to one another, "Who will roll away the stone for us from the entrance to the tomb?" When they looked up, they saw that the stone, which was very large, had already been rolled back. As they entered the tomb, they saw a young man, dressed in a white robe, sitting on the right side; and they were alarmed. But he said to them, "Do not be alarmed; you are looking for Jesus of Nazareth, who was crucified. He has been raised; he is not here. Look, there is the place they laid him. But go, tell his disciples and Peter that he is going ahead of you to Galilee; there you will see him, just as he told you."

> (Mark 16:1–7)

Had it ended this way, it would be only a bit odd for Easter—no sudden appearance, no encounter on the road. But the final, omitted last verse of the Gospel makes things all the more peculiar:

So they went out and fled from the tomb, for terror and amazement had seized them; and they said nothing to anyone, for they were afraid.

(Mark 16:8)

Mark seems to have left it there. The question hangs in the air: what will these women do? They have not found Jesus where they expected to find him. The heavenly messenger did not console them but confused and terrified them. Overawed and in terror, they flee—and worst of all, they are silent and say nothing. Mission abandoned, just as it starts. Nothing more is said in the Gospel according to Mark.

These women are, in other words, much like Arjuna, sunken in doubt and confusion, unable to act. As in the *Gita*, the solution is not simply the Lord's words, the good news—they have all the words and wisdom they need—but how these women receive it, hear it, understand it, let it sink in, choosing or not to let it change them and send them, no longer afraid, on mission.

The *Gita* ends with Arjuna saying that he will return to the work given him. Mark seems to be saying, Well, what happened to these women? As if to add: You know what happened—you are in the very church, after all, that preserved this Gospel. If you want to know what happened next, he is suggesting, look to your community, look into yourself and figure out how the confused, fearful, and depressed rise up to speak the word given to them. It is here, not in the book but in life, that the story concludes.

At Easter 2015, we too are being challenged to rise up: to believe, even if we've seen nothing, had no apparitions, and perhaps find ourselves less certain than we were at Lent's beginning. By taking the word to heart, we can come out the other side of our fears and doubts, depression and despair, and do what we are called to do. Or not.

The *Gita* helps us to realize the remarkable event of resurrection: the miracle, today, is our own rising up.

Prana, Yoga, Spirit, Pentecost

May 15, 2016

Cambridge, MA. (This reflection was written on Pentecost Sunday, after Mass and after pondering the sunlit trees shaking their bright leaves in the morning breeze.)

If, on this feast of Pentecost, we delve into the technical language of Trinitarian theology—Trinitarian processions, Filioque, and the rest—we may find the terminology of the Trinity and, all the more, of the Holy Spirit somewhat intimidating, perhaps very dry indeed. But because it is Pentecost, a day of inspiration and imagination, we do well first to remind ourselves how simple and vivid is the basic symbolism of the Spirit. Whenever the wind blows, though we cannot see it, we feel it and see the trees moving in the wind; when we open a window after the long winter, we feel the fresh air flow into the room; when we quiet down and pay attention to how we are, we notice the in-breathing and out-breathing that keep us alive. Breath, wind, spirit, and Spirit are everywhere. Thus we begin to appreciate Pentecost by recognizing the freedom and "everywhere" motion of the Spirit—or just by paying attention, on a spring morning like today.

Much of reality reminds us of the Spirit, unseen, everywhere. We confirm this instinct when we look at the rich set of readings available for Pentecost and its vigil (which suggests no fewer than four opening readings), we can see at work the play of images of God's spirit: in Ezekiel 37, the spirit comes upon the dry bones and brings back to life that which was dead; in Joel 2, the spirit descends upon the people: "Thus says the Lord: I will pour out my spirit upon all flesh. Your sons and daughters shall prophesy, your old men shall dream dreams, your young men shall see visions; even upon the servants and the handmaids, in those days, I will pour out my spirit"—and of course these are the words Peter quotes in Acts 2 to describe the descent of the Spirit. In 1 Corinthians 12, it is the Spirit that brings the community together as a living organism: "As a body is one though it has many parts, and all the parts of the body, though many, are one body, so also Christ. For in one Spirit we were all baptized into one body, whether Jews or Greeks, slaves or free persons, and we were all given to drink of one Spirit." Just as a living body is whole and one but disintegrates into pieces when the breath leaves it, so too the church: without the Spirit, it is merely the sum of members competing and distrusting one another. When, in John 20, Jesus breathes on his disciples in the upper room, they are given the power to bind and to loose, but also, more simply, to be at peace—as if to say: calm down, take a deep breath, be at peace.

And, of course, the theme of prophecy and speaking aloud in the name of Jesus—the famous Pentecost scene itself—is at its most basic level also grounded in breath, for it is breath marvelously finding its way to articulation in our mouths—throat, tongue, teeth—that yields the marvel of speaking. No speech without breath, neither ordinary everyday words or the most exalted words of testimony. No breath, no fire.

The very idea of spirit, Spirit, invites meditation further afield. I cannot help but think here of the *prana*—breath or vital force—so often spoken of in ancient India, in the Upanishads and then too in the texts of yoga. This *prana* is the life force, breath itself, but also more broadly, inner vitality. The ancient Brihadaranyaka Upanishad, for instance, speaks of the *prana* well over one hundred times. Near its beginning, in 1.3, a competition of the senses leads to the obvious conclusion that while sight or hearing, though invaluable, are not essential to life, without the *prana*, life ends quickly; because revelation existed in a recited form, *prana* was basic, too, to the very life of that revelation as heard in this world. In provocative though not quite Trinitarian language, the Upanishad goes on to meditate on *prana* as a cosmic and divine and human power:

> [In the beginning], three he designed for himself: the mind, the organ of speech and the *prana*; these he designed for himself. These are the three worlds. The organ of speech is this world, the mind is the sky, and the *prana* is that world. . . . These are the father, mother and child. The mind is the father, the organ of speech the mother, and the *prana* the child.

. . . Whatever is unknown is a form of the *prana*, for the *prana* is what is unknown. The *prana* protects him (who knows this) by becoming that (which is unknown). . . . Heaven is the body of this mind, and that sun is its luminous organ. And as far as the mind extends, so far extends heaven, and so far does that sun. The two were united, and from that the *prana* emanated. It is the Supreme Lord. It is without a rival. A second being is indeed a rival. He who knows it as such has no rival.

(1.5.3–12; trans. Swami Madhavananda, adapted)

This is no place for an exposition of the large topic of the role of *prana* in yoga, but we can recall *pranayama*—breath control, the focusing of the breath—and there are many sites online that explain *pranayama* in yoga. For instance, look at the resources at a site such as Yoga Basics or at the Christians Practicing Yoga site. See also my post during Lent in 2013. For the feel of its teaching, here are the low-key, instructive sutras of Patanjali on the topic of the *prana* (breath, in- and out-breath):

After a steady position is established, then comes control of breath, interrupting the motion of in-breath and out-breath. Breath control's motion can be external, internal, and stopped, and these are closely observed according to time, place, and number. Such breaths are long or subtle. A fourth state of breath control puts aside both external and internal breath movements. After this, the obscuration of light is destroyed, and there is fitness of mind for acts of focusing.

(*Yoga Sutras* 2, 49–53)

Once we are paying attention, practicing, learning, we can then again look for parallels closer to home in the Ignatian *Exercises*. For example, Patanjali's instructions on breathing may well enhance the third method of prayer recommended by Ignatius in the *Exercises*:

The Third Method of Prayer is that with each breath in or out, one has to pray mentally, saying one word of the Our Father, or of another prayer which is being recited: so that only one word be said between one breath and another, and while the time from one breath to another lasts, let attention be given chiefly to the meaning of such word, or to the person to whom he recites it, or to his own baseness, or to the difference from such great height to his own so great lowness.

Patanjali might find the words and the pairing of breaths and thoughts unnecessary—just breathe, that is God's spirit—but for those of us who are Christian, it is worthwhile too to give voice to the presence of this spirit as we know it, the Spirit sighing with us, leading us in the Son to the Father.

Practice is key, but theology is important too, and at this point one could go deeper, looking into how various theologies of the Holy Spirit do (or do not) open paths of interreligious learning and exchange. This is because the Spirit—always the Spirit of Christ—is at work everywhere in the world, certainly beyond the bounds of explicit Christianity. I recommend here looking into the writings of Jacques Dupuis, SJ, who wrote eloquently and daringly on the importance of the Spirit to the Christian understanding of other religions. But for now it will suffice to quote Jesus in John 3: "The wind blows where it chooses, and you hear the sound of it, but you do not know where it comes from or where it goes. So it is with everyone who is born of the Spirit."

At Pentecost, let us keep looking within us and around us and in the most vital possibilities of church and world to celebrate God's Spirit.

At Pentecost the Spirit Blows, Interreligiously

May 22, 2010

Cambridge, MA. As you know from many "fusion" blogs, I do not neatly separate out my weekend ministry as a priest and my work as a Catholic theologian who tries to learn deeply from Hinduism. Another crossover moment is our current feast, Pentecost. As we hear in the first reading, the Spirit comes as wind, and then as tongues of fire—and then the men and women gathered in the upper room begin to speak aloud, recounting the great deeds of God. Not only is their Spirited speech not mysterious or unintelligible, but it is stressed that each listener hears the message in their own language. Clear understanding is a fruit of this Holy Spirit.

As a scholar of Hinduism, I cannot help but think of all kinds of parallels in the Hindu tradition, and here I will mention just two. First, perhaps tapping also into a natural insight into how speech works, ancient Hindu texts emphasize a deep connection between breath—life's breath (*prana*)—and sacred speech. No breath, no spirit, no speech—breath, spirit, is for the sake of speech. This is clear in the oldest Upanishads, such as the (rather difficult) section 1.3 of the Brihadaranyaka Upanishad, where everything that we do and see and say begins in that sacred breath. Later Upanishadic texts shift the emphasis from breath to the inner self (the *atman*, what we might call soul), but even that *atman* too is a breath of life. This seems an insight quite friendly to what we celebrate on Pentecost: breath is for speech; when we are alive, we speak, and the world of sacred practice lies in the fruitfulness of breath, speech. Just as wind and fire are hard to pin down as "my wind" or "your fire," it is probably helpful for us, as a starting point, to avoid worrying too much about who owns the Holy Spirit, which "blows where it will."

Second, Abhirami Bhattar, the eighteenth-century devotee of the Goddess Abhirami (The Beautiful), was pushed by the local king to prove that his faith was real and that he was not insane. When he was about to fall into a fire and perish, his Goddess appeared to him, and he too burst into song, singing the one hundred verses of his *Abhirami Antati*, that begins this way:

> Rising, bright, radiant,
> auspicious mark on high,
> jewel prized by the discerning,
> pomegranate bud,
> splendid vine praised by the woman on the lotus,
> pool of fragrant kumkum paste—thus is Your form described, Abhirami,
> ever my best help. (1)
> My help,
> the divinity I worship,
> my own mother,
> the sacred word's branch, shoot, spreading root,
> in Your hands, a fresh-flower club, cane bow, tender net, goad:
> O beautiful lady of the three cities,
> You're all I know. (2)

What is of interest to me is that these Hindu saints found themselves surprised by God, infused with divine presence, and thereafter sung beautiful verses with great eloquence—just as the disciples in the upper room, on fire with the Spirit, spoke with far greater power and eloquence than they knew they had.

We could, of course, start thinking of Biblical examples: Miriam, sister of Aaron, who sings praises of God when Israel has been delivered from Pharaoh (Exodus 15); Deborah, who sings a song of triumph after Israel is delivered from Canaanite enemies (Judges 5); Hannah, who praises God when her son Samuel is born (1 Samuel 2); Mary, who bursts into the Magnificat when greeted by Elizabeth (Luke 1). To experience God's power firsthand is to find a voice by which to sing a new song, as did the Tamil saints.

None of the above is expressed with theological precision; we would have to sort out more deeply how the Spirit, which we believe to be the Spirit of Jesus, is the Spirit alive in these Hindu saints too—as the Spirit of God, not in a merely second-class way. Lots of conundrums to ponder. Rather, what I have written here is simply what occurs to this priest who is a Catholic theologian who studies Hinduism. But the main points for all of us now, this Pentecost, are two: First, we must reflect deeply on what we are asking for in praying for the Spirit. That Spirit can be many things for us, of course, but in keeping with the outpouring of Spirit and speech in Acts 2 and in these examples from Hinduism, we should at least expect that when we are touched by the Spirit, we will receive the gift to speak boldly of God's great deeds. Second, this seems not to be a narrow Spirit, as if only we can be touched by it: songs that come from within are a gift, and at Pentecost it would seem stingy to imagine that only we receive the Spirit and sing by its fire. So we need to pray, speak, and even listen for a Spirit that blows where it will.

In Ordinary Time: The Sermon on the Mount, a Hindu Reading I

January 29, 2011

Cambridge, MA. It is the start of the new semester at Harvard, and these weeks are more than ordinarily busy—even as the relative quiet of the weeks between semesters and our sixty-plus inches of snow make hibernation seem a better idea than robust activity. Classes have begun, and I am team-teaching a challenging course, Theories and Methods in the Study of Religion as Relevant to Students in Preparation for Ministry; we are reading admissions files for the graduate programs; the Center for the Study of World Religions is beginning its full program of events for the semester; the lectures I need to prepare and things I need to write form a mass that never really diminishes. It is all too much, but luckily I enjoy almost all of it.

But what I want to write about beginning today is the Sermon on the Mount in the Gospel according to Matthew, which we begin hearing at Mass on January 30, the fourth Sunday of the year, and will continue hearing through the first Sunday in March, just before Lent begins. The Sermon is, of course, a prime teaching worthy of our meditation at the start of our (ever new) encounter with Christ, as Matthew intended. It is also a Gospel text that has gained great favor among Hindu readers. Mahatma Gandhi said of it, "Christ's Sermon on the Mount fills me with bliss even today. Its sweet verses have even today the power to quench my agony of soul." He also believed that Indians could delve very deeply into its meaning: "The Sermon on the Mount left a deep impression on my mind when I read it. I do believe with you that the real meaning of the teachings of Jesus will be delivered from India." As you know, I agree, to the extent that we can always learn our own faith more deeply by learning what people of other faiths have to say about our texts and traditions.

Although Gandhi never wrote a commentary on the Sermon, one Hindu Swami did—Swami Prabhavananda (1893–1976), longtime head of the Ramakrishna Vedanta Society of Southern California, published in 1964 a small book entitled *The Sermon on the Mount according to Vedanta*, the fruits of his actual preaching on the Sermon.

Prabhavananda prefaces his teaching with two interesting insights. First, he indicates that like other great teachers, Jesus offered a more demanding and esoteric teaching to his serious disciples, and a more common, simpler teaching to the crowds. Surprisingly, he counts the Sermon as the advanced teaching of the inner way for disciples and those who are ready to advance spiritually; it is too hard for many people. Second, in keeping with Hindu instincts about the spiritual path, he seems to be reading the Beatitudes as a kind of spiritual ladder, so that one needs to advance upward through all eight beatitudes. This is rather different from the view that each beatitude is for a different kind of persons, or all of them, in whatever order, for all of us all at once. Let us follow his teaching (as I read it).

Thus, being (1) "poor in spirit" is the necessary starting point, since unless we are humble, we cannot learn, and nothing else can follow. Similarly, being (2) one of those who mourn indicates a necessary detachment from this world, a deep sense of lack that can only be filled with God.

(3) Meekness, by Prabhavananda's reading, is an abandonment of ego: "It is to live in self-surrender to God, free from the sense of 'me' and 'mine.'" We are God's servants, entirely dependent—yet once we thus renounce ego and possessions, "we find that in the truest sense everything belongs to us after all." So too, (4) "hunger and thirst for righteousness" must be understood in its Biblical context, as a hunger and thirst for absolute righteousness—for God alone. He refers to a familiar story, wherein the teacher shows the disciple in a simple way what it means really to desire God: when they are wading in a lake, the teacher suddenly holds the disciple's head under water until he is gasping for air; letting go, he explains: "When you feel that intensely for God, you won't have to wait long for his vision."

In turn, (5) mercy is the fruit of this desire for and attachment to God, a kind of yogic radiance of inner calm, by which one is now able to feel and share the joys and sorrows of those around us, as ours too. Prabhavananda develops (6) "purity of heart" at greater length, for he sees this as the ongoing process of purification that enables us to receive God's revelation to us. He notices that it is very hard to think of God, since we instinctively think of everything but God.

The purification then is a matter of calming the mind and simplifying it, that it may attend to God alone.

Being (7) a peacemaker is another fruit of increasing union with God. Admitting that he himself had always gained peace simply by the presence of a holy teacher, Prabhavananda quotes a classic scripture, the *Bhagavata Purana*: "He in whose heart God has become manifest brings peace, and cheer, and delight wherever he goes." Perhaps Prabhavananda is a little puzzled as to why last of all we have the blessing on those who are (8) persecuted and reviled, but for him this too is a test of and fruit of turning ever more intensely to God. People to whom God is not central cannot understand the person focused on God—and therefore lash out at her. Prabhavananda insists though that here too a kind of peacemaking is at stake: this advanced soul does not respond angrily to those who persecute and revile but only responds with mercy and compassion.

Should you hear the Beatitudes in church this Sunday, think of Prabhavananda's approach and hear the text holistically, as one message charting a single path: all eight beatitudes apply to all of us. Underlying his reading, of course, is a universalist view: this teaching, at the heart of Christianity, is for everyone, a gift leading all on the path to God. The Sermon is not a text by which God speaks only to Christians. See what you think; it depends on how you read all of Matthew. Don't depend on my summation, of course, which is brief and quickly done. You can purchase the Swami's book rather easily or find it in a library; much of it at least is available on Google Books.

Salt and Light: Swami on the Sermon II

February 3, 2011

Cambridge, MA. As the churches continue to read the Sermon on the Mount at Sunday Eucharist until the beginning of Lent, I continue my series on Swami Prabhavananda's reading of the Sermon in *The Sermon on the Mount according to Vedanta*. This Sunday's portion is brief enough to quote:

> You are the salt of the earth; but if salt has lost its taste, how can its saltiness be restored? It is no longer good for anything, but is thrown out and trampled under foot. You are the light of the world. A city built on a hill cannot be hidden. No one after lighting a lamp puts it under the bushel basket, but on the lampstand, and it gives light to all in the house. In the same way, let your light shine before others, so that they may see your good works and give glory to your Father in heaven.

(Matt 5:13–16 NRSV)

Prabhavananda sees Jesus's first words, regarding the salt, as reminders to his listeners as to their identity: "In India, when a disciple comes to a teacher, the teacher tries first of all to give him a firm faith in himself, and a feeling that weakness and cowardice and failure have no part in his true nature." This is how Krishna began his teaching in the *Bhagavad Gita* and how Jesus awakens his disciples here. Lack of confidence must be overcome if we are to grow spiritually. So Jesus's insistence, "you are the salt of the earth," is meant to awaken a sense of our power "to unfold the divinity latent within us." This is a matter not, Prabhavananda insists, of personal ego but of discovering God within: "A person who has surrendered everything to God has no ego in the ordinary sense. He cannot be vain or proud. He has strong faith in the true Self within him, which is one with God."

Turning to "the light of the world," Prabhavananda shifts emphasis, wishing now to speak about how teachers teach their students. It is "by actual transmission of spirituality" that the good teacher "actually illumines the hearts of his disciples and makes them the light of the world." We become light by contact with the Light dwelling in every heart. (Swami might have quoted Psalm 36:9 here: "For with You is the fountain of life; in Your light we see light.") Only people who are thus illumined, who have seen God (as Ramakrishna put it), can teach the word of God.

To explain this point, Prabhavananda distinguished, in accord with traditional Vedanta theology, between the lower and higher knowledge. The lower knowledge is *what* we know, including science, philosophy, and even the content of Scripture—even the content of the Sermon, perhaps. But the higher knowledge "is the immediate perception of God. A man who is enlightened by this higher knowledge does not need encyclopedic information in order to expound the scriptures; he teaches from inner experience," from the light shining forth.

Consequently, the enlightened teacher effortlessly attracts disciples who are seeking instinctively for the light; his presence "naturally" turns their thoughts to God, even if the teacher is talking about something else. This is the sequence intended, Prabhavananda says, in this Gospel's closing words: "In the same way, let your light shine before others, so that they may see your good works and give glory to your Father in heaven."

Once again, my goal in introducing you to Swami Prabhavananda's teaching is not that we need agree entirely with the Swami, nor decide whether his interpretation mirrors Matthew's intent. Of course there are innumerable ways of reading this Gospel passage in the Christian tradition, and we need not turn to a Swami to find what we might find in any biblical commentary. Rather, what Prabhavananda adds, with his Indian and Hindu sensitivity, is a focus on the dynamics of teaching: Jesus as teacher, enabling his listeners to hear, learn, and become teachers. On the surface, it makes little sense merely to tell us that we are the salt of the earth and light of the world; even good theology, reminding us of our identity as God's children, does not make this salt and light potent realities. We can read the Sermon over and over and not change much at all.

Prabhavananda's contribution here is therefore that he expands our attention from what Jesus says to the fact that he is the one saying these words. In order to hear, the people have come and sat in his presence; even as he speaks, they taste the salt, they radiate the light. How good it would be for this to happen to us in church this Sunday!

Jesus the Avatar: Swami on the Sermon III

February 12, 2011

Cambridge, MA. For any preacher, this Sunday's portion of the Sermon on the Mount poses great challenges. It is quite long, a full twenty verses (Matt 5:17–37). It is also full of difficult ideas: Jesus is the one who comes to fulfill, accomplish, the Law in its every detail. If the Pharisees are thought of as overly concerned about obeying the Law, then, Jesus says, outdo them in righteousness, neither breaking the Law nor encouraging others to do so. Not a Jesus most of us like to think about. And then there are the four examples that Jesus gives, each worthy of at least one Sunday homily: not only do not kill, but do not get angry; not only do not commit adultery, but do not lust in your heart; not only expel your wife from your house *only* in accord with legal restrictions, but do not do that at all; not only be honest in swearing oaths, but do not swear at all, simply tell the truth. Each of these gets complicated when we ponder its meaning for the church and society today. Either it is obscure or, on the contrary, so simple as to make us uncomfortable. Key is to not treat any of the four instances as entirely different (as if to say: the Sermon means that divorce is always wrong, but killing and getting angry, etc., can be okay.)

So it is no surprise that Swami Prabhavananda takes a full twelve pages in his *Sermon on the Mount according to Vedanta* to comment on this section. It may be surprising that more than half his comment is on the opening section,

Do not think that I have come to abolish the law or the prophets; I have come not to abolish but to fulfill. For truly I tell you, until heaven and earth pass away, not one letter, not one stroke of a letter, will pass from the law until all is accomplished. Therefore, whoever breaks one of the least of these commandments, and teaches others to do the same, will be called least in the kingdom of heaven; but whoever does them and teaches them will be called great in the kingdom of heaven. For I tell you, unless your righteousness exceeds that of the scribes and Pharisees, you will never enter the kingdom of heaven.

(Matt 5:17–20)

But his interest in this portion makes sense when we realize that this text reminds Swami of the words of Krishna in the *Bhagavad Gita*, and so he fixes on them, in turn giving an unexpected teaching on the meaning of the incarnation.

For it is here that Jesus explains *why* he came, the purpose of his particular *avatara* (descent into the world). Recall that for the Swami (and for most Hindus) there is no problem at all in recognizing that Jesus is God come into the world. The problem, as he explains here at length, has to do with uniqueness: "Christians believe in a unique historical event, that God was made flesh once and for all time in Jesus of Nazareth. Hindus, on the other hand, believe that God descends as man many times, in different ages and forms." Even declarations of uniqueness simply remind Prabhavananda of other such declarations; Krishna says in the *Bhagavad Gita*, "I am the goal of the wise man, and I am the way. I am the end of the path, the witness, the Lord, the sustainer. I am the place of abode, the beginning, the friend and the refuge." So too, Swami adds, the Buddha can be accepted as an *avatara*.

Why so many *avataras?* The world has its ups and downs, righteousness is often forgotten, neglected, and so God comes again to restore order in every particular case. In fact, Jesus's words remind Prabhavananda of the famous words of Krishna in the *Bhagavad Gita*: "Whenever goodness grows weak, When evil increases, I make myself a body. In every age I come back, To deliver the holy, To destroy the sin of the sinner, To establish righteousness." Yet, Prabhavananda adds, it is always the "same supreme Spirit" manifest in the *avatara*. He knows that Christians will resist this idea of recurrent descents of God into the world, but he suggests that we need not be afraid. As in this Sermon passage, Jesus came to teach the truth, but "if, in the history of the world, Jesus had been the sole originator of the truth of God, it would be no truth; for truth cannot be originated," that is, begin to be true at some particular time. Interestingly, Swami supports his view by quoting Saint Augustine: "That which is called the Christian religion existed among the ancients, and never did not exist from the beginning of the human race until Christ came in the flesh, at which time the true religion, which already existed, began to be called Christianity" (from his *Retractions*).

Prabhavananda then goes on, much more briefly, to comment on new, interiorized values—be one who is not angry, or lustful, or hard-hearted and legalistic toward one's wife, or truthful only in accord with external words and oaths. We cannot go into detail—read it for yourself—but can only notice the main point. Righteousness is about "entering the kingdom of Heaven," it is a pathway to God. As we unite ourselves with God, who is beyond all "relative good and evil," we too "transcend relative righteousness." But the path is long, and we must first learn to "abstain from harming others, from falsehood, theft, incontinence, and greed; we must observe mental and physical purity, contentment, self-control, and recollectedness of God." This is what Jesus is teaching by his call for righteousness greater than external observances. He is, in essence, arguing that Christian holiness begins in the same basics—external and internal discipline (*yama, niyama*)—that yoga teaches: the ending of anger; the embrace of chastity as a positive virtue and not simply self-denial; a simple truth telling that needs no oaths because it is simply conformity to God: "'Not I, not I, but thou, O Lord!' The more we become established in this idea, the more we renounce the thought of self, the greater will be our attainment of peace." (Swami seems to say nothing about Jesus's command "not to put away one's wife." Not sure why!)

So there is much here to consider, about who Jesus is, as teacher and giver of a new interior righteousness. A key question for us will be whether we can learn by agreeing in part with Prabhavananda, in part disagreeing. If we want to insist that Jesus is not an *avatara* like Krishna or the Buddha, will we still be able to learn from the remainder of this Hindu teaching on the righteousness taught in this Sunday's Gospel? Distinguishing the teacher and message is never easy. Which is more important? I would say the teacher in this case, but perhaps Swami's view is not entirely foreign to what Matthew intends.

Nonviolence for Some: Swami on the Sermon IV

February 18, 2011

Cambridge, MA. The Gospel for Sunday, February 20, includes two famous and challenging teachings of Jesus: The first is "You have heard that it was said, 'An eye for an eye and a tooth for a tooth.' But I say to you, Do not resist an evildoer. But if anyone strikes you on the right cheek, turn the other also; and if anyone wants to sue you and take your coat, give your cloak as well; and if anyone forces you to go one mile, go also the second mile" (Matt 5:38–41). The second is "Be perfect, therefore, as your heavenly Father is perfect" (Matt 5:48). In this fourth in my series on Swami Prabhavananda's *The Sermon on the Mount according to Vedanta* geared to our Sunday Gospels until Lent, I consider his view of radical nonviolence, and in a fifth (soon to follow), his view of Jesus's call to perfection.

I mentioned at the start of this series that, contrary to how we often think about the universality of Jesus's message, Prabhavananda thinks the Sermon is for advanced disciples, not for a crowd hearing Jesus for the first time. This is why Jesus can put this "highest truth" of nonresistance (or nonviolence) before his listeners, even if it is "nearly impossible to understand and follow." While we can see instances of great saints who live out such nonresistance, "few people struggle to achieve the lofty spiritual state which would enable them to practise this non-resistance." Moreover, Prabhavananda adds (quoting Paul Elmer More) that the world would come apart if we applied "the laws of the spirit to the activities of this earth." We must admit that beings are at various grades of spiritual advancement, most not ready for the nonviolence Jesus teaches: "Non-resistance is therefore recognized by

Vedanta as the highest virtue, but all people under all circumstances are not expected to live up to it in its highest form." Some are violent, or cowardly, or lazy—and must deal with these defects before they imagine living out the nonviolence Jesus teaches.

Prabhavananda illustrates this by telling the story of two disciples of his own guru, Ramakrishna. A disciple overhears people speaking ill of Ramakrishna and reacts heatedly, threatening to upset the ferry on which they ride; Ramakrishna scolds him for his anger and his lack of detachment. A second disciple, hearing similar gossip, does nothing—and Ramakrishna scolds him for his lack of loyalty to his teacher. The point, says Prabhavananda, is that Ramakrishna was teaching each differently, in accord with where he was on his spiritual ascent. This is why, he adds, Jesus can teach nonviolence to his advanced disciples, while Krishna in the *Bhagavad Gita* counsels detached action, duty, and even warfare when speaking to the warrior Arjuna, who has not yet renounced the world.

There is no value, Prabhavananda says, in allowing people to push us around or harm our families. Resistance, free of hatred, is necessary for most of us, much of the time. But "the devotee of God who perseveres in his spiritual practices eventually reaches a state in which non-violence in thought, word, and deed is natural to him. Then, with mind absorbed in God and heart purified by devotion, he does spontaneously what Christ asks of him—he loves his enemies, blesses those that curse him, does good to those that hate him, and prays for those who persecute him."

I know that some readers will resist the idea that Jesus taught different listeners differently, depending on their capacity. We tend to be democratic, believing Jesus had one message for all. But perhaps here at least the Swami is right. If we act as if radical nonviolence really is mandated for everyone, then when that does not happen, we are watering it down to a kind of soft inner disposition (just as we don't seriously expect everyone to give all their possessions to the poor).

But if we take Jesus's command literally, we may judge nearly the entirety of our society as drastically disordered—not just in the violence of warfare or the militarized state or the abomination of proliferating handguns, but also in the failure of individuals to turn the other cheek in all situations of violence small and large. A Gospel for all, all the time, could be rather ineffective: if not too soft, then too hard.

While reserving the command to radical nonviolence to a small group of advanced souls sounds terribly elitist and may seem to let the rest of us off the hook, Prabhavananda is suggesting that this is nonetheless the deep, concrete realism that undergirds Jesus's most demanding teaching. It is a spiritual advance in itself to admit when you cannot, in fact, live up to the teachings of Jesus.

On Being Perfect: Swami on the Sermon V

February 18, 2011

Cambridge, MA. This Sunday's Gospel prompts two considerable reflections by Swami Prabhavananda, the first regarding nonviolence (which I treated in my last post) and the second regarding the command, "Be perfect, therefore, as your heavenly Father is perfect" (Matt 5:48). As for this second text, if you have been following this series, you will not be surprised that here too the Swami finds a deep philosophical and spiritual insight. He takes it to be "the central theme of the Sermon on the Mount" and indeed the theme that is "at the heart of every religion: Seek perfection! Realize God!" Divine perfection—being like God to the limit—has no real parallel in this world, impermanent and unsatisfactory as it is. It is easier, he says, to say what God and God's perfection are not than what they are.

In his Vedanta tradition, this perfection is expressed in the language of perfect nondualism: the Self (*atman*) and Ultimate Reality (*Brahman*) are entirely one. "To discover this true being, or divinity, which lies hidden within oneself, is to become perfect." But Christ too is pointing to the divinity within us, as in John, "I in them and you in me, that they may become completely one" (John 17:23a), or in Paul, "Do you not know that you are God's temple and that God's Spirit dwells in you?" (1 Cor 3:16), or in the mystic Angelus Silesius, "Christ may be born a thousand times in Bethlehem, but if he be not born anew within your own heart, you remain eternally forlorn."

The task of the spiritual life, then, is to realize this truth, make it real in one's own life. There is something to be done. Hence Jesus's command, "Be perfect as your heavenly Father is perfect." The

Swami then offers a fairly standard modern Hindu understanding of how one becomes perfect: by the paths of service or knowledge or devotion. He suggests, too, that these ways of perfection are present in the teachings of Jesus, who poses to us the example of service, an awareness of the frailty and limits of his world, and the necessary transition from praying to the Father to realizing "I and the Father are one."

Or, still more practically, Prabhavananda concludes, the path of perfection has three steps: First, "wherever the unruly senses and mind wander, we must try to see the Lord." Second, "we are to practice the ethical virtues taught in the scriptures—virtues such as compassion, non-violence, and chastity." Third, "we must set aside regular hours for the exclusive practice of prayer and worship," as Saint Paul says, "praying without ceasing." Such practices awaken and deepen love of God and allow "the thought of the beloved Lord to be continually in one's consciousness," until "the love, lover, and beloved become one." The end point is the fulfillment of Jesus's command in this Gospel passage: "The man who experiences this unitary consciousness enters into the kingdom of heaven and becomes perfect even as the Father in heaven is perfect."

One could write a book or more deciphering Prabhavananda's Vedantic understanding of the relationship of Jesus and the Father, and of Christians with Christ, and then distinguishing this understanding from other (less nondualistic) Hindu understandings of the goal of existence. It may also occur to many a reader that Jesus could not possibly have meant all this in commanding that his disciples be perfect as God is perfect.

But even so, we are left with the question, What did Jesus mean in challenging us to be perfect as God is perfect? Prabhavananda's reading at least has the merit of taking up the challenge with the utter seriousness such a command deserves: the only real human perfection is to enter into the perfection of God—be perfect. Think about it when you hear the Gospel in church.

Do Not Be Anxious: Swami on the Sermon VI

February 23, 2011

Cambridge, MA. Readers will not be surprised to learn that Swami Prabhavananda, in *The Sermon on the Mount according to Vedanta*, has a straightforward reading of the first part of the Gospel for Sunday, February 27: "No one can serve two masters; for a slave will either hate the one and love the other, or be devoted to the one and despise the other. You cannot serve God and wealth" (Matt 6:24). For the Swami, it is obvious that a choice has to be made, since "we cannot become absorbed in God as long as we are slaves to cravings such as lust and greed. . . . If you really want God, you must give up mammon [wealth]." The real renunciation is interior, since the things we possess are less of a problem than the instinct to possess and accumulate; in traditional Hindu ascetical terms, you must let go of "I" and "mine."

Consequently, given this starting point and the Swami's sense of a small audience that is ready for this teaching, the major part of this Gospel passage follows smoothly: "Therefore I tell you, do not be anxious about your life, what you will eat or what you will drink, or about your body, what you will wear. . . . If God so clothes the grass of the field, which is alive today and tomorrow is thrown into the oven, will he not much more clothe you—you of little faith?" (Matt 6:25–30). These words are practical—for the few. He even suggests that it is the wandering renunciants of Hindu tradition, having no possessions at all, who "prove that Christ's teaching of perfect renunciation can be followed without any compromise." Prabhavananda admits, however, that even his master, Ramakrishna, was scolded for encouraging the young to embrace this renunciant life instead of doing something useful. But Ramakrishna held in his message the same balance Jesus maintained: "He knew that all people cannot live the ideal of total renunciation, and he asked perfect self-denial only from his future message-bearers [apostles]. But his householder-disciples also were expected to practise renunciation and self-surrender."

At this point, a person is at peace in the hands of God, unable to be hurt even by injuries others inflict. Prabhavananda parallels the ends of Jesus's teaching—"But strive first for the kingdom of God and his righteousness, and all these things will be given to you as well" (Matt 6:33)—with words from the *Bhagavad Gita*: "If a man worship me, and meditate upon me with an undistracted mind, devoting every moment to me, I shall supply all his needs, and protect his possessions from loss." In the end—shifting to a vocabulary most Christians probably would not accept—he adds that once a person "has become spiritually illumined, he recognizes that body and mind are separate from the Atman [Self]; and his purified heart experiences the infinite happiness which exists beyond the grasp of the senses."

Thus Swami's teaching on this Sunday's Gospel, in very short form. Since there will be just one more installment in this series before Lent begins, it is not too early to reflect on the whole of his interpretation. Prabhavananda's reading may be Hindu, but it is not shockingly other or strange. As your comments have shown, and other blogs indicate too, not every Christian would read the Sermon as does the Swami. His focus may be too ascetic, even monastic, too much for the few who have advanced far along the path, too much a combination of a very high ideal, though with plenty of room for the rest of us to do the best we can, even when it is less than Jesus's ideal. His commentary is full of references to the Buddha, to Rama and Krishna, and to his own tradition's master, Ramakrishna. While he does believe that all the great teachers have to have basically the same message, he is not writing to establish a pluralist theology. He knows many religions, and knows that his readers know them too; he wants to draw on that diversity not to relativize Jesus but to help his readers to focus on the message of Jesus, taking it seriously as likely to transform our lives.

So while you probably won't have been hearing Prabhavananda's version of the Sermon on Sundays, listening to him seems to be a wise—and Christian—thing to do.

Jesus, Spiritual Master: Swami on the Sermon VII

March 3, 2011
Cambridge, MA. Lent is upon us, our Sunday readings from the Sermon on the Mount come to an end on March 6, and so we must take leave of our series on Swami Prabhavananda's *Sermon on the Mount according to Vedanta*. Three passages from his commentary on chapter 7 of Matthew (of which we hear only part in church) beg for special notice.

First, he comments on Jesus's admonition, "Enter through the narrow gate; for the gate is wide and the road is easy that leads to destruction, and there are many who take it. For the gate is narrow and the road is hard that leads to life, and there are few who find it" (7:13–14). As throughout, this confirms for Swami that Jesus's teaching is not for the idly curious or beginners: "Jesus warns us that realization of God is not easy. Purity of heart can only be achieved after great struggle. In the *Katha Upanisad* we read, 'Like the sharp edge of a razor, the sages say, is the path. Narrow it is, and difficult to tread!'"

To confirm this admonition, Prabhavananda moves in an unexpected direction, explaining the "narrow gate" by appealing to spiritual advancement charted in accord with the seven yogic/tantric "centers," the chakras: "At the base of the spine a reserve of latent spiritual energy is situated which, awakened by spiritual practices and devotion to God, flows upward through the narrow channel of the sushumna [nerve]." The narrow gate is marked physically and psychologically by the narrow channel up the spinal cord, along which one advances by transformation on all levels. What are we to think of this? While the language is unfamiliar, it gives a substantive meaning to our belief that Jesus manifest in his physical form the truth of his spiritual reality, experiencing to the limit possibilities latent in every human's physical and spiritual being.

Swami then surprises us by adding that Jesus himself manifest the highest ascent up that channel in realizing his true identity, unity with the Father. To confirm this striking idea, he appeals to Jacob Boehme in the Christian mystical tradition: "When the flash [of the Spirit] is caught in the fountain of the heart, then the Holy Spirit rises up, in the seven unfolding fountain spirits, into the brain, like the dawning of the day, the morning redness." At that point, Boehme adds, "From this God I take my knowledge and from no other thing; neither will I know any other thing than that same God."

More quickly, Prabhavananda takes the occasion of Jesus's next admonition—"On that day many will say to me, 'Lord, Lord, did we not prophesy in your name, and cast out demons in your name, and do many deeds of power in your name?' Then I will declare to them, 'I never knew you; go away from me, you evildoers'" (Matt 7:22–23)—for another unexpected teaching. True religion does not lie in good deeds. Yes, work for our fellow humans, but no, that is not the essence of religion: "We must do this [service], not as philanthropy or service to mankind, but as service to God out of love for God." He adds, following his teacher Swami Vivekananda, that it is absurd to think, in helping others, that they need our help in particular, as if we are saviors.

Rather, give all into God's hands and be a channel of God's grace whether you succeed or fail in your acts of service: "Do what good you can, some evil will inhere in it; but do all without regard to personal result. Give up all results to the Lord, then neither good nor evil will affect you." Or, simply as Jesus says, it is the doing of the will of God that enables one to enter the kingdom of heaven.

And finally, skipping other fascinating insights (read the book!), I note the Swami's comments on the end of the Sermon, "Now when Jesus had finished saying these things, the crowds were astounded at his teaching, for he taught them as one having authority, and not as their scribes" (Matt 7:28–29). Jesus was not passing along others' insights or secondhand reports. Rather, in Swami's view, he is like the Buddha and Ramakrishna in simply witnessing to what he himself has seen. So too, listening to Jesus reaches fruition only if we, settled on that rock, see what Jesus has seen: "Religion is something we ourselves have to do, and be, and live—or else it is nothing."

This reading of the Sermon is not an easy one, for many reasons, but it is a word from a Hindu brother encouraging us to take the Sermon to heart as serious, powerful, transformative. Here is a particular form of dialogue, less newsworthy and more enduring than formal, staged events, being taught from outside, as it were, about the core of our faith, learning to hear Jesus anew because of what a Hindu swami (or a rabbi or an Imam or a Santeria priestess, perhaps) tells us about this Jesus we follow.

I will close with a passage from Vivekananda that Prabhavananda ends with—as if to startle us once more, right at the end:

> Jesus had no other occupation in life, no other thought except that one, that he was Spirit. He was disembodied, unfettered, unbound Spirit. And not only so, but he, with his marvelous vision, had found that every man and woman, whether Jew or Gentile, whether rich or poor, whether saint or sinner, was the embodiment of the same undying Spirit as himself. Therefore, the one work his whole life showed was calling them to realize their own spiritual nature.

A Hindu Response to
"Swami on the Sermon"

March 19, 2011

Cambridge, MA. Readers may remember that in the season between Epiphany and Lent, I offered a series of seven reflections on Swami Prabhavananda's Vedanta Hindu commentary on the Sermon on the Mount, our Gospel text at Sunday Mass. I did so because his comments are insightful and spiritual and because I wanted to exemplify a deeper and longer-term interreligious exchange, such as would also contribute immediately to what we would be hearing and reflecting on in the Christian context each Sunday. But of course, another side of such interreligious learning is to hear from Hindu practitioners themselves, and for this purpose I am delighted to be able to post here an elegant and personal reflection by Pravrajika Vrajaprana, a Hindu nun in the Vedanta tradition who was a disciple of Swami Prabhavananda. She and I welcome further comments from readers. FXC

Pravrajika Vrajaprana writes:

Santa Barbara, CA. As a disciple of Swami Prabhavananda and a Vedanta nun for over thirty years, it has been with great interest that I have read Francis X. Clooney's "Swami and the Sermon" and the readers' responses to it. Like Swami Prabhavananda, I, too, have found my life profoundly enriched by the life and teachings of Jesus, and like Father Clooney, I have found genuine insights into my own tradition by learning from a religious tradition different from my own.

Swami Prabhavananda took the teachings of Jesus seriously, and he had a particular love for the Sermon on the Mount. In fact, it was through

him (and his predecessor, Swami Vivekananda) that I learned to love and deeply appreciate Jesus and his teachings, finding (to my young astonishment) much more relevance there than I had expected.

I was a young, disaffected teenager in the 1960s, who—like many others during those times—was ready to throw the baby out with the bathwater when it came to religion. To my hypercritical and cynical eye, American Christianity reeked of hypocrisy—there was all too much interest in a dissociative "Sunday religion" or, alternately, in feverish social action, yet little was offered to salve a disheartened but yearning soul. Like all too many others, I was ready to dismiss Christianity as a spiritual dead end.

It was then, at the ripe age of fifteen, that I encountered Swami Prabhavananda and his Sermon on the Mount according to Vedanta. *I read the book and saw how puerile and spiritually indefensible my easy dismissals were. The book was published out of a series of lectures that Prabhavananda gave on the Sermon, and he chose the topic because of his love for it and because he found in the Sermon a potent source for spiritual transformation. Taken seriously, and Swami did take them seriously, following the precepts of the Sermon would lead a spiritual seeker to the highest spiritual realization.*

According to the Vedanta tradition, the goal of life is to have the direct experience of God. Not to "believe" in God, not to subscribe to any creed, but to have the direct experience of God. As Swami Prabhavananda saw it, the central theme coursing through the entire Sermon was that very assertion and he saw in the Sermon a blueprint to achieve that goal: "Be ye therefore perfect, even as your Father which is in heaven is perfect." To Swami's mind this translated as: "Seek perfection! Realize God!"

In reading the readers' comments on "Swami and the Sermon," there has been some lively discussion concerning Prabhavananda's assertion that the Sermon was an advanced teaching, directed to Jesus's most serious and committed followers. The teachings are too hard for many, perhaps for most, people to practice. This has led at least one reader to suggest: "I believe it is a serious misreading of the Sermon on the Mount as if it is not for the ordinary Christian. It is a terrible dichotomy which encourages mediocrity in the followers of Christ. As if the Sermon on the Mount is unrealistic."

Swami Prabhavananda would, I think, contest this. He would reply that just because something is difficult, doesn't mean it shouldn't be done. In fact, it's all the more reason why it should be done. Much of spiritual life is, after all, an uphill battle: we are battling our own egotism, laziness, self-centeredness, fearfulness, and sheer bullheadedness in order that we may attain genuine love for God and our fellow beings; in order for us to gain compassion, humility, sincerity, truthfulness, and purity. And that's just the short list.

While the teachings of the Sermon are clear, they are not so easy to implement. "Blessed are the pure in heart, for they shall see God." The follow-through: we must be pure in heart to see God. Does that mean because it's difficult to become pure in heart that we should not bother to struggle to do so? Hardly. Does that mean that most people will falter on the way or think that it's an unachievable goal? Perhaps. As Father Clooney wrote in his third installment: "It is a spiritual advance in itself to admit when you cannot in fact live up to the teachings of Jesus." To which I say, Amen.

The teachings eternalized in the Sermon on the Mount are no more unrealistic than any other lofty ideal. Whether or not these ideals are difficult to attain does not in the least affect the fact that they remain the highest ideals to which humanity can aspire. Most, perhaps, will not make these ideals, and the goal of achieving these ideals, the purpose of their lives. But those who have, have done more to save and serve the world than the tens of millions of others who haven't bothered to try.

So in this holy Lenten season, let us remember these teachings of Jesus—teachings that have inspired people from every religious tradition the world has known. And let us thank Father Clooney and Swami Prabhavananda for bringing these much-needed ideals to our attention once again.

Another Hindu Response to "Swami on the Sermon"

March 20, 2011

Cambridge, MA. In my previous blog, I mentioned that in light of my series on Swami Prabhavananda on the Sermon on the Mount, I welcomed a Hindu response from Pravrajika Vrajaprana. I am delighted to be able to post now a second such response, this one from Swami Tyagananda of the Vedanta Society in Boston.

Swami Tyagananda writes:

The series on "Swami on the Sermon" has provided me much food for thought, and I am grateful to Francis X. Clooney for sharing his insights and thoughts with us, and grateful also for his invitation for me to contribute. As I read the seven reflections, one after another, I found myself continually nodding in agreement.

I thought of the two books that Swami Vivekananda (1863–1902) carried during his several years as a wandering monk: the Bhagavad Gita *and* Thomas à Kempis's The Imitation of Christ. *In Vivekananda's lectures, he often quoted from the New Testament, and the one sentence that appears with amazing frequency in his lectures and writings is from the Sermon on the Mount: "Blessed are the pure in heart, for they shall see God." This is what Vivekananda said about this profound teaching: "In that one sentence is the gist of all religions. If you have learnt that, all that has been said in the past and all that it is possible to say in the future, you have known; you need not look into anything else, for you have all that is necessary in that one sentence; it could save the world, were all the other scriptures lost. A vision of God, a glimpse of the beyond never comes until the soul is pure"* (Complete Works of Swami Vivekananda, 4.26).

In his Works, *Vivekananda's interpretation of "purity," "heart," and what it means to "see God" is obviously influenced by his own Hindu tradition and Indian culture. He is offering it not as a universal explanation but as a personal understanding that has enriched his own life. The point here is not so much to agree or disagree with him but (as Fr. Clooney so insightfully pointed out in part 1) "we can always learn our own faith more deeply by learning what people of other faiths have to say about our texts and traditions."*

In that spirit, I found both Fr. Clooney's observations and the readers' comments educative, especially those that reflected their views of Hinduism and Hindu society. I was intrigued by the readers' comments about nonviolence and about who the target audience of the Sermon is. As I understand it, an ideal—any ideal—is clearly something that is yet to be attained; once attained, it can no more be considered an "ideal," it then becomes the reality of one's life and experience. So while perfect nonviolence of the highest kind may be the "ultimate goal," we need several "intermediate goals" to be attained before we reach the summit, so to speak. Like most things in life, violence has its gross and subtle aspects. We can begin with avoiding gross violence, and then work, with patience and perseverance, to eliminate the subtle aspects of violence, verbal (hurtful speech, for instance) and psychological (jealousy, hatred, anger).

The Sermon on the Mount, like all great teachings, is clearly for everybody, but at any given time we can only take in what we are ready for. I like to view spiritual life as a struggle to acquire and increase our readiness (Sanskrit, adhikara*). When I am fully ready—and one day every one of us will be—the complete significance of the Sermon on the Mount will be revealed to me. It will then cease to be merely a scriptural text to be "studied." It will become a living reality in my life and it will be expressed, spontaneously and effortlessly, through the way I live; that is, it will shine through my thoughts, words, actions, and relationships. This is the way my mind, colored by its Hindu training and upbringing, thinks about it. For me personally, "Blessed are the pure in heart, for they shall see God" is the most compact statement of the highest truth expressed in theistic terms and comparable to the statement from a Hindu text that is expressed in nondualistic terms—"This Atman (the reality within the individual) is the same as Brahman (the reality behind the universe)" (Brihadaranyaka Upanishad, 2.5.19).*

One closing thought and I am done. When we undertake the study of religion, one's own or others', a study focused on a religion's theology, history, sociology, or politics using texts or through fieldwork, it may be good to keep in mind that religion is more than merely a set of ideas, concepts, traditions, beliefs, doctrines, and rituals. Religion is, above all, a living reality in the hearts and minds of people all over the world. The spirit transcends the limitations inherent in all human struggle and effort, and it is the spirit—the mysterious presence of God—that beckons us all. Every one of us may respond to it differently. What matters in the end is not who is right or who is wrong. Who, after all, is authorized, and by whom, to make that judgment? What matters ultimately is whether our response to the call of the Spirit brings us the peace, the love, the purity "that passeth understanding." No conflicts torment the person who dwells in that ethereal peace, love, and purity. From that vantage point, all criticisms look foolish, all disagreements look petty, all quarrels look pointless. Until that blessed state is reached, the drama of the world will continue to fascinate and frustrate us.

Additional Experiments in
Interreligious Reading

How I Preach, after Hindu Learning:
The Example of the Gospel of the Ten Lepers

October 9, 2016

Cambridge, MA. As many readers will know, I have been studying Hinduism for over forty years, since I first visited Kathmandu, Nepal, in 1973 to teach at St. Xavier's School. Over the years, people have asked me what difference this study has made for me. I have always had to give a complicated answer: "not much, and everything." I live here, in the United States, not in Nepal or India, and at best am a missionary in reverse, bringing Hinduism to the attention of American Christians. I have not become a Hindu; I am still a Catholic priest and a Jesuit. I am not a pluralist who believes that all religions are varying affirmations of the same truth; I prefer to go deep in my own tradition to interpret pluralism. I am a Catholic theologian, just a slightly different kind. People sometime persist: how then has Hinduism made a difference in my practice of Catholicism, as a priest? Often enough, I add that I almost never mention India or Hinduism in my homilies in my Sunday parish (where I've helped for over nineteen years)—but that my study of Hinduism has changed how I preach, what I am looking for, and what I find in the readings of any given day. It is hard to explain how this works out, to be deeply influenced by Hinduism in preparing my homilies, while yet almost never mentioning Hinduism from the pulpit.

But I found today that my reading of the Gospel deeply resonated with my study of Hinduism, and that it perhaps serves as a good example. Let me explain this by several general observations and then several particular comments on the Gospel read in church today, the ten lepers.

On the general level: First, I think it quite in keeping with Hindu tradition that I never mention Hinduism from the pulpit: the point of a homily, religious speech before a gathered religious community, is to address listeners where they are, in the tradition to which they belong, without disturbing them by complicated new information. One finds God where one is, not by going somewhere else. So why would I preach on Hinduism to Catholics? Simply explain the words of the Bible to Catholics, that is enough. If one preaches to Hindus, I suppose, words from a Hindu scripture would be enough. Second, Hindu teachers tend to read texts without much reference to historical context or to current events: they dwell in the story at hand and bring its details to life. I am not much of a storyteller anyway, I am sure, but I am always content likewise simply to go inside the readings of the day, letting the words roll over me, so to speak, to become, for the moment, all that matters. So one goes deep inside a Gospel passage, for instance, and sees what one finds. This is all that matters for speaker and listeners on a Sunday morning. Third, sacred texts are *texts*; the ideas may be fine, but the transformative power of the text lies in each and every word, so one must read very closely and carefully. All one needs to do is help us all to really hear the words. To preach well depends a lot on simply reading slowly and attentively; Hindu teachers too often simply go over a text, word by word.

I had pondered today's simple Gospel all week long:

On the way to Jerusalem Jesus was going through the region between Samaria and Galilee. As he entered a village, ten lepers approached him. Keeping their distance, they called out, saying, "Jesus, Master, have mercy on us!" When he saw them, he said to them, "Go and show yourselves to the priests." And as they went, they were made clean.

Then one of them, when he saw that he was healed, turned back, praising God with a loud voice. He prostrated himself at Jesus' feet and thanked him. And he was a Samaritan. Then Jesus asked, "Were not ten made clean? But the other nine, where are they? none of them found to return and give praise to God except this foreigner?" Then he said to him, "Get up and go on your way; your faith has made you well."

(Luke 17:11–19)

Having read so many Hindu texts, my expectation usually is that the message is in the details. So with my congregation, I began with a question: Why does Jesus send them on their way to the priests before he heals them? We may be misled by the end of the passage, into thinking that only the Samaritan had faith. Yet all ten were people of faith, willing to expose themselves and risk everything by going to the priests, even unclean; obey, even when there were no visible reasons to. It was only on the road that they were cleansed of their disease. Their faith came first, before any signs of a cure.

Given my interreligious learning, I am also alert to the danger of making one religion look good at the expense of another: so even here, there is no point in making it seem as if Jews are ungrateful and the Samaritan leper the example of gratitude. All ten risked everything in going to the priests; the nine Jewish lepers (if they were all Jewish) were obeying the command of Jesus to go first to the priests. Obedience too is a virtue. It could hardly be surprising that a Samaritan leper would be the one to consider that encounter with the priests less important—the priests are presumably Jewish, and he is not; what does he have to lose in turning back? This is not a Gospel that makes Jews look bad and Samaritans look good. I have known too many Hindus to want to make one religion look good at the expense of another.

But what then is special about this tenth leper? He praises God on the way back and might just as well have praised God on his way home to Samaria. So why is he special? It is here that a Hindu instinct comes to the fore, since anyone who has studied Hinduism will immediately resonate with what the Samaritan actually does: "He prostrated himself at Jesus' feet and thanked him." Thanks yes, but the posture of surrender, prostration, jumps out as the perfect gesture: for it is there, where Jesus is, that the healing actually takes place. To be at the feet of the Lord Jesus, a Hindu teacher will tell us, is the perfect place to be, the highest goal in life. This is a superlative act of great love that any Hindu would recognize.

It is also a sacramental moment—the words are not enough, praising God is not enough, nor even thanking Jesus or "keeping his distance" as at the start of the story. "Here and now" would also resonate with most Hindu readers. And so, in my homily, I detoured briefly to the first reading from 2 Kings, where Elijah cures Naaman, commander of the army of the king of Aram. I went there not because of the leprosy, surely the intention of those compiling the Sunday readings, but because of what Naaman wants as he leaves:

Then Naaman said, "If not, please let two mule-loads of earth be given to your servant; for your servant will no longer offer burnt-offering or sacrifice to any god except the Lord."

(2 Kings 5:17)

Two mule-loads of earth—it is hard to imagine being more material, physical, local, than this. Naaman wants the very soil of Israel, that he might stand on it for his prayer—not just to thank God, or praise the God of Israel, but in a rather primal fashion, to abide on the soil of Israel for his worship. This too—an idea with Biblical roots, to be sure—makes perfect sense in light of my understanding of Hinduism: God here and now, such that one can prostrate before God, and in a holy place, on sacred ground, because God was here. God, who is everywhere, is especially present in some holy places. Both Catholics and Hindus appreciate material, holy, tangible things.

Such was the substance of my reading of the text. Readers may observe that there is no proof here, no claims about the influence of Hinduism on the Bible, and no claim about a reading of the Gospel that could not have happened otherwise. All this is true. But my point is subtler: what I noticed and noted in the Gospel moved away from the theme of "thanksgiving" but later returned to it in a heightened fashion. I became sensitive to certain odd dynamics—the command to go to the priests before the cure occurred, the praise of the Samaritan who had no real reason to go to the priests and who easily turned back, and the event of his prostration—because I have read so many Hindu texts that resonate with such turns and eventualities.

Still, of course, one might expect more, if one wishes for a Hindu reading of a Gospel. But there is more power that goes deeper and lasts longer in the subtle and simple. I doubt if I would have noticed what I did in the Gospel without my study of Hinduism. That study has brought out the power of this tale of thanksgiving as utter devotion, here and now. And that is the point: studying another religion helps us to find in our own what we would not have ever noticed there.

The *Study Quran* and the Battle
against Ignorance

December 8, 2015

Cambridge, MA. If there was any doubt, it should be clear now that Donald Trump lacks the moral quality required of a politician who would become our president. He has offended both morality and practicality by his rants against Mexicans, his call to deport all illegal immigrants, his bullying, and his disrespect for those who dare to argue with him. His new call to ban all Muslims from entering the United States is another singular instance of his lack of credentials, moral as well as intellectual, that would make a person a serious candidate for our highest office. His call to exclusion is not only deeply offensive to Muslims, it is an abomination to people of other faith traditions as well. Indeed, it is hard for me, a Catholic priest who knows the Bible reasonably well, to imagine how any Christian who respects the word of God can in good conscience support or vote for Donald Trump, especially after his mean-spirited and dangerous call to ban Muslims who would enter the country.

But underlying his rant against Muslims seems to be a deep ignorance of Islam and the loud pretense that such ignorance is not a problem. ISIS and similar violent organizations likewise seem to manifest ignorance regarding what Islam is really about, how to interpret—as one must —its original texts and its traditions. Ignorance and violence, verbal and physical, travel together.

And so those of us who can need to make determined efforts to cut through the ignorance of this dangerous moment. As a professor—and as a priest—I suggest that one thing we can do is study Islam and learn more of this religious tradition. (In another context, I might urge *all* people of religious faith to study each other's scriptures; no religious community can imagine itself exempt, as if interreligious knowledge is optional or unimportant for its true believers.)

There are many ways to study Islam, of course, and reliable textbooks exist regarding Islam's history, its theology, and its acculturation to new environs over the centuries. But some of us—*particularly* those of us, such as myself, who have no particular expertise regarding Islam—should seize the opportunity just now made available to us of purchasing, or borrowing, from a friend or the library, *The Study Quran: A New Translation and Commentary* (New York: HarperOne, 2015) and studying it carefully. To see this new volume as a timely resource today is hardly a novel idea, and many have already noted that in a time when ignorance is rampant and violent, this can be a book of great value.

It is a very impressively put together volume. The fresh translation of each of the 114 suras (chapters) of the Qur'an is accompanied by copious notes, frequently more than half of the page, and sometimes even several full pages of commentary on some few verses. These notes are rich in necessary historical and linguistic information and in detail from the many commentaries on the Qur'an through the ages. The editors of this volume take very seriously the task of "study," and want to give readers everything they require for this work.

A general introduction by Seyyed Hossein Nasr, chief editor, precedes the translation, along with some initial advice. Fifteen essays by distinguished scholars conclude the nearly two-thousand-page volume, with titles such as: "How to Read the Quran" (Ingrid Mattson), "The Quran in Translation" (Joseph Lumbard), "The Islamic View of the Quran" (Muhammad Mustafa al-Azami), "Quranic Commentaries" (Walid Saleh), "Quranic Ethics, Human Rights, and Society" (Maria Massi Dakake) and "Conquest and Conversion, War and Peace in the Quran" (Caner K. Dagli).

This volume is, then, something like a combination of the *Oxford Annotated Bible* and the *Jerome Biblical Commentary*. Much to read, much to learn, all the more important when the ignorant are the loudest.

Of course, even I recognize that the media moves quickly, ideas and diatribes fly back and forth at great speed, and few of us (even busy academics at the end of the semester) actually have the time to sit down and read the two thousand pages of this volume carefully. Trump and company will not care for such learning but continue on their path of exaggeration, fearmongering, and violent rushes to judgment. Politics trumps all. Terrorists, violent under the guise of Islam, will likewise have no time for the quiet reading of the text—wisdom is the most fearsome enemy of terror, after all. But we must sit down and we must read, and we must share what we learn, to push back the waves of ignorance about Islam by a good dose of knowledge. Of course, knowledge does not predictably serve a single purpose, and it may be that in our study we also come up against ideas or sentiments in the Qur'an that we do not agree with. But we will be much better off if our disagreements are grounded in close reading and articulated with respect to specific points.

Studying the Qur'an as a Catholic II

December 11, 2015

Cambridge, MA. Ironically, sadly, just when Donald Trump wants to close the door on Muslims, Pope Francis is opening the holy door in St. Peter's Basilica, insisting that divine mercy is never a closed door. Indeed, as he insisted back in April when he announced the Holy Year of Mercy, this is truth shared widely with Jews, Muslims, and people of other faiths. After offering a strong affirmation of God's mercy in Jewish tradition, he turned to Islam:

> Among the privileged names that Islam attributes to the Creator are "Compassionate and Merciful." This invocation is often on the lips of faithful Muslims who feel themselves accompanied and sustained by mercy in their daily weakness. They too believe that no one can place a limit on divine mercy because its doors are always open. So let us begin there, with the first words of the Qur'an itself: "In the name of God (Allah), the Compassionate (al-Rahman), the Merciful (al-Rahim" (1.1). These words open every chapter of the Qur'an except one, the ninth ("Repentance," al-Tawbah), which speaks of repentance but also of fierce contest with idolaters; more on that difficult chapter another day. Here, in the very first chapter, the next verses echo the same theme: "Praise be to God, Lord of the worlds, the Compassionate, the Merciful."

> (1.2–3)

The Study Quran—a wonderful Christmas gift for studious friends and family in all its magnificent two thousand pages—invites us to simply read the chapters of the Qur'an itself, or to ponder any given verse with commentary, or, as I have begun to do, to look into the fifty-seven page index, to follow a word across the many chapters. But surely the basic point is simple: right from the first verses of the first chapter, we begin to learn much about God's compassion and mercy. We are confronted with it, surprised by it, drawn into it. This is a core truth of Islam, repeated over and over, and neither the bigoted nor the violent can obscure the fact.

The first chapter of the Qur'an is only seven verses long, but the commentary in *The Study Quran* extends for nearly seven pages and is full of insights for beginners like myself. "God, the Compassionate, the Merciful": the divine essence (Allah, God), the unity of all divine attributes (Compassionate), and the unity of divine acts (Merciful). "The Compassionate" is a divine name that no other can bear, since "it connotes the Loving-Mercy by which God brings forth existence." "The Merciful" indicates "the blessing of nourishment by which God sustains each particular being." Compassion is like the sun, mercy is the ray of sunshine warming and vivifying every given thing on earth. The first (Compassion) brings the world into being, the second (Mercy) "is that by which God shows Mercy to those whom He will, as in 33:43, 'And He is Merciful unto the believers,'" enabling them to endure as they were created to be. And that Mercy is, in turn, the wellspring of other divine names: the Kind, the Clement, the Beautiful.

We learn later on, in 21:107, that the Prophet Mohammad is sent by God as an act of mercy: "And We sent thee not, save as a mercy unto the worlds." The commentary here explains the subtlety of the Arabic: "The grammar of the verse allows it to be understood to mean either that the sending of the Prophet Mohammad was a merciful act by God or that the Prophet is himself a mercy that God sent. It can signify that the Prophet is a possessor of mercy, is merciful, or is himself a mercy." This is, the comment continues, a manifestation of the mercy to which the Law tends, and a mercy for all, the whole "world," and not just believing Muslims. Even those who do not believe in the Prophet experience his mercy, which wards off doom even from those who reject him; he will intercede for all, on the day of judgment.

And finally—I cannot go on too long—this mercy brings peace and harmony to men and women, who find their partners by divine mercy: "And among His signs is that He created mates for you from among yourselves, that you might find rest in them, and He established affection and mercy between you" (30:21). This, we are told in the commentary, is "an address to both men and women, telling of the manner in which God has extended His own Love and Mercy to them through the love and mercy that they manifest toward one another." One could continue tracing "the Merciful" for a long time; God is invoked this way well over one hundred times in the Qur'an (or so my counting in the index suggests).

The comments are, we are told, drawn from the forty-one traditional commentaries listed at *The Study Quran*'s beginning. One thousand five hundred years of wisdom across the bottom of the page. Like most of you reading this, I cannot go and check those original sources for myself, but it seems that the illuminations of every word of every verse are rooted in the consensus of a long lineage of earlier readers. We read the Qur'an not on its own but with those who have gone before us. Is this not the Catholic faith, too?

And, as I have just shown, mention of the opening of the Holy Door of Mercy by Pope Francis, seen by him to be an act that will resonate with Jews and Muslims and believers in other traditions, leads easily and smoothly into these passages from across the Qur'an. *The Study Quran* makes it so very easy for us to meditate on God's mercy, the reality that shames and extinguishes hatred among people of different faiths. In the same declaration I cited at the start of this post, Pope Francis makes an appeal for a merciful encounter among believers, the very opposite of fear and discrimination, hatred and violence against the outsider:

> I trust that this Jubilee year celebrating the mercy of God will foster an encounter with these religions and with other noble religious traditions; may it open us to even more fervent dialogue so that we might know and understand one another better; may it eliminate every form of closed-mindedness and disrespect, and drive out every form of violence and discrimination.

Granted, his words do not, and my words certainly will not, suffice suddenly to change the reckless tone of our politics and extinguish the international infatuation with violence. Last night, I listened to a moving conversation at the Harvard Divinity School with Pastor Dr. James Movel Wuye and Imam Dr. Muhammad Nurayn Ashafa, as part of the HDS Religions and the Practice of Peace initiative. Such courageous figures have opened doors to reconciliation between Muslims and Christians in Nigeria, and their work is more immediately important than the study we do. But learning, studying, and teaching are fundamental to living faith in any tradition, part of the human race's spiritual DNA, essential to our survival in a world that spirals downward when ignorance prevails. Pray, study, and act.

Violence in the Qur'an

December 15, 2015

Cambridge, MA. I continue here my brief series on the Qur'an, how the new *Study Quran* can be an aid to interreligious understanding in the necessary battle against the twin evils of ignorance and violence. One might similarly look at *The Jewish Study Bible*, which includes the Jewish Publication Society Tanakh Translation, or *The New Oxford Annotated Bible with Apocrypha*. We need to be studying each other's holy books, and we can, and we should.

It is important to remember that my concern here is the study of the holy book itself, rather than all the important contextual issues that must also be addressed. I admit, as always, that the study of the text does not replace other "infinite paths of learning": the study of one's own deepest self, the study of the surrounding social and political conditions, and, finally, our unending encounter with God. The study of the text is only a small part of the larger wisdom required of us, but it is an irreplaceable part. That it is easy enough to do should shame those who refuse to actually study other religions before judging them. *The Study Quran* means that this vastly influential holy book is now more easily available for our study, open and ready, and my posts are meant to be examples of this study, by a reader who is not an expert on Islam.

In my last post, I reflected on the God of mercy, the compassionate and merciful Lord of whom we hear again and again in the Qur'an—and who is very much in the forefront of the consciousness of Catholics during Pope Francis's Year of Mercy. I did intend now to move on to Mary and Jesus in the qur'anic tradition but thought that perhaps skeptical readers would charge that I'd taken the easy path: Who can object to the idea that God is merciful? So I thought it wiser to stop for a moment to ask a difficult question: What then does the Qur'an say about violence?

One place to start is Caner Dagli's masterful article in *The Study Quran*, "Conquest and Conversion, War and Peace in the Quran." Citing key but disparate texts, Dagli reminds us that at various points in the Qur'an, the political context makes the teaching seem to incline toward either peace or the taking up of arms. Each sura (chapter) and the key verses in each sura need to be studied and read in context. While at a deep level the Qur'an is perfectly consistent, one cannot retrieve its teachings by citing just one passage or another.

But here I can consider just two passages. First, consider these verses in the second sura, "The Cow":

> God, there is no god but He, the Living, the Self-Subsisting. Neither slumber overtakes Him nor sleep. Unto Him belongs whatsoever is in the heavens and whatsoever is on the earth. Who is there who may intercede with Him save by His leave? He knows that which is before them and that which is behind them. And they encompass nothing of His Knowledge, save what he wills. His Pedestal embraces the heavens and the earth.
> Protecting them tires Him not, and He is the Exalted, the Magnificent. There is no coercion in religion. Sound judgment has become clear from error. So whosoever disavows false deities and believes in God has grasped the most unfailing handhold, which never breaks. And God is Hearing, Knowing. God is the Protector of those who believe. He brings them out of darkness into the light. As for those who disbelieve, their protectors are the idols, bringing them out of the light into the darkness.

(2:255–57)

This magnificent passage will remind us of similarly lofty words in the Psalms or the Prophets of Israel, and we can benefit from meditation on them. Of course, we naturally seize upon the words, "No coercion in religion," which seems to leave matters of faith and belonging in God's hands. The children of the light and darkness are allowed to go their own way, by God's mysterious will, and humans are not to interfere. Yes, the passage is also judgmental, speaking of false deities (any deity but the Lord) and idols (anything one worships as equal to God), and what is needed is a twenty-first-century Islamic theologies of religions.

The Study Quran's commentary on the verse, a full page, fills out our understanding. It points us to parallels, for example at 10:99–100 and 18:29. It also explores a variety of traditional interpretations and asks how the verse was originally applied, even perhaps in the context of "mixed marriages" with Jews or Christians. One needs to go back to the original social and political context to understand how it is to be read, since out of context it can easily be misread, misused. In brief, though, the commentary concludes, "The fighting Muslims carried out was motivated by political circumstances and not the desire to convert."

My second text, from the ninth sura, "Repentance," serves to bring out another side of the matter. As the commentary suggests, it might even be taken as superseding the passage we have just read:

> And an announcement from God and His Messenger to the people on the day of the great hajj: that God and His Messenger have repudiated the idolaters. So, if you repent, it would be better for you. And if you turn away, then know that you cannot thwart God.
>
> And give the disbelievers glad tidings of a painful punishment, save for those idolaters with whom you have made a treaty, and who thereafter commit no breach against you, nor support anyone against you. So fulfill the treaty with them for its duration. Truly God loves the reverent. Then, when the sacred months have passed, slay the idolaters whereso-ever you find them, capture them, besiege them, and lie in wait for them at every place of ambush. But if they repent, and perform prayer and give the alms, then let them go their way. Truly God is Forgiving, Merciful. And if any one of the idolaters seek asylum with thee, grant him asylum until he hears the Word of God. Then convey him to his place of safety. That is because these are a people who know not.

(9:3–6)

The words are certainly strong: again, judgment is passed on the "idolaters" and "disbelievers"; if they break treaties one must ambush them, capture them, slay them. And yet—there is always more—if they repent of their treaty violations, they can be allowed to go their own way.

Idolaters can be granted asylum, safe haven. Here, too, the commentary tells us, we will have to learn about the politics of the early Islamic world and the Prophet's efforts to hold his community together, defending it against hostile neighbors; not every word is meant for application in every time and place. My own impression—after preliminary study—is that we find here a sanction of force, but force constrained within the context of diplomacy and treaties, and in the end, ever open to peace, since God, who repudiates idolatry and has no patience with treaty violators, also "loves the reverent" and is ever "Forgiving, Merciful."

So what do we conclude? All is in God's hands; peace is at the core of Islam; there have been and are times when believers have to fight fiercely; people who believe differently are in God's hands, not ours; divine mercy is never exhausted. All this is very complicated, and perhaps I confuse readers by offering a few insights rather than a full study of such themes. But the point is that further study is needed not just by the experts but by you and me. Hence the value of *The Study Quran*. In the short run, read Caner Dagli's essay, mentioned above, and then, when you have time, start reading passages such as the two I have cited, and then, using the commentary and the index, start flipping back and forth and noting down all the other passages one must read.

To say that all this is complicated is not to evade hard questions but to insist on hard study. We do not get to judge the Qur'an without studying it, nor can we walk away from it with some handy verse that suits our friendly or hostile purposes. With any sacred scripture, our own or another, we push back the forces of ignorance and violence if we engage the whole, in all its depth and complexity, insisting on slow study in the face of impatience, fear, anger, and ignorance.

Maryam, Mother of Jesus, in the Qur'an

December 18, 2015

Cambridge, MA. I began this series because of my sharp disagreement with Donald Trump's call to close our borders to all Muslims and my distress at how others seem to approve of the idea. His call for this is, in my judgment, wrong, unworkable, and also ignorant. I felt it timely to urge my readers to push back against this dangerous ignorance and literal exclusion of people of another faith tradition, in part by informing ourselves about each other's religions. For those of us who are not Muslim, the recently released *Study Quran* presents a fine opportunity to make the case for study and learning, and so I have offered this short series, A Catholic Reads the Qur'an during Advent.

I appreciate the considerable interest among readers of these posts, many by personal email and some posted at the *America* site. Excepting a few commenters who appear too eager to draw conclusions—about Islam, about me—I appreciate the posts, including those who want to read the Qur'an differently, with differing views on mercy or violence in the Qur'an. (I am also grateful to the reader who pointed out that the volume does contain an essay toward an Islamic theology of religions, Joseph Lumbard's "The Quranic View of Sacred History and Other Religions," a beautiful essay worthy of close reading.)

As I have said each time, my point is not that we agree but that we who are not Muslim educate ourselves on these matters, resist caricatures of Muslims, and be open, ideally also entering into conversation with Muslim neighbors likewise open to studying the Bible. While such a community of readers will not push aside headlines dominated by the Trumps and the ISIS supporters of this world, we will in the long run make the greater difference.

Given that we are deep into Advent, I thought it fitting now to explore *The Study Quran* on the theme of Mary, Mother of Jesus. The ample index tells us that there are more than fifty references to Jesus in the Qur'an and more than fifteen to Mary. They are mentioned in the editors' commentary many more times, as the index shows us. The editors point out that Mary is the only woman named in the Qur'an; while most such named figures are prophets, there is debate about Mary's status, some listing her among the prophets, others preferring to say that she is "an exceptionally pious woman with the highest spiritual rank among women" (763).

They add that in a hadith (traditional saying), "the Prophet names Mary as one of the four spiritually perfected women of the world," (763) who will "lead the soul of blessed women to Paradise" (143). In Sura 66 (Forbiddance), Mary is evoked again respectfully, "the daughter of Imran, who preserved her chastity. Then We breathed therein Our Spirit, and she confirmed the Words of her Lord and His Books; and she was among the devoutly obedient" (66:12). One commentator, Fakhr al-Din al-Razi, takes this to mean that Mary "believed in all previous revelations."

I need not deny that other passages diverge further from Christian faith, yet without disrespect for Mary and Jesus. In Sura 5 (The Table Spread), for example, we read, "The Messiah, son of Mary, was naught but a messenger—messengers have passed away before him. And his mother was truthful. Both of them ate food. Behold how We make the signs clear unto [the People of the Book]; yet behold how [those signs] are perverted." The commentary notes that the Prophet Mohammad is described in the same way in Sura 3:144: "Mohammad is naught but a messenger; messengers have passed before him."

The commentary adds,

"The assertion in this verse that both Mary and Jesus ate food is meant to affirm their full humanity and refute those who see them as divine. Of course, Christian theology also sees Christ as 'fully human' and 'fully divine,' and the Qur'anic view of Jesus as fully human is consistent with certain verses of the New Testament, such as Luke 18:19 and Philippians 2:6–8, which stress Jesus' humanity in relation to God." That Mary was "truthful" places her in the company of the prophets; she is the one who testifies to "the truth of Jesus' prophethood and message."

In Sura 3 (The House of Imran), Mary is introduced as the daughter of Imran and his wife, who prays, "I have named her Mary, and I seek refuge for her in Thee, and for her progeny, from Satan the outcast" (3:36). Mary is then placed by the Lord under the care of Zachariah, father of John. This version of the Annunciation follows:

> And (remember) when the angels said, "O Mary, truly God has chosen thee and purified thee, and has chosen thee above the women of the worlds. O Mary! Be devoutly obedient to thy Lord, prostrate, and bow with those who bow."

(3:42–43)

She is twice chosen: as the pious girl dwelling in the temple and as the mother of Jesus. A few verses on, the angelic message is put this way,

> "O Mary, truly God gives thee glad tidings of a Word from Him, whose name is the Messiah, Jesus son of Mary, high honored in this world and the Hereafter, and one of those brought nigh. He will speak to people in the cradle and in maturity, and will be among the righteous." She said, "My Lord, how shall I have a child while no human being has touched me?" He said, "Thus does God create whatsoever He will." When He decrees a thing, He only says to it, "Be!" and it is. And He will teach him the Book, Wisdom, the Torah, and the Gospel. And (he will be) a messenger to the Children of Israel.

(3:45–48)

Finally, Sura 19 (Maryam) treats Zachariah and John at its start, Abraham and Moses later on, and in between (19:16–36) recounts again the story of Mary and how she came to give birth to Jesus. Mary, exiled in the desert and alone, prays to a mysterious figure who comes to her: "I seek refuge from thee in the Compassionate, if you are reverent" (19:18). He is an angel, a messenger, who tells her about the son she will bear. Mary consents, but after conceiving the child, she is again alone and bereft, and cries out in words that refugees worldwide may be tempted to use even today: "Would that I had died before this and was a thing forgotten, utterly forgotten!" (19:23). The angel shows her the running water and date palm tree that the Lord has provided for her, and she survives. When confronted by her gossiping neighbors when she returns home with her newborn child (there is no Joseph, no Bethlehem, in this account), Mary chooses to be silent (as Zachariah was by force) and lets the child speak for himself:

> He said, "Truly I am a servant of God. He has given me the Book and made me a prophet. He has made me blessed wheresoever I may be, and has enjoined upon me prayer and almsgiving so long as I live, and (has made me) dutiful toward my mother. And He has not made me domineering, wretched. Peace be upon me the day I was born, the day I die, and the day I am raised alive!"

(19:30–33)

The commentary fills most of several pages on this account. It highlights Mary's initial desperation: "She wished he could have died before the onset of the difficulties she now faced as a woman giving birth to a child alone, without a husband, including both the physical pain of labor and the embarrassment about what people would think of her." She almost prefers oblivion, though some traditional commentaries see her as "expressing the ultimate victory against the worldly ego," to forget the world and be forgotten by it. That Jesus speaks, even as an infant, shows his resolve, as newborn prophet, "to absolve his mother of any blame or suspicion." That is to say, to be a prophet (even today) is to speak up on behalf of the excluded, downtrodden, helpless.

The commentary reports how this sura on Mary and Jesus and other prophets once helped save the lives of Muslim refugees under the protection of the Christian negus (king) of Abyssinia. A Makkan delegation had come and demanded that the refugees be turned over for execution. The negus asks that first a sura of the Qur'an be recited. When part of this sura is recited, "the Negus and the religious leaders of his court began to weep profusely and refused to hand over the Muslims, indicating that the religious teachings of the Qur'an were deeply related to those of the Christian faith." Is it not so very right that scripture might inspire those in power to protect rather than abandon those in dire need, even if they are of another faith?

The commentary also points out the stylistic unity and harmony of this sura; it is one that you may wish to listen to, if you have never heard qur'anic recitation. You can find many sites online that offer examples of recitation.

That I highlight in this way some of the passages dealing with

Mary in the Qur'an is by no means a novel idea. Readers interested in more on Mary, Jesus, and other biblical figures in the Qur'an, can turn to John Kaltner's *Ishmael Instructs Isaac: An Introduction to the Qur'an for Bible Readers* (1999). That Mary can even today be a powerful protector and nurturer of Muslim and Christian unity was well expressed in 1996 by Cardinal William Keeler in "How Mary Holds Christians and Muslims in Conversation." Similarly, Fr. Miguel Angel Ayuso, secretary of the Pontifical Council for Interreligious Dialogue, in his 2014 "The Virgin Mary in Islamic-Christian Dialogue," highlighted the great importance of Mary in Muslim-Christian dialogue.

Can we not imagine that in this Jubilee Year of Mercy, Mary will help refugees across closed borders and open the hearts of gatekeepers who would close the door on people who live by the holy Qur'an? As Pope Francis wrote (in *Misericordiae Vultus*) when he declared the Jubilee Year of Mercy,

> Chosen to be the Mother of the Son of God, Mary, from the outset, was prepared by the love of God to be the Ark of the Covenant between God and man. She treasured divine mercy in her heart in perfect harmony with her Son Jesus. Her hymn of praise, sung at the threshold of the home of Elizabeth, was dedicated to the mercy of God which extends from "generation to generation" (Luke 1:50). We too were included in those prophetic words of the Virgin Mary. This will be a source of comfort and strength to us as we cross the threshold of the Holy Year to experience the fruits of divine mercy.

Jesus in the Qur'an: Pious, Obedient, Favored Servant of God

December 21, 2015
Cambridge, MA. Then God will say,

> O Jesus son of Mary! Remember My Blessing upon thee, and upon thy
> mother, when I strengthened thee with the Holy Spirit, that you might-
> est speak to people in the cradle and in maturity; and when I taught
> thee the Book, the Wisdom, the Torah, and the Gospel; and how thou
> wouldst create out of clay the shape of a bird, by My Leave; and how
> though wouldst breathe into it, and it would become a bird, by My
> Leave; and thou wouldst heal the blind and the leper, by My Leave; and
> thou wouldst bring forth the dead, by My Leave; and how I restrained
> the Children of Israel from thee, when thou didst bring the clear proofs,
> and those disbelieved among them said, "This is naught but manifest
> sorcery." And when I inspired the apostles to believe in Me and in My
> messenger, they said, "We believe. Bear witness that we are submitters."

(5:110–11)

When the apostles said,

> "O Jesus son of Mary! Is thy Lord able to send down to us from Heaven
> a table spread with food?" [Jesus son of Mary] said, "Reverence God,
> if you are believers." They said, "We desire to eat from it, so that our
> hearts may be at peace, and we may know that thou hast spoken truth-
> fully unto us, and we may be among the witnesses thereto." Jesus son of
> Mary said, "O God, our Lord! Send down unto us a table from Heaven
> spread with food, to be a feast for us—for the first of us and the last of
> us—and a sign from Thee, and provide for us, for Thou art the best of

providers." God said, "I shall indeed send it down unto you. But whoever among you disbelieves thereafter, I shall surely punish him with a punishment wherewith I have not punished any other in all the worlds."

(5:112–15)

And when God said,

"O Jesus son of Mary! Didst thou say unto mankind, 'Take me and my mother as gods apart from God?'" [Jesus son of Mary] said, "Glory be to Thee! It is not for me to utter that to which I have no right. Had I said it, Thou wouldst surely have known it. Thou knowest what is in my self and I know not what is in Thy Self. Truly it is Thou Who knowest best the things unseen. I said naught to them save that which Thou commanded me: 'Worship God, my Lord and your Lord.' And I was a witness over them, so long as I remained among them. And Thou art Witness over all things. If Thou punisheth them they are indeed Thy servants, but if Thou forgiveth them, then indeed Thou art the Mighty, the Wise."

(5:116–18)

There are many passages in the Qur'an to look at if one wants to understand the role of Jesus in the eyes of the Prophet and early Islam. See in particular, and most easily, passages cited by Joseph Lumbard in his essay in *The Study Quran*, "The Quranic View of Sacred History and Other Religions" (particularly pages 1777–82; e.g., 19:16–21, 3:45–47, 3:49). See also some of the books he refers to, such as *Qur'anic Christians* (1991) by Jane McAuliffe, former dean at Georgetown and now president of Bryn Mawr College, and Mahmoud Ayoub's 1995 essay, "Jesus the Son of God: A Study of the Terms Ibn and Walad in the Qur'an and Tafsir Tradition." John Kaltner's book *Ishmael Instructs Isaac* remains valuable here, too, as is a 2013 essay on Mary and Muhammed in the *Journal of Ecumenical Studies* by my Harvard doctoral student Axel Takács. One can also search through the detailed index of *The Study Quran*, which lists more than fifty references to Jesus with many more in the commentaries.

A lot to read. Indeed, the multitude of such passages is part of the point: confronted with the mysteries of God and of ourselves, and guided by our traditions and Scriptures, there is still much room for study and close, complex reading; there is room for learning in the face of the monumental ignorance tormenting us today. Violence wins in the short run, truth in the long run. A humble contribution to this great work of learning is what my posts have been about, including this one. We are not doing theology in any completed sense in this study, but we are making ourselves the literate persons who will be capable of theologies worth reading. I am therefore encouraged by the many comments on my posts, particularly from those who read closely what I write. May the study continue long after this fifth and last post is forgotten.

Not wanting my always-too-long posts to be even longer, I had to choose one passage about Jesus to write about, and the passage cited above from sura 5 (The Table Spread) seems beneficial and illuminating. Sura 5 is difficult as it incorporates several different Christian and Muslim views of Jesus, and requires cross reading with many other qur'anic passages. The passage falls into three parts. Verses 110–11: God's declaration to Jesus of what he has done for him, through him, both deeds such as we find in the Gospels and the account of the miraculous clay birds we find in the infancy gospel of Thomas. The people's refusal to accept Jesus is in God's hands, as is the divine protection of Jesus kept from their hands. This is God's direct address to Jesus, after addressing a wider group of prophets. Verses 112–15: The heavenly meal that God sends down, possibly after a Ramadan fast, showing to ambivalent disciples the effective intercessory power to Jesus. Verses 116–18: Jesus's testimony, when questioned by God, that as God already knows, Jesus did not ask his listeners to worship him (and his mother) as deities apart from God, since his message is always, "Worship God, my Lord and your Lord."

The passage, nine verses, is accompanied by about five pages of small-print commentary, not to be skipped. Regarding verses 110–11, for instance, we learn of the Islamic tradition's teaching on the Holy Spirit as either the Archangel Gabriel or the Spirit arising from God's command, the "Spirit of the Holy." Jesus is well-versed in all the sacred books; the "Book" may be taken as God's word, perhaps first of all the uncreated Qur'an before its worldly revelation and then too the Torah as well (see also 2:129, 3:3–4, 48–53). His disciples are "submitters," true "Muslims." Regarding 112–15, even when these apostles believe, they also balk and demand a sign, a meal from Heaven—or, it is because of their faith that they hunger for the meal from Heaven. Jesus can bring down this heavenly food; Jesus is the one to whom God will listen, whose requests God honors. Noting that Christian readers will see here hints of Jesus's multiplication of the loaves (and, I would add, a distant gesture toward Jesus himself as the Bread from Heaven), the commentary notes that it also prompts in Muslim readers a sense that Jesus and his apostles were sharing a meal after a fast like Ramadan; or, it is the Christian 'id, joyful meal from Heaven, perhaps even the Eucharist, a meal of faith, grounded in the piety and obedience of Jesus.

And finally, regarding the most difficult, 116–117: Perhaps, the commentary says, this section is prompted by the mention of disbelief in the previous section. True belief knows that Jesus directed worship only to God, not to himself. Perhaps the Prophet had the impression from Christians he observed that Mary too was worshipped, and so that piety too is restrained here: "Jesus indicates that he bears no responsibility for such exaggerations of his or his mother's status, but rather than directly denying that he commanded his disciples to take him and his mother *as gods apart from God*, he demonstrates an attitude of proper comportment before God by offering a response of perfect humility, saying he had *no right* to utter such a thing." God knows Jesus, but even Jesus does not know his God as God knows him. In leaving judgment in God's hands—punishment and forgiveness mark God's justice and mercy—Jesus leaves the door open, the commentary says, to God's patience with those who see Jesus as God, a confusion, in the qur'anic way of thinking, that is not the grievous sin of idolatry.

In the previous two paragraphs, I have stated all too briefly some complicated matters and touched on issues that Muslims and Christians, and those dedicated to Christian-Muslim dialogue, have debated and written about for centuries. My summary, meant to give a taste of the book itself and of *The Study Quran*'s notes to readers without the text in front of them, does not substitute for the necessary personal study—study that, I am suggesting, must come before a return to doctrinal disputes, and that through learning will leave no space for border-closing bigotry and interreligious violence that stresses only differences, replacing divine mercy with human zealotry.

The Jesus we discover in Sura 5:110–18 is not the Jesus of the New Testament and Christian faith; and yet—in the text's strong sense of God, God's providence, God's special relationship to Jesus, and Jesus's own utter fidelity and obedience to the word of God he came into the world to witness—we are not as far from Christian faith as one might have thought. We encounter here the piety of Jesus, a Jesus reverenced in the Qur'an with his mother, beyond the Christian communities of the time. We who are Christian can, in light of this text—and the many others in the Qur'an—prayerfully return to the Gospel with a fresh eye, not to abandon our faith, but to recognize that instructed by the Prophet, we become able to see more of Jesus than we had seen before. If Muslims do the same, and study the Gospels with open hearts, we will all be better off, and ignorance will lose another battle.

Merry Christmas to all; peace be upon all God's people; may the borders remain ever open to God's mercy.

Reading the Book of Mormon, Part I

September 14, 2012

Cambridge, MA. As readers will know, I am hopeful about the possibility of our learning across religious boundaries. I have repeatedly explained that this has nothing to do with losing Christian faith, or learning things that are wicked and harmful; it is a matter of seeking truth where it is to be found, finding God in all things, and without undue fear, welcoming wisdom where I find it. I do however also believe that this learning has to be done in small doses. Keep away from vast generalizations about the faith traditions of others, study carefully, and attend to what you learn. Reading can get you quite far in interreligious learning, respect, and wisdom—and hence in being a better Christian too.

I am not a scholar of the Latter-Day Saints; I have previously only skimmed the Book of Mormon, and the copy I have is from a hotel room. Since this is a blog, I also cannot take vast amount of time for this series. I have also learned that much of what one might want to know about Mormons is not actually in the Book of Mormon but in later sources, traditions about Joseph Smith, Brigham Young, and later figures.

One cannot directly explain Mitt Romney by reading the Book of Mormon. One cannot explain everything everyone has heard about Mormons by reading the Book of Mormon. I also learned that one cannot assume that all Mormons have studied the book carefully; it is difficult reading, boring, something like reading First and Second Chronicles. Somewhere I read the words of a Mormon who cheerfully confessed that many a Mormon has fallen asleep trying to read through the Book: "If you were to take all the Mormons who have fallen asleep reading the Book of Mormon and lay them down, head to toe—they'd be more comfortable."

But one must start somewhere. I can read, think about what I read, and so I have; and it is this minimal learning that I will share. I delved into the book, with a bit of help from online sources (I use the online version, posted by the LDS), and from the seven little volumes that comprise *The Reader's Book of Mormon* (Salt Lake City: Signature Books, 2008). I decided that I would focus on the Third Book of Nephi (hereafter 3 Nephi). This is, as far as I can tell, one of the best places in the Book of Mormon for a Christian reader to begin. I encourage you to read it for yourself. If there are Mormon readers of this blog, I welcome their insights and corrections into what follows.

The Third Book of Nephi stands near the end of the Book of Mormon. If one can trust the little introductions to each chapter that one finds in the online version, the events in the book occur just after the death and resurrection of Jesus, during the time when he appears to his scattered disciples. The early chapters (and several later chapters) recount the fickleness, internecine violence, and eventual return to faith of the Nephites, who are basically good, over against their dark enemies, the Lamanites. Heroes and villains come and go, bearing the most exotic names. (Nephi is a simple name, compared to Giddianhi, Zemnarihah, and Gidgiddoni.) It seems that Nephi was a prophet from among the Nephites, who seem to be one of the (additional) tribes of Israel. On and off they are faithful and terrible sinners, and they live and suffer through a history and lives parallel to the Israelites of the Bible. In this parallel Nephite story, they meet Jesus and hear his preaching. At this point they may not yet be in North America, but they will be there in the near future.

Nephi speaks in part of 3 Nephi, and Mormon himself also speaks on occasion. Mormon, a witness to everything, begins writing down what happens and the words of Nephi—with a devotion to Christ that seems typical of 3 Nephi:

> Therefore I have made my record of these things according to the record of Nephi, which was engraven on the plates which were called the plates of Nephi. And behold, I am called Mormon, being called after the land of Mormon, the land in which Alma did establish the church among the people, yea, the first church which was established among them after their transgression. Behold, I am a disciple of Jesus Christ, the Son of God. I have been called of him to declare his word among his people, that they might have everlasting life. And it hath become expedient that

I, according to the will of God, that the prayers of those who have gone hence, who were the holy ones, should be fulfilled according to their faith, should make a record of these things which have been done. . . . I am Mormon, and a pure descendant of Lehi. I have reason to bless my God and my Savior Jesus Christ, that he brought our fathers out of the land of Jerusalem, (and no one knew it save it were himself and those whom he brought out of that land) and that he hath given me and my people so much knowledge unto the salvation of our souls.

(5:10–20)

Nephi also speaks for himself:

And it came to pass that Nephi—having been visited by angels and also the voice of the Lord, therefore having seen angels, and being eye-witness, and having had power given unto him that he might know concerning the ministry of Christ, and also being eye-witness to their quick return from righteousness unto their wickedness and abominations; Therefore, being grieved for the hardness of their hearts and the blindness of their minds—went forth among them in that same year, and began to testify, boldly, repentance and remission of sins through faith on the Lord Jesus Christ.

(7:15–16)

But what to make of all this so far? First, it is very complicated and seemingly realistic about the violence and evils of human life. Second, it is a history that is parallel to the biblical accounts; the Book of Mormon seems to strive to be a complement and parallel, rather than an alternative to either the Old or New Testaments. Too much? Think at least of the words ending John 20: "Now Jesus did many other signs in the presence of his disciples, which are not written in this book." Third, the drama seems designed to point to Jesus as the center of it all. By the time we reach chapter 9, amid all the violence endlessly ravaging the land of Nephi, it is also known that in Jerusalem Jesus has died on the cross and, it seems, risen. It is here that Jesus begins to speak to the Nephites, in words meant at least to echo, if not to repeat, Gospel words:

Behold, I am Jesus Christ the Son of God. I created the heavens and the earth, and all things that in them are. I was with the Father from the beginning. I am in the Father, and the Father in me; and in me hath the

Father glorified his name. I came unto my own, and my own received me not. And the scriptures concerning my coming are fulfilled."

(9:15–16)

Reading Mormon II:
When Jesus Came to America

September 22, 2012

Cambridge, MA. I tell my students that one way to figure out what one thinks is to start writing, and to a large extent that is my experience with my short and sporadic study of 3 Nephi in the Book of Mormon these past weeks. My hope is to convince some readers of this blog at least that one can begin with no knowledge of another religion, clear one's mind and heart for a moment of all one's heard, and by quiet reading get quite far in beginning to understand it and learn from it. Yes, it is correct, as pointed out by those who commented on my first blog, that there are many other ways to study the Latter-Day Saints. But those are harder ways, and often superficial ways. I have never found it all that easy to sort through historical documents, oral traditions, and various popular accretions to a tradition; Googling rumors is hardly the way to trace the life of a lived religion. And so I stay with the text—to each his own—and return here to 3 Nephi.

I must first express my gratitude to Grant Hardy, a distinguished scholar of the Book of Mormon, for emailing me and making several good suggestions. Key is his work in editing *The Book of Mormon: A Reader's Edition* (Urbana: University of Illinois Press, 2003), an edition that makes the (unchanged basic) text of Mormon so much easier to read. You can still consult the online edition and the *Reader's Book of Mormon*, which I mentioned last time, but if you want just one book, buy Dr. Hardy's edition. He also pointed out to me that Krister Stendahl, a distinguished New Testament professor at Harvard, dean, and later bishop of Stockholm, wrote "The Sermon on the Mount and Third Nephi," a very interesting and learned essay, particularly regarding its use of the Sermon on the Mount (you can find it online and in *Reflections on Mormonism* [1978]). So there it is: I am the second Harvard professor, also not a Mormon, to zero in on 3 Nephi as the place for a Christian reader to start.

Last blog I ended with the Nephites hearing the voice of Jesus: "Behold, I am Jesus Christ the Son of God. I created the heavens and the earth, and all things that in them are. I was with the Father from the beginning. I am in the Father, and the Father in me; and in me hath the Father glorified his name. I came unto my own, and my own received me not. And the scriptures concerning my coming are fulfilled" (3 Nephi 9:15–16). This voice of Jesus scolds the people for their incessant violence and commands them to come to him. This appeal is followed by a great silence across the land, after which the people, further rebuked, repent. Mormon offers an aside to the reader, as it were, to point out that all of this fulfills the old prophecies: it is all true, it is all happening right here (3 Nephi 10).

Chapter 11 is rather beautiful. The people "were marveling and wondering one with another, and were showing one to another the great and marvelous change which had taken place" (11:1). There follows another heavenly voice, but this time, though the voice (as it were) pierces them, at first they do not understand it at all. Only on the third time do they understand the words, "Behold my Beloved Son, in whom I am well pleased, in whom I have glorified my name—hear ye him." But then Jesus himself comes down into their midst and stands right there before them. He invites them to see the nail holes in his hands and his feet and the cut in his side. Bolder than Thomas, they put their fingers in the holes and know that it is indeed Jesus. And then the mission begins.

Jesus calls Nephi to him, who bows down and kisses the feet of Jesus. After this, Jesus calls a group of twelve to whom he gives the mission to preach, baptize, and teach, though without any rancor: "And there shall be no disputations among you, as there have hitherto been; neither shall there be disputations among you concerning the points of my doctrine, as there have hitherto been. For verily, verily I say unto you, he that hath the spirit of contention is not of me, but is of the devil, who is the father of contention, and he stirreth up the hearts of men to contend with anger, one with another. Behold, this is not my doctrine, to stir up the hearts of men with anger, one against another; but this is my doctrine, that such things should be done away" (11:28–30). In her introduction to this volume of the *Reader's Book of Mormon*, Linda Hoffman Campbell comments that here "the text spoke to me more directly than any other passage ever had in the volume. I thrilled at the personal, intimate invitation for each person to come, one by one, to touch the Savior's wounds" (xxii).

What to make of all this? Remember, all this occurs in the new world, after the ascension. The risen, ascended Jesus has come here to speak even to this scattered tribe in this far-off place. Unusual. But it is clear that the author wants to stress continuity: this is the same Jesus who is the Son of the Father, who died on the cross, and whose mission has not changed at all. The point seems not to privilege this group of Nephites in America as possessed of a special revelation that goes beyond the Bible, but to say that they too received "the same revelation" that is described in the canonical Gospels.

Now it is true that few of us reading a blog for *America*, the magazine, will be able to imagine that Jesus appeared in America, the land, in 34 CE or so. But many of us have believed that the same Jesus who lived and died and rose and taught in Palestine in those days does, as it were, truly visit us here and now. Like these Nephites, we believe ourselves to encounter the risen Christ and to hear not a new revelation, our own secret teaching, but the same message that reverberates through the ages, for those who will come to Christ when his voice finally makes sense to them. This is, in a way, what the *Spiritual Exercises* are all about too. It may seem very odd to think that Jesus came to America several millennia ago, but I know people, as do you, who believe it very odd to think that Jesus visits us in our times of prayer, or that we can converse with Jesus in our heart of hearts. In its own way, the Book of Mormon creates the space, albeit as somewhat literal space, for this. Even if 3 Nephi takes a step too far for most of us, we should be able to be sympathetic with its conviction that Jesus is here, now.

That 3 Nephi is all about "the same experience" and "same teaching" occurring all over again is confirmed in chapters 12–18—and for this I rely on Grant Hardy's clear subheadings—where, in Jesus's long teaching to the gathered crowd, he first (in chapters 12–14) repeats large portions of the Sermon on the Mount (Matthew 5–7). See Stendahl on this very point. In my next blog, I will say a bit more on this teaching and the added chapters of teaching, blessings, and the instruction on the Eucharist that fill out chapters 12–18—after which, "it came to pass that when Jesus had touched them all, there came a cloud and overshadowed the multitude that they could not see Jesus. And while they were overshadowed he departed from them, and ascended into heaven. And the disciples saw and did bear record that he ascended again into heaven" (18:38–39).

Reading Mormon III:
The Sermon on the Mount Reimagined

October 6, 2012

Cambridge, MA. As I was preparing this third reflection on the Book of Mormon, it became clear to me that working in smaller scale—just a focus on 3 Nephi, just this one of all the books in the Book of Mormon—is indeed giving me more work, not less. Reading closely does open new vistas—all of it becomes interesting—and gives many insights and raises many questions. There is certainly no exception here, as I face the prospect of saying something about the three appearances and three sermons of Jesus in 3 Nephi. (Once again, I recommend Grant Hardy's *The Book of Mormon: A Reader's Edition*, and likewise his *Understanding the Book of Mormon*.)

Here I will comment just on the first of Jesus's three teachings. In 3 Nephi 12–14, Jesus in essence repeats the Sermon on the Mount (Matthew 5–7). I mentioned last time that Krister Stendahl wrote a learned article on the similarities and subtle differences between the Sermon in Matthew and the Mormon version of the Sermon. No very large change stands out, but small changes appear frequently enough. I suggest that you read these chapters with your New Testament nearby, using Hardy and Stendahl as aids. If you read closely, you will appreciate both the continuity and changes. In my own brief study—a start, though hardly decisive—I did not discover any smoking gun, such as would prove something decisive about Mormons or about the use of the New Testament in the Book of Mormon.

It is interesting that 3 Nephi then puts the Sermon in a new, broader context. In chapter 15, Jesus explains in more detail how he fulfills yet does not terminate the Law and the Prophets; that the Prophets still matter seems particularly important, because some of the prophecies have yet to be fulfilled. In any case, it is all Christocentric, as he declares, "Behold, I am the law, and the light. Look unto me, and endure to the end, and ye shall live; for unto him that endureth to the end will I give eternal life. Behold, I have given unto you the commandments; therefore keep my commandments. And this is the law and the prophets, for they truly testified of me" (15:9–10).

In the same chapter Jesus explains in some detail the meaning of John 10:16 ("I have other sheep that do not belong to this fold . . .") These words are taken to be coming true in accounts such as 3 Nephi, where Jesus is now visiting and teaching a wider set of listeners, beyond those reported in the Gospels: "And verily, verily, I say unto you that I have other sheep, which are not of this land, neither of the land of Jerusalem, neither in any parts of that land round about whither I have been to minister. For they of whom I speak are they who have not as yet heard my voice; neither have I at any time manifested myself unto them. But I have received a commandment of the Father that I shall go unto them, and that they shall hear my voice, and shall be numbered among my sheep, that there may be one fold and one shepherd; therefore I go to show myself unto them" (16:1–3). After further teachings on the scattered people of Israel and the gentiles, Jesus drives home the point by quoting Isaiah 52:8–10 ("The Lord has bared his holy arm before the eyes of all the nations; and all the ends of the earth shall see the salvation of our God"). According to 3 Nephi, this good news will, in a rather direct manner, reach all nations, including in the "new world," among the Nephites.

In chapter 17—quite unusual, but by my tastes also quite beautiful—Jesus heals the sick and then blesses the children. The latter rather tender scene ends in a rather dramatic fashion:

> And he spake unto the multitude, and said unto them: Behold your little ones. And as they looked to behold they cast their eyes towards heaven, and they saw the heavens open, and they saw angels descending out of heaven as it were in the midst of fire; and they came down and encircled those little ones about, and they were encircled about with fire; and the angels did minister unto them.

(17:23–24)

In chapter 18, Jesus feeds the people with bread and wine, urging them likewise to do the same in memory of him. He exhorts the crowd to prayer, to letting their light shine forth, and to allowing strangers to join their community. With even stronger words to his chosen disciples, he again recommends a cautious openness to the admission to outsiders and strangers to the community.

And then he departs:

> And it came to pass that when Jesus had made an end of these sayings, he touched with his hand the disciples whom he had chosen, one by one, even until he had touched them all, and spake unto them as he touched them. And the multitude heard not the words which he spake, therefore they did not bear record; but the disciples bare record that he gave them power to give the Holy Ghost. And I will show unto you hereafter that this record is true. And it came to pass that when Jesus had touched them all, there came a cloud and overshadowed the multitude that they could not see Jesus. And while they were overshadowed he departed from them, and ascended into heaven. And the disciples saw and did bear record that he ascended again into heaven.

(18:36–39)

Make of all this what you will. These further sayings and activities of Jesus seem not to be meant to be sensational, nor to outdo and marginalize traditional Christians—the rest of us. This first extended teaching of Jesus is interesting to me because the whole of it represents a way of maintaining continuity with the Gospels even while seeking to authenticate—spiritually, by teaching—the message to this new community in the new land. Obviously, there is no need for a Christian reader, such as me or most of you, to be won over by this imagined arrival of Jesus with his new/old teaching and actions. But neither do I see any reason why we cannot listen, learn, and benefit from what we hear.

After all, it is in the Gospel of Mark, not the Book of Mormon, that we hear these words:

> John said to him, "Teacher, we saw someone casting out demons in your name, and we tried to stop him, because he was not following us." But Jesus said, "Do not stop him; for no one who does a deed of power in my name will be able soon afterwards to speak evil of me. Whoever is not against us is for us."

(Mark 9:38–40)

Reading Mormon IV:
Prophecies and Ecstasies

October 9, 2012

Cambridge, MA. This is the fourth of five reflections on 3 Nephi, the book within the Book of Mormon in which Jesus most prominently appears. My goal from the start has been to show that one can pick up a book of another religious tradition, read it carefully, and draw some meaning from that reading, and that this reading does not require a lifetime of study, such as I have devoted to Hinduism. I expect careful reading but try not to impose too highly elite standards. These blogs are about careful amateur reading. I don't mind the range of comments on my previous entries, even those that have been fierce and daunting. I am indeed irenic in my reading, because that is my approach and also fits with what I have been finding in 3 Nephi. Since over and again I have recommended that readers do their own reading—the text is available in many forms—I am by no means pretending to monopolize how 3 Nephi is to be read. I read with a certain peacefulness, but others can read in the opposite way if they wish: is "polemic" still the opposite of "irenic"? I have only recently come across *Third Nephi: An Incomparable Scripture* (2012), edited by Andrew C. Skinner and Gaye Strathearn, and also *A Tale of Two Cities: A Comparison Between the Mormon and the Catholic Religious Experiences* (1980) by William Taylor.

After the long first sermon that incorporates most of the Sermon on the Mount, Jesus departs, and the community dedicates itself to prayer for a time. Jesus returns (3 Nephi 19:15) and commands them to pray all the more intensely, even as he steps aside and prays for them to his Father. The result is a greater intensity in prayer:

And it came to pass that when Jesus had thus prayed unto the Father, he came unto his disciples, and behold, they did still continue, without ceasing, to pray unto him; and they did not multiply many words, for it was given unto them what they should pray, and they were filled with desire. And it came to pass that Jesus blessed them as they did pray unto him; and his countenance did smile upon them, and the light of his countenance did shine upon them, and behold they were as white as the countenance and also the garments of Jesus; and behold the whiteness thereof did exceed all the whiteness, yea, even there could be nothing upon earth so white as the whiteness thereof. And Jesus said unto them: Pray on; nevertheless they did not cease to pray.

(19:24–26)

In turn, this prayer is followed by another multiplication—or creation—of bread and wine for a Eucharist, which seems to move the assembly to a kind of ecstasy—as if in the Spirit, though the Spirit seems unmentioned—in the presence of Christ: "Now, when the multitude had all eaten and drunk, behold, they were filled with the Spirit; and they did cry out with one voice, and gave glory to Jesus, whom they both saw and heard" (20:9).

At this point, Jesus quotes a number of passages from the Hebrew Bible/Old Testament: Isaiah 52, Micah 5, Isaiah 54, and Malachi 3–4. It is not possible or necessary to quote extensively from these texts to get a feel for the teaching communicated here—check your Bible—but two may be of help. Jesus quotes fierce, dire words from Micah 5 on the coming vengeance and fury, including these:

And I will cut off the cities of thy land, and throw down all thy strongholds; And I will cut off witchcrafts out of thy land, and thou shalt have no more soothsayers; Thy graven images I will also cut off, and thy standing images out of the midst of thee, and thou shalt no more worship the works of thy hands; And I will pluck up thy groves out of the midst of thee; so will I destroy thy cities. And it shall come to pass that all lyings, and deceivings, and envyings, and strifes, and priestcrafts, and whoredoms, shall be done away. For it shall come to pass, saith the Father, that at that day whosoever will not repent and come unto my Beloved Son, them will I cut off from among my people, O house of Israel; And I will execute vengeance and fury upon them, even as upon the heathen, such as they have not heard.

(Mic 5:11–15, as quoted in 3 Nephi 21:15–21)

He then adds some new words of hope for those who repent:

> But if they will repent and hearken unto my words, and harden not their hearts, I will establish my church among them, and they shall come in unto the covenant and be numbered among this the remnant of Jacob, unto whom I have given this land for their inheritance. And they shall assist my people, the remnant of Jacob, and also as many of the house of Israel as shall come, that they may build a city, which shall be called the New Jerusalem. And then shall they assist my people that they may be gathered in, who are scattered upon all the face of the land, in unto the New Jerusalem. And then shall the power of heaven come down among them; and I also will be in the midst.

(21:22–25)

At the end of Jesus's quotation of the prophecies, he concludes with Malachi 3–4, the text that stands at the end of the Old Testament in the Christian ordering of the text, ending with the words: "Behold, I will send you Elijah the prophet before the coming of the great and dreadful day of the Lord; And he shall turn the heart of the fathers to the children, and the heart of the children to their fathers, lest I come and smite the earth with a curse" (Mal 4:5–6, as cited in 3 Nephi 25:5–6).

Now it may seem most peculiar to the Christian reader that Jesus is quoting the prophets, and quoting them as predictive of the future, not simply as finished, fulfilled in himself. But in the "ecstatic" context of this second teaching by Jesus in 3 Nephi 19–26, the point seems to be that none of the words of the Bible are merely past; they continue to voice the future, the ups and downs of the human race, the patience and wrath of God with his people, and the never-quite-extinguished hope for salvation. This reminds me of many a retreat I have been on over the years, and the many more Sunday readings I have heard, in Advent and throughout the year, that use ancient prophecies to illumine our present and our future: the "old words" of Scripture are ever new, telling us about where we and our world are going "today." The old texts, if truly the word of God, are always about the future too. 3 Nephi deflects one criticism—that Jesus is somehow superfluous, as if nothing has changed—by picturing him as speaking the words: all the prophecies are his words, words of the Word. 3 Nephi does not intend to leave Jesus behind.

3 Nephi 26 brings the second sermon (there is a brief third one, which I will not get into here) to a conclusion with several interesting

points. First, there is a powerful confession of the totality of the revelation given by Jesus:

> And he did expound all things, even from the beginning until the time that he should come in his glory—yea, even all things which should come upon the face of the earth, even until the elements should melt with fervent heat, and the earth should be wrapt together as a scroll, and the heavens and the earth should pass away.

(26:3)

There follows a prediction of a last judgment, but then another confession of how overwhelming the teaching of Jesus is: "And now there cannot be written in this book even a hundredth part of the things which Jesus did truly teach unto the people" (26:6). There is a Johannine aura to many of the words of Jesus in 3 Nephi, and these particular protestations seem to echo the end of the Gospel according to John:

> This is the disciple who is testifying to these things and has written them, and we know that his testimony is true. But there are also many other things that Jesus did; if every one of them were written down, I suppose that the world itself could not contain the books that would be written.

(John 21:24–25)

Mormon, recording all this, repeats this idea in his own words:

> And now there cannot be written in this book even a hundredth part of the things which Jesus did truly teach unto the people; But behold the plates of Nephi do contain the more part of the things which he taught the people. And these things have I written, which are a lesser part of the things which he taught the people; and I have written them to the intent that they may be brought again unto this people, from the Gentiles, according to the words which Jesus hath spoken.

(26:6–8)

The chapter ends with the spectacle of the children testifying:

> And it came to pass that he did teach and minister unto the children of the multitude of whom hath been spoken, and he did loose their tongues, and they did speak unto their fathers great and marvelous

things, even greater than he had revealed unto the people; and he loosed their tongues that they could utter.

(26:14)

And this in turn seems to echo Jesus's words in the Gospel:

> But when the chief priests and the scribes saw the amazing things that he did, and heard the children crying out in the temple, "Hosanna to the Son of David," they became angry and said to him, "Do you hear what these are saying?" Jesus said to them, "Yes; have you never read, 'Out of the mouths of infants and nursing babies you have prepared praise for yourself'?"

(Matt 21:15–16)

Enough of quotes within quotes in this very long, too long blog. But I hope to have given the willing reader enough to think about, even as you may—as you should—read 3 Nephi yourself and assess what I've included and left out. I will offer just a few concluding comments in my next and very last excursion into 3 Nephi; the book is often called, a reader pointed out, "the Holy of Holies of the Book of Mormon."

Reading Mormon V:
To the Future

October 19, 2012

Cambridge, MA. This is the last of the reflections I am posting on 3 Nephi, the book within the Book of Mormon where Jesus appears three times, shortly after the resurrection, to a remnant community in a new land that is taken to be (though of course never named as) America. This study—not my field—has been a rewarding if arduous experience, with a real learning curve indeed. As professors are wont to do, I've accumulated new books: several editions of the Book of Mormon (be sure to use Grant Hardy's *The Book of Mormon* if you intend to read it); Hardy's *Understanding the Book of Mormon*; *Third Nephi: An Incomparable Scripture*, edited by Andrew Skinner and Gaye Strathearn, which is a set of lectures and studies by committed Mormon scholars, meant for readers within the church itself; and for a comparative perspective, Rev. William Taylor's *A Tale of Two Cities: A Comparison between the Mormon and the Catholic Religious Experiences.*

I've said nothing about this year's presidential election, the prospect of a first Mormon president, but I think we are better off for knowing what is inside texts such as 3 Nephi before speaking on the topic. Previously I had nothing much to say when asked whether it would be good to have a Mormon president; now I have something to say. Yes, it is true there is much to know about the Latter-Day Saints not contained in the Book of Mormon, and yes, one cannot predict the policies of a politician today simply from reading sacred texts of her or his tradition; after all, no Christian president's policies have been simply the teachings of Jesus in the Gospels. But I feel more certain of myself when I find myself in conversation about religion and the elections now that I know something of substance from within the Mormon tradition. If a President Romney were to serve the American people while conscientiously following the teachings of Jesus in 3 Nephi, we would have a foundation both for understanding Mr. Romney's policies, and then, if we have doubts, for shaping a substantive religious-political dialogue—and argument—about those views alongside the many other views that inspire people of faith in today's America. So think of reading 3 Nephi before you vote.

But I will finish by turning to the closing chapters of 3 Nephi. After the departure of Jesus and the testimonies of the children at the end of 3 Nephi 26, Jesus appears yet again in chapters 27–28 for a further teaching to the leaders of the community: they are to preach the gospel, be gathered in a church named by the name of Jesus, and remain faithful to the teachings he has given on these three visits. Nine of the twelve apostles are granted the prospect of a swifter end to their ministries on earth, whereas three remain to perform their ministries and preaching for a much longer time. In the end, the fate of these three is rather mysterious, a kind of twilight presence near but not quite in this world, and as if to come again:

> And now behold, as I spake concerning those whom the Lord hath chosen, yea, even three who were caught up into the heavens, that I knew not whether they were cleansed from mortality to immortality. But behold, since I wrote, I have inquired of the Lord, and he hath made it manifest unto me that there must needs be a change wrought upon their bodies, or else it needs be that they must taste of death. Therefore, that they might not taste of death there was a change wrought upon their bodies, that they might not suffer pain nor sorrow save it were for the sins of the world. Now this change was not equal to that which shall take place at the last day; but there was a change wrought upon them, insomuch that Satan could have no power over them, that he could not tempt them; and they were sanctified in the flesh, that they were holy, and that the powers of the earth could not hold them. And in this state they were to remain until the judgment day of Christ; and at that day they were to receive a greater change, and to be received into the kingdom of the Father to go no more out, but to dwell with God eternally in the heavens.

(3 Nephi 28:36–40)

In chapter 29, after the departure of Jesus the third time, Mormon offers his own stern exhortation that all must hear and take to heart all that has been said here. The brief chapter 30 is a final word, an exhortation to the Gentiles to listen and repent:

> Hearken, O ye Gentiles, and hear the words of Jesus Christ, the Son of the living God, which he hath commandeth me that I should speak concerning you, for, behold he commandeth me that I should write, saying: "Turn, all ye Gentiles, from your wicked ways; and repent of your evil doings, of your lyings and deceivings, and of your whoredoms, and of your secret abominations, and your idolatries, and of your murders, and your priestcrafts, and your envyings, and your strifes, and from all your wickedness and abominations, and come unto me, and be baptized in my name, that ye may receive a remission of your sins, and be filled with the Holy Ghost, that ye may be numbered with my people who are of the house of Israel."

(3 Nephi 30:1–2)

From a critical theological and spiritual perspective, none of this is beyond question; we need not merely accept this harsh dismissal of the gentiles—as if to be a gentile is to be wicked—and we can disagree and raise questions without shifting from accepting everything to rejecting everything. Certainly, I learned from my Jesuit high school and the Jesuit novitiate on that we honor our own faith and our own scriptures and traditions in part by respectful but insistent questioning. Today, we can similarly honor and respect one another's traditions by a serious learning across religious borders that nonetheless leaves room for real questions. One might conclude from these last words in 3 Nephi that the gentiles are merely a sinful lot who need to be saved but have nothing to teach and show. But this is no more a solution to the challenges of religious pluralism than any single Christian judgment on other religions might be. But here too, the conversation, including the challenges and difficult learning, occur after and not before respectful consideration; disagreements are best when they are specific, and one of the very best ways to become specific is to read, study, and take to heart the texts that have come down to us. The Third Book of Nephi has much to teach every *America* reader and, I venture to add, the Latter-Day Saints too will benefit when people like you and me pick up 3 Nephi and read it respectfully and intelligently.

PART II

In Dialogue

So What, If Barack Hussein Obama
Were a Muslim?

May 23, 2008

Cambridge, MA. I cannot resist a quick comment on the debate about Barack Obama's religion, particularly regarding those who attack him by implying he *is* a Muslim, and those who defend him by vigorously assuring us that he is *not* a Muslim. Granting that we need to be sensitive to people's religious commitments and make neither too much nor too little of their religious belonging, and granting that Mr. Obama definitely is a Christian, we should still be asking: why would it be a problem if he were a Muslim? I think it would be a fine thing for the United States, and for Christians in the United States too, if one day soon we elect a Muslim president.

Yes, it goes without saying that Islam and the West have had a troubled history, some Muslims have not lived up to the best of their tradition, and some Muslims, however devout, should not be elected to high office. But yes too, it also goes without saying that the Christian West has had a troubled history with respect to the rest of the world, some Christians have not lived up to the best of their tradition, and some Christians, however devout, should not be elected to high office. But good men and women of every faith should be welcomed to compete for and win the presidency. It would be a fine thing to have a Muslim president. Perhaps someday we will also have a Hindu president, a Jewish president, and presidents belonging to other larger and smaller faiths.

But for now, while recognizing and welcoming the fact that Mr. Obama is a practicing Christian, let us not think or speak as if being a Muslim would somehow diminish a candidate's readiness or worthiness for office. Being a Muslim politician is a good thing, needing no apology. In fact, I suggest that there are no good reasons for wishing to exclude Muslims from our highest office.

The Hindus Are—Here!

July 2, 2008

Cambridge, MA. June 27–30 I was in Orlando, Florida, for the Seventh International Conference of the World Association of Vedic Studies (WAVES). This is a meeting of Hindus who meet every second year for a conference that is in part a cultural event, in part a confidence-building gathering, and in part an academic conference. Most of those who came reside in the United States, including a good number of young Hindus born in the West, but some participants came all the way from India. Some are professors in religious and philosophical studies, while others are professionals in other fields but nonetheless deeply committed to their religion's well-being. I was there because I was invited to give the keynote address on the first night, on how the Hindu community can contribute to religious life here in America. I stayed the entire weekend, knowing that I would enjoy the gathering and also learn much from the papers given and from the conversations at meals and between sessions. As an event, WAVES is a sign of a community that has "arrived" and is big enough to sponsor serious conferences, and yet is stilling finding its way.

The Hindu community is well established in the United States, and is largely very successful in business, technology, and the sciences; there are now Hindu temples in most large and medium-sized American cities, as well as many educational organizations, cultural centers, publications, websites, and so on. If one also counts yoga as a practice most closely connected to Hinduism, we can say that Hinduism is already having a great impact in the United States, and this influence is destined to increase in the next decades. In saying this, I realize that some readers will be not used to thinking about the Hindu community, since we usually think of Islam and Buddhism as the "newly arrived" religions that are having the most influence on our society. Perhaps it is a blessing, though, that Hindus are simply here and flourishing, without any great fanfare or headlines. But of course, with success there are also growing pains. One underlying theme of the weekend was the need to keep continuity between Hindu life and values in India and here in America—a problem that surely every immigrant group has faced. How do the venerable values of Hindu traditions still matter in today's world? More implicitly, there seemed to be an underlying concern to sort out a love-hate relationship with the West: there is the legacy of colonialism, of centuries of Christian attacks on idolatry, paganism, and the perceived deficiencies of the Hindus, and a feeling that even today, Indian culture and religion are little appreciated and understood in the West.

So how to become increasingly American, while yet having doubts about the goodwill and welcome of the West and its Christian majority? How to fit in, while keeping traditional values? Should the community keep its distance from the American mainstream? Should Hindus try to build their own educational system, as did Catholic immigrants in the nineteenth century? Do temple worship and other ancient traditions need in some way to be "Americanized"? The major point I tried to make in my opening address was that Hindus are now well placed to play an important role in the religious life of the United States for reason such as these: They come from India, a large, diverse democracy in which many religions have long been present, and so our religious diversity is less of a shock than it is for many others. Hindus bring with them cultural and religious traditions that are complete, rich in literature and poetry, philosophy and theology, ritual and art, and so can remind us of how to live an integral familial and cultural life. The Hindu traditions are intellectually as well as religiously rich, and Hindus can bring intelligence to American conversations on religion and spiritual vigor to the intellectual life. Although Hindu beliefs cover a wide spectrum of views about the divine, many of the largest and most vigorous are theistic traditions, dedicated to a supreme God, or Goddess, or supreme divine couple; so despite expectations to the contrary, they can share with Christians a sense of God as Person and of God's will, grace, and salvific involvement in the world. Everything is in a sense different, of course, and there will be points of real contrast, but Hindus and Christians who believe in God can talk to one another on many levels.

So, I said, it is possible and important for Hindus to make themselves heard in American life, showing that their beliefs and values are not exotic but quite relevant as we look to the future. I concluded by admitting that we—Americans and Catholics too—can learn much from Hindus, and together we can work to make our country a better, healthier, more spiritual environment. Over the weekend, I had many conversations with individuals, and we did in fact find much to talk about. It helped, of course, that I have studied Hinduism for many years, but it was clear that we really did have something in common. My being a Catholic priest and Jesuit was a plus, not a negative, in part because Indians have great respect for the Jesuit educational institutions of India, and also because they have the highest respect for Jesus as a divine teacher. I would like to think that my experience over the weekend and similar positive encounters across the country indicate that Hinduism is an underestimated blessing in American culture, and that we should not neglect Hindu-Christian relations even when other interreligious relationships seem to press upon us more vigorously. The Hindu-Christian dialogue is, in a way, the neglected dialogue that promises to teach us much about ourselves and America and about our Hindu sisters and brothers; I am confident it will grow during the decades to come. Note to the reader: if you do not know much about Hinduism, you might start with Vasudha Narayanan's *Hinduism: Origins, Beliefs, Practices, Holy Texts, Sacred Places* and her edited collection (with Jack Hawley) *The Life of Hinduism*.

Contra Interreligious Ignorance

October 13, 2008

Cambridge, MA. The *New York Times* for Monday, October 13, 2008, caught my eye three times over with items of sadness that pertain to interreligious relations and interreligious thinking. On the front page, one article talked about the campaign dedicated to spreading the rumor that Barack Obama is a Muslim. A second frontpage story recounted the ongoing violence against Christians in Orissa and efforts to "reconvert" Christians to Hinduism. Inside, a third report narrated recent violence against the tiny Christian minority in Iraq, in the town of Mosul.

Each story is of course a world unto itself, and each case requires a different kind of analysis. But among other things, they all show us how ignorant people can be of other people and their religions and, in these cases at least, the apparent unwillingness—rooted in ignorance—even to imagine properly the religious worlds of others. The campaign against Barack Obama may be nothing but a deliberate effort to confuse voters—since Mr. Obama is a lifelong Christian—but it also bears with it the unexamined presupposition that there is something wrong with being a Muslim, or that it would be bad for the United States to have a Muslim president. The violence in Orissa is certainly not simply a matter of misunderstanding, but there is a duty—not just now, when the fires are burning, but as a regular part of life—for people who live as neighbors to understand the faith and practices of those neighbors. Majorities in particular are obliged to learn from religious minorities, not just tolerate, to some extent, their existence. The same applies to the situation in Iraq. It is very good for communities to live without fighting, but it is not enough, since such a "peace" today may erupt in warfare tomorrow. It is necessary to keep banishing ignorance by learning from one another, allowing the ideas, images, practices of our neighbors to enter deep inside us, so that we will find it very hard, perhaps impossible, to treat the other as a stranger, threat, or enemy.

Yes, it is also obvious that no amount of book learning guarantees that ill will, violence, and lying will not occur. Sin is not reducible to ignorance. But since we can learn and can open our minds, it becomes culpable ignorance not to keep learning about one another. If Christians and Hindus and Muslims—in these particular stories—knew more of one another's traditions in detail and close-up, we would surely be more disposed to respect one another and resist the sin of interreligious animosity.

Of course, this applies to the people we read about in the newspapers, but it applies as well to us when we may be tempted to judge those we are reading about, "as if" we understood how they think, what they believe. If we are Christians, in particular, we have much to learn from our Hindu and Muslim neighbors, and we need not to judge them on the basis of the violence of the few.

Karl Barth, Thomas Merton:
Forty Years Later

December 5, 2008

Cambridge, MA. It is the end of the semester and a busy season, but I cannot help but interrupt to remember two great Christian intellectuals and writers who died forty years ago, on December 10, 1968: Karl Barth and Thomas Merton.

Karl Barth (1886–1968), one of the greatest Christian theologians of the twentieth century, was a Swiss Protestant theologian in the Reformed tradition. In a series of weighty tomes—most importantly his commentary on Saint Paul's Letter to the Romans and his vast *Church Dogmatics*—he sought to rethink Christian identity in radical fidelity to the word of God while rejecting all the distractions and cultural detours into which European Christianity had fallen in the twentieth century.

Thomas Merton (1915–1968), perhaps Catholicism's greatest spiritual writer in the twentieth century, captivated a generation by the story of his conversion and journey into monastic life, *The Seven Storey Mountain*. During his years in the Trappist monastery of Gethsemane in Kentucky, Merton returned to writing, winning readers everywhere with his poetry, his meditations on the spiritual life, his search for the true grounding of the Christian life in contemplative wisdom, his growing concern in the 1960s for a socially just Christian witness, and finally, at the end of his life, his turn to the East, his growing interest in the religions of Asia, particularly Buddhism.

Barth and Merton shared a deep Christian concern, a dissatisfaction with bourgeois Christianity, and a sense that we must be radical, given over to faith, if we are to be alive spiritually at all. And, of course, they are different in so many ways: Barth was Protestant, a professor who died at the end of a long and fruitful life, a stubborn witness to the uniqueness of Christianity; Merton, who become Catholic, died tragically in an accident in Bangkok, Thailand, when he was only fifty-three, a stubborn witness to our need to let go, to go forth from our comfortable Christian security, to find God in real spiritual abandonment, freedom, even beyond what the church has imagined possible. Barth, though thoughtful and complex in his reflections on religion and the religions of the world, seemed to hold back at the prospect that God could really work in and through people of deep faith in other religions; Merton kept pushing us to be deep enough spiritually that we might be spiritually alive, meeting one another across religious boundaries, unafraid.

And both died on December 10, 1968. Looking back forty years, I think it true to say that we need both these versions of Christian witness: deeper, radical Christian commitment and a fearless going forth into interreligious encounter. Our world today does not need simply a repeat of Barth's view of the word in the world, while reading Merton without reading Barth leaves us in danger of skipping lightly over the radical paradox and scandalous particularity of Christian faith.

2008 is a different world. But on Wednesday, let us honor the memory of both of them by taking bolder, riskier Christian steps into interreligious learning, without expecting Barth or Merton to tell us what comes next in our moment of history.

The Loud Silencing of Roger Haight, SJ

January 24, 2009

Cambridge, MA. Just after Christmas I splurged online, searching used-book sites for the seven volumes of Hans Urs von Balthasar's *Glory of the Lord*, his wonderful and extensive reflection on the aesthetic element in our theological and spiritual knowledge, our apprehension of the beautiful in our encounter with God. Since I had previously collected the five volumes of the *Theodrama* and the three volumes of the *Theologic* (all in English, I confess), I now have the entirety of this grand work. I love pulling a volume off the shelf and reading what Balthasar says about one of the Christian tradition's great monastic or lay writers, mystics or theologians. I hope this interest of mine is not surprising. I am, as you will know by now if you have been reading me at this site over the past year and more, a comparative theologian, and I spend a good part of my time studying classical Hindu literature. To some, surely, this means that my tastes are liberal. But in fact, my study of India has only deepened my respect for our classical tradition, and so too for solid, serious, deep theologians such as Balthasar among the Catholics and Karl Barth among the Protestants.

I mention this because I have felt the need, for weeks now, to say something about the recent Vatican decision to bar Roger Haight, SJ, from teaching and writing. I am sure you know about the case against his *Jesus Symbol of God* and the Notification several years back. Since then, Fr. Haight moved from teaching at the (then) Weston Jesuit School of Theology, has continued his writing, and also taught at Union Theological Seminary in New York, a Protestant seminary. But now, he is barred from further theological writing and from teaching, even at Union. The reason, it seems, is that he is not willing to recant and disown what he wrote in *Jesus Symbol of God*.

Now, as I have just said, it is Balthasar I love to read, and he is the one I find inspiring to me in my interreligious, comparative theology. While I admire the solidity and clarity of Fr. Haight's writing, *Jesus Symbol of God* but also his other works too, it is not the kind of theology that helps me very much in the work I do. I also recall that when Fr. Haight's book came out, it quickly became a hot topic in theology, and the early reviews of it were quite varied, some positive and some quite critical of this or that aspect of the book. I recall hearing Fr. Haight speak about reactions to the book at the Catholic Theological Society annual meeting one year. Even at that point, there were some twenty-five or thirty reviews of it (the author in me dies of envy), and many of them engaged in the academic delight and duty of giving Fr. Haight a hard time. I have taught the world religions chapter of it in my classes, first at Boston College and now at Harvard, and while there are things I admire greatly in the chapter, both my students and I found cause to quarrel with the book and the way in which Fr. Haight explains the relation of Christ, Christianity, and the world religions.

I think the mixed reaction to the book was a fine thing, and am fairly sure that Fr. Haight himself had no problem with it. Such are the ups and downs of academe, and it is through this critical exchange, sometimes gentle, sometimes harsh, that our work gets done. And so I was disappointed years ago by the investigation of the book and its author, by his dismissal from the seminary faculty, by the Notification, and now by this silencing. Even though I do not agree with all that Fr. Haight wrote, I thought the academic give and take was the best way to sift out the good and the bad, what would endure and what would be forgotten, in *Jesus Symbol of God*. The Notification was quite clear; the issues were known and widely discussed. I had hoped that with this clarity we had all moved on, Fr. Haight to other writings and the rest of us to our own ways of reflecting on Christ today, wiser by this whole experience. But silencing?

Silencing can be a terrible thing, but not always. In Hinduism, for millennia it has been a way of spiritual discipline, a hard practice by which a sage (*muni*) goes down inside themselves and finds still deeper and more lasting insights into reality. Such sages, by their austere penance of silence, were known to build up a terrible inner heat (*tapas*), which could erupt at the most unpredictable moment. Perhaps Fr. Haight, who has taken the silencing with seeming equanimity, will likewise accumulate *tapas* for all of us. Global warming, indeed.

But on the larger scale, there are two things I really want to say. First, silence is one thing, being silenced another. It is true that I have no inside information on the Vatican, no connections, no influence, and cannot pretend to speak as an expert on Vatican matters, and it is not my place to imagine telling Rome what to do. But it does seem to me counterproductive to have silenced Fr. Haight at this point, all the more drawing attention to him and his work. He shall be remembered forever, in theological circles, for this event too. Perhaps there are places in the church where the silencing will produce a desired caution and even fear in theologians, but here in the United States, my guess is that it is mainly the Vatican that comes off looking bad; such is our media and how we instinctively take sides with the underdog in disputes like this. Correct me if I am wrong in guessing this outcome. It would have been better, wise, kinder, more productive, more charitable, to let Fr. Haight write what he wants and teach at Union, letting the rest of us, who do really care about Jesus and his meaning for us, judge whether Fr. Haight is to be in our bibliographies and on our reading lists or not. Silencing simply interrupts and delays the necessarily slow process of making up our minds on his writing; there is simply no way to substitute for the learning each of us must do, sooner or later.

Second, and although, again, I really do love reading Balthasar and will go back to reading him and the Hindu theologian Ramanuja (about whom I wrote in Advent) once I am finished writing this blog, I am all the more and endlessly edified by Fr. Haight as intellectual, writer, teacher, and Jesuit. He wrote what he thought, in simple and austere honesty, working out his ideas step by step. He wrote, as he saw it, for the church and for his students. It is, I would think, impossible in his eyes to take it back, to recant, to change what he wrote. And so, without "going public" with denunciations to the press or media campaigns or inflammatory websites, Fr. Haight has simply accepted this austerity of silence. As if to say, without saying, something like this: "I accept the decision of the Vatican, I will be silent. I cannot unwrite what I wrote or unthink what I thought, but neither is it my place to change the rules so late in the game. I stand by my book, and I will not speak." In this way, Fr. Haight, whose ideas

I share only somewhat, is all the more one of my intellectual heroes. We need to think and write honestly, as if everything is at stake, no matter what the cost. Fr. Haight doing this, and taking all this so seriously (as has the Vatican, to be sure), upgrades the value of what all theologians do and reminds us of what is at stake in our daily thinking, writing, praying, teaching. It is important enough to fight about and to suffer for.

I do hope the silencing ends soon, even as Fr. Haight's *tapas*, the fruit of his silence, sets us all ablaze. But for now, what he does not say has become the most eloquent way for him to keep teaching us.

The Death of a Swami, and His Bliss

May 8, 2009

Cambridge, MA. On May 3, Swami Sarvagatananda, a senior monk of the Ramakrishna Vedanta Society and longtime head of the Vedanta Society in Boston, died at the age of ninety-six. While his death did not make national headlines, it is good to reflect for a moment on his life and its meaning, so I will tell you something about him and what his life can mean for us.

First, the facts, succinctly detailed in the notice I received:

Born in 1912, Swami Sarvagatananda joined the Ramakrishna Order in 1935, received mantra-diksha [an initiation akin to first vows] from Revered Swami Akhandananda Maharaj in the year 1936, and sannyasa [final vows] from Revered Swami Virajananda Maharaj in 1944. He came to the United States in 1954 to assist Swami Akhilananda Maharaj. He became the head of the centers in Providence and Boston in 1962, and continued in that position until 2001 (Providence) and 2002 (Boston). Even after his formal retirement from active work, he continued to meet with devotees and to guide them. His untiring service to the Vedanta work in Boston and Providence, his unbounded love for devotees and, above all, his sterling spiritual life have been, and will continue to be, a source of inspiration to all.

The record in itself is impressive: more than seventy years as a monk and more than fifty years of unbroken service to the members of the Vedanta Society and a wider mix of Hindus who came to the Boston and Providence Centers. It would be very hard to count up the number of Sunday services, weekday classes in basic Hindu and Vedanta texts, classes at Harvard and MIT for interested students and staff—plus the many hours of counseling he offered to anyone coming to seek his guidance.

Yet still more can be said about this compassionate, joyful, and loving man. There is a 1996 volume that was published in Swami's honor, *The Lamplighter: Swami Sarvagatananda in the West*. It contains about fifty reminiscences from friends and disciples who knew Swami over the years: testimonies to his wisdom, love, sense of humor, and his great joy and perennial hope for the spiritual advancement of the human race in its quest to realize God. It is clear that he was able, again and again, to communicate divine love and joy to people of all kinds and backgrounds. (I was honored to contribute my own reflection to the book.)

Reflection on Swami's legacy reminds us to keep our balance in reflecting on pluralism. The diversity of religions is of course a major factor facing all of us today, and we know that discussions of religious diversity have been delicate and difficult in most Christian churches. Even if almost all of us admit by now that diversity will be with us for a very long time—it shows no sign of waning, quite the opposite—we still and rightly want to avoid a mindless relativism, and we do not want to settle for a merely tepid witness to our faith. So we need to think carefully about diversity and how we are to interpret our faith amid the many religions.

But even as we take both our own and other religions seriously, it is important to admit more simply that there are all around us graced persons who radiate wisdom and compassion, in their own words in their own religions. We need to study the theologies and great texts, indeed, but we need also simply to recognize and honor the presence of saintly persons who in some simple but most evident way witness to divine love. Swami, in his very long life and ministry in Boston, is one of these persons: however we explain Christ and the world religions, we have to be diligent in our gratitude for persons such as Swami Sarvagatananda. Our faith must make room for his faith.

Swami invited me to preach at the Center three times, and I found it a moving spiritual moment to be with him at those Sunday services. In turn, I invited him to the Boston College campus as well, and each time he came, even when he was quite elderly, he made a powerful impression on our students. His message was simple and stressed the value of knowledge of the self, the possibility and value of spiritual progress, the presence of God everywhere, and the harmony of religions.

I remember one time when a student asked him if he thought there would ever be a single world religion, Hindu or other. He replied simply, "I hope not! The ways to God are rich and varied, we learn about God and ourselves by enjoying all the many ways people seek and find God. May there always be thousands of paths to God!" It seemed to me that he really did live up to the charism of Sri Ramakrishna, the nineteenth-century mystic and saint who found God—his Mother, Kali—in all things and was the inspiration for the Vedanta Society to which Swami gave his life. Swami also lived up to his name, Sarva-gata-ananda: "He whose bliss (*ananda*) reaches (*gata*) all things (*sarva*)," or perhaps better, "He whose bliss is in the One who has reached everywhere." Or, as a Jesuit might say, "He who finds God in all things."

I close with a prayer found in *The Lamplighter*:

We offer our salutations to the All-Loving Being who endows all beings with consciousness. We meditate on the Lord, who is the origin of the universe. Lord, you abide in all. You are all; You are Existence, Knowledge, and Bliss. Salutations unto You! May the World be peaceful. May the wicked become gentle. May all creatures think of mutual welfare. May their minds be occupied with what is spiritual and abiding. May our hearts be immersed in selfless love for the Lord. Peace, peace, peace be unto all.

A Hare Krishna Swami Tells All

May 21, 2009

Cambridge, MA. I recently wrote a remembrance of a very old swami, Swami Sarvagatananda of the Ramakrishna Vedanta Society. This time, I write of a middle-aged swami who is by all accounts still very active in his ministry.

A while back, I was sent a copy of *The Journey Home: Autobiography of an American Swami* and asked if I could review it for a journal. I declined to do an academic review of the book since (a) it would be difficult to describe and assess for an academic journal so vivid a first-person account; (b) the scholar to do it would have to be expert in the era of spiritual journeys to the East and all kinds of details of religious places and practices in North India, as I am not; and (c) the book is documentary in a way, and one would also have to draw on the skills of an investigative reporter to report responsibly on what one read. But I trusted the person sending me the book, and I promised that instead I would call your attention to the book in this blog.

It is certainly an interesting story, the spiritual journey of one Richard Slavin who, born in 1950 in Chicago in a Jewish family, goes on a pilgrimage through India when he is about nineteen—one among many seekers who went to India in the 1960s and 1970s. His trip was most eventful, and he had numerous adventures that are strikingly and entertainingly recounted in the book: large animals, unfriendly policemen, dubious and saintly teachers, exotic spiritual sites, robberies, mishaps on the road, friendships made and lost. Like many a spiritual autobiography, the external events and details turn out to be the setting for the author's inner quest. His journey is a humbling, learning-to-be-poor series of tests that push him toward living by faith alone.

Like any pilgrim, he does not see all of this along the way, but in retrospect sees how he was being quietly, insistently drawn toward God all the time.

After and through it all, he discovers the spiritual path he has followed since, becoming a dedicated swami—an ascetic, teacher, and leader—thereafter to be known as Radhanath Swami. The photographs in the book make all this clear, reminding us of a series of gurus and swamis such as Swami Rama (founder of the Himalayan Institute of Yoga), J. Krishnamurti (wise man, teacher, writer), and Maharishi Mahesh Yogi (who guided the Beatles, among others). He is also pictured with Mother Teresa in one photo and with the Dalai Lama in another.

Radhanath seems deliberately—in the preface, on the cover—to be quiet about the fact that he is a swami in the International Society for Krishna Consciousness (ISKCON), the Hare Krishna. Not that he hides the fact, since the climax of the book is, after all, his encounter with A. C. Bhaktivedanta Swami Prabhupada, charismatic founder of ISKCON. It is wise in a way not to make much of this connection on the cover and instead to highlight the fact of this very human journey of spiritual discovery and grace. Readers might be distracted too soon by the overlay of an exotic tradition that remains ill-understood by most Americans. But to me, it is worth noting that ISKCON is by now a rich spiritual and theological tradition that, despite its difficulties and growing pains along the way, is maturing as a community true to its ancient Indian roots. Thus my decision to draw attention to the ISKCON connection in the title of this piece. Radhanath gives flesh and blood and spirit to ISKCON; this book is a good way to begin to understand what it means to be a Hare Krishna—willing to devote oneself to praise of God (Hare! Krishna!) who is present as Krishna, young, so very near in flesh and blood, loving as he is loved.

I must confess too that the book enabled me to think back on my own spiritual journey; he and I are the same age, and by eighteen, right in New York City, I had ventured my own lifelong commitment to God, a great gift I received. In a way, we were both saved by a spiritual insight into the love of God that carried us through those tumultuous years and kept us going. In other ways, our lives have obviously been very different: born a Catholic, I am still a Catholic; I have never really been on a quest for God, who seems to have been there—here—from the start. I am a professor, and my many visits to India have been by comparison extremely low-key and uneventful;

readers of my autobiography would have to put up with descriptions of bookstores, research centers, and pictures of me sitting first at a typewriter, now at my computer.

There is much to be said about Christ and Krishna, of course. For centuries, books have been written on the topic, and Radhanath's book does not seek to resolve the theological questions that arise when two great monotheistic traditions meet (for I do think ISKCON is a monotheistic form of Hinduism). In such an encounter, however reverently and graciously engaged, those of us who are Catholic will still have tough questions to ask ourselves, about God's work outside the visible church, in persons and in traditions. Reflective swamis too will want to ask about the meaning of God's work in the lives of faithful Christians. But it will help all of us to hear each other's stories, how God was found, how God finds us when we are young and keeps after us for a lifetime. We should imagine a kind of dialogue—not of religions or theologies this time—but of women and men of different traditions who, upon reaching a certain age, tell their stories with a certain wisdom and humor and in that way speak to one another across religious boundaries. In particular, Radhanath's account invites us baby boomers (readers of this blog included) to look a little deeper into how we found, lost, kept, gave away, were given (back) the faith—how we managed to find the 1960s a time of grace and wonder. For this invitation, we can all be grateful to Swami Radhanath. But judge for yourself; take a look at the book, see what you think.

Pope Benedict's Most Generous Interreligious Vision

June 2, 2009

Cambridge, MA. Years ago, when I was a young professor, I was asked by a journal editor if I wished to review a certain scholarly book in my field. It was the 1980s and email was not yet common, so I duly checked off "yes" on the postcard the editor had sent me and mailed it back to him. The book did not come, and I assumed he had found another reviewer. It was only two years later that I received yet another note from the same editor, calmly asking, "Did you decide yet if you want to review that book?" Apparently, the postcard had gone astray. So I did the review, and within two more years, it was in print. No rush, at least in certain halls of academe. I recall this story in self-defense because it is only now, with the semester done (and Harvard's graduation finally upon us), that I am getting around to writing a few comments on one of the addresses Pope Benedict gave during his tour of the Middle East a month ago. You will find no breaking news in blogs I write, to be sure, but I do have a good memory for things to go back to for a second reading.

You can find all or most of the speeches from his trip at the Vatican website, and I recommend you go back and read them. But the one that caught my eye is from May 11, "Meeting with Organizations for Interreligious Dialogue," held at the Notre Dame Center in Jerusalem. Addressed to a group of leaders of different religious organizations dedicated to dialogue—all men, it seems—the speech is irenic and welcoming, entirely ecumenical. It is, in essence, an appeal to people of all religions to remain confident in the positive power of religion, the value that religions and faith bring to society, and the need for people of faith, committed to the truth revealed in their traditions, to speak confidently in the public realm.

It is remarkable how inclusive the address is. God, who spoke to Abraham, is ever involved in the world. His word irrupts in our world, and he calls us all on a journey of faith, whether we belong to "the synagogue, church, mosque or temple." We, all of us, are invited into "a culture not defined by boundaries of time or place but fundamentally shaped by the principles and actions that stem from belief." We need to focus on the truth, and not be blind to the many ways in which it appears: "Although the medium by which we understand the discovery and communication of truth differs in part from religion to religion, we should not be deterred in our efforts to bear witness to truth's power." Obedience to the truth and serious reflection on it open us up rather than narrowing our horizons: this obedience "in fact broadens our concept of reason and its scope of application, and makes possible the genuine dialogue of cultures and religions so urgently needed today."

Even when differences among religions are evident, "they need not overshadow the common sense of awe and respect for the universal, for the absolute and for truth, which impel religious peoples to converse with one another in the first place." While God gives us the truth, we do not necessarily receive it all, all at once: "Although the medium by which we understand the discovery and communication of truth differs in part from religion to religion, we should not be deterred in our efforts to bear witness to truth's power." Differences are an opportunity: "they provide a wonderful opportunity for people of different religions to live together in profound respect, esteem and appreciation, encouraging one another in the ways of God."

Throughout, the pope is intent upon speaking in the most inclusive terms. Indeed, it is amazing that while "God" is referred to thirteen times, the words "Jesus" and "Christ" do not appear at all in the address. Surely the pope is no relativist, but here he is quite comfortably speaking of God and truth without mention of Jesus Christ.

What can we draw from all this? While we ought not to exaggerate its importance—it is just a speech, not an official teaching—neither can we imagine that the pope was merely catering to his audience and saying merely politic words. These practical, heartfelt words, spoken to a diverse religious group, must be taken as characterizing how Benedict thinks we ought to speak in a pluralistic setting: there is truth, there is God, there is a power in our many forms of faith that we must welcome and share. What divides us is less important than what brings us together.

The skeptical reader might say that the pope is speaking to a limited audience—Jews, Muslims, and Christians—and that he does not mean to suggest that we share faith and the experience of God with Hindus, for instance. What he really means, it might be said, is that "God" is "our Jewish, Muslim, Christian God," not "their God." But so narrow an interpretation is wishful thinking, since we cannot take the words with which he concludes as excluding believers in still other religions: "Prompted by the Almighty and enlightened by his truth, may you continue to step forward with courage, respecting all that differentiates us and promoting all that unites us as creatures blessed with the desire to bring hope to our communities and world. May God guide us along this path!" There are certainly Hindus who strongly believe themselves to be monotheists, and a straightforward reading of Benedict's words indicate that he agrees: our God "irrupts" into our world over and again, and what a lost and weary world needs most is more and not less faith. We—who believe in God, in "the synagogue, church, mosque or temple"—must speak the truth God gives us. No believer in God is excluded from this "we." Or, even more simply, perhaps no one at all can be excluded.

That is to say, it is now perfectly clear that the post-Vatican II openness to religions is real, true, and irreversible. While we will continue to quarrel about the details, and necessarily keep probing deeper into the mystery of Christian witness in a world of many religions, there is no turning back. The basic question may come in several forms, but a very good formulation of it is the one the pope asked in Jerusalem: "Can we then make spaces—oases of peace and profound reflection—where God's voice can be heard anew, where his truth can be discovered within the universality of reason, where every individual, regardless of dwelling, or ethnic group, or political hue, or religious belief, can be respected as a person, as a fellow human being?"

A Hindu-Christian Conversation Begins

October 2, 2009

Cambridge, MA. I have been blessed with many Hindu friends over the years, and many of them have also challenged me and raised difficult questions that were good for me to answer. Well, now is a chance for a bit of online dialogue with a new Hindu friend. One person has commented occasionally on my posts as simply MMK—but through emails he and I have had some great conversations. It occurred to me that as a kind of experiment, we could share some of our dialogue with you. So let us introduce ourselves.

You know me already, I hope—Catholic, Jesuit, priest, Harvard professor. My partner in dialogue is Sri Murali Manohar. He is a Hindu in the United States and, like many of his generation in their thirties and forties, is an engineer who has more than a passing interest in religion and the dialogue among religions. But I now turn things over to Mr. Manohar, to introduce himself:

My interest in dialogue is shaped by many factors—my personal background, one shaped by a religious family and a technical education; my witness to the "religious others" characterization of aspects of Hinduism, positive and negative; my reception and response to academic scholarship of traditions; and questions about theological implications of pluralism and dialogue.

I seek to gain an understanding of dialogue, with concerns that are distinct from the Christian concerns and presentation of dialogue—a view of dialogue that is usually framed by Christians where the ground rules preserve a nonnegotiable place for Christ and where the emphasis significantly privileges texts, textual comparison, and Christian doctrinal matter. By contrast, much of Hinduism is embodied in its domestic, oral, performative, artistic, and visual representations—in addition to texts.

I also seek to understand the ultimate individual value of dialogue beyond its important and practical value of social goodwill. My conversations with Professor Clooney start with these important questions that are not merely theoretical but of the sort that one encounters in very real, reflective, jarring, and comical ways in a country like India, as well as among Hindu and Christian friends in the United States.

This blog is the introduction, and the next will be a post by Mr. Manohar. In turn, I will respond to him, and then in the fourth, possibly final, post he will respond again to me.

A Hindu-Christian Conversation II:
A Hindu View of Dialogue

October 9, 2009

Cambridge, MA. For the next several weeks, I will share this space with Sri Murali Manohar, who has kindly agreed to share with me a conversation on matters of interest to Hindus, Christians, and, hopefully, to a wider range of readers interested in religion today. What follows is Mr. Manohar's first entry. After a week or so, I will respond to him. We will also be watching for your comments to see what you think.

Mr. Manohar writes:

In this post, I will present some of my questions and understanding of two aspects of dialogue—pluralism and theological value. I will press forward with the provisional acceptance of the importance of dialogue itself; it is to discover the "why" and "how" that I like to dig deeper. While at it, I do recognize that there are both scholarly and visceral responses that question the importance of dialogue itself; there are those who believe that dialogue is passé and has reached a stalemate of sorts, and there are those who believe—as one of the comments, from Siva, on the introductory post shows—that it is futile and perhaps even corrosive. To be sure, there is a kind of dialogue where conversion, apologetics, or self-definition is the objective. I wish to focus on different questions first.

Let us begin with deeply religious people. There are many deeply religious people in India who are scholars, but not in the way that Western academia looks at scholarship in religion. When theological dialogue is not academic or scholarly, it usually presents itself as little more than an introduction to the other or a romanticized travelogue. What of deeply religious people who don't care about theological dialogue? Are they just unenlightened laggards? If not, why not? Popular presentations of dialogue and pluralism also assume that the reader readily accepts—or at least ought to accept—the universal importance of dialogue and tends to talk down to those who don't, those whose concerns may be personal sadhana (spiritual discipline), not dialogue. Many learned scholars are content to stay away from any such theological dialogue for fear of superficiality and distraction. How should we articulate the value of dialogue to the individual, beyond platitudes and appeals to social goodwill, so that we may sincerely seek to be enriched by the engagement of such religious people in theological dialogue?

Next, let us consider the issue of learning from the other. What are the epistemic implications and consequences of dialogue and studying texts of the other? There are two kinds of charges that this leads to. One of need and adequacy, the other of misappropriation.

What is it of value that we seek to learn, that is to be found from the other, if our own system is complete and adequate? We often encounter this argument: our belief already has a privileged, if not exclusive, means of salvation; in such a situation, isn't it a mere distraction to spend time studying world scripture? We also see a different form of this charge—that we tend to read a lot more into the tradition of the other than is due. Indeed, there are many who have tried a contrived higher narrative of religions, and often such dialogue is viewed with caution. One encounters in such dialogue an enthusiasm to show a transcendent unity of religion. There is quite a wide range of this attitude, from deeply reflective and philosophical essays where the authors freely borrow or import ideas from Hinduism to Christianity and vice versa (see, for example, works of Ananda K. Coomaraswamy) to popular TV dramas where "Om" is chanted the way Christians say "Amen" at the end of something significant. This leads to the charge of misappropriation. How does one defend against the charges of misappropriation of theologies and practice? Many Hindus charge inculturation with such misappropriation, but even more broadly, much of the new age relativism stems from such misappropriation of theologies.

And finally, how far should dialogue go? As we study texts and traditions of the other, we immediately begin to see the aesthetic, allegorical, and hermeneutic aspects of that tradition. Should dialogue go just as far as joint study? As neighbors and friends, we often participate in the reli-

gious festivals of each other. Should this be the boundary of dialogue, where we are comfortable with each other's customs? What about praying like the other? There are many charismatic preachers and gurus who include public universalistic prayer—prayers that include chants and hymns from many traditions—as part of their rituals. Is a sincere and serious acceptance of such universalistic prayer possible in personal life? After all, prayer is one's deeply personal response or appeal. What of visits to the other's place of worship—beyond the initial novelty of how the other prays, is it anything other than a tourist attraction or a political statement? In the end, when it comes down to the individual, how is this useful to one's bhakti *[devotion],* upasana *[meditation], or* sadhana *[way of spiritual practice], to one's personal spiritual discipline in one's own tradition?*

A Hindu-Christian Conversation III:
A Christian Reply

October 13, 2009

Cambridge, MA. In the last entry in this blog, Mr. Murali Manohar offered some very thoughtful and perceptive reflections on interreligious learning, definitely worth your reading. So please read his remarks before proceeding with this entry. Here I take up just a few of his major points. First, one reminder: while I do think and write and, indeed, live as a Roman Catholic, I do not speak for the church in any official sense, nor even for most Catholics. I speak rather as one Catholic who has devoted much time and energy to reflecting on Hinduism and writing from that experience. But this is not to say that the Catholic context is unimportant. It helps me do what I do. In recent decades, the church has made it clear that God's salvation is available to all and does not teach hell or damnation for non-Christians. Yes, that salvation is mysteriously mediated through Jesus Christ, but it is, really, for all. The intellectual tradition of Catholicism is actually open, curious about the world around us, and even a believer's mind does not merely stop at particular religious borders. As a Jesuit, I have been taught to find God, to expect to find God, everywhere, including in religions other than my own. But now for some brief comments in response to Mr. Manohar, as just one Catholic respondent:

Mr. Manohar writes, *"What of deeply religious people who don't care about theological dialogue? Are they just unenlightened laggards?"* I agree that there are people, deeply religious, who are not interested in interreligious learning; there is no reason to be condescending toward them. It is only when people state that there is nothing to be learned from other religions that I question them back, since often we work with stereotypes about the other and find excuses not to learn. But if a person simply chooses not to undertake interreligious learning for personal reasons, I respect that choice.

"How should we articulate the value of dialogue to the individual, beyond platitudes and appeals to social goodwill, so that we may sincerely seek to be enriched by the engagement of such religious people in theological dialogue?" I can think of at least three answers. First, learning interreligiously is like other learning; being religious is no reason not to learn, to become wiser as we get older, and it would be most odd to learn in every area of life except religion. Second, being Christian does have an outward push to it: go to all nations—and if we go, we cannot go simply to teach without learning, talk without listening. Are there no good Hindu reasons for learning from people in other religious traditions? Third, many people, myself included, have found that this learning can be liberative, life-giving, able to help us to see and understand our own faith anew as we see it through the eyes of another tradition. Isn't it possible for a Hindu to profit on a deep spiritual level from another religion?

"What is it of value that we seek to learn, that is to be found from the other, if our own system is complete and adequate?" One model for interreligious learning is motivated by dissatisfaction, a sense that something is missing from what I have. Mr. Manohar is quite right—I can be perfectly happy in my own faith, finding the truth there, and interreligious learning would be difficult if it meant dishonoring the truth of my own tradition. But I do not believe that God wants us to close down our minds and not keep learning; nor do I believe that all of us have to "stay home" and learn only from our own. Truth does not begrudge truth; learning newly does not dishonor the truth we hold.

"Many learned scholars are content to stay away from any such theological dialogue for fear of superficiality and distraction." Yes indeed! It is hard enough to study one's own religion in depth, and learning across religious boundaries is very demanding. But if it is worthwhile and important, surely some of us must try.

How far should interreligious learning go? Here Mr. Manohar asks a series of wonderful questions: *"Should dialogue go just as far as joint study? As neighbors and friends we often participate in the religious festi-*

vals of each other. Should this be the boundary of dialogue, where we are comfortable with each other's customs? What of visits to the other's place of worship—beyond the initial novelty of how the other prays, is it anything other than a tourist attraction or a political statement?" This is a difficult set of questions. On the one hand, traditions obviously have their limits and do not want outsiders intruding on precious places and rituals, nor do they wish to see words, images, and acts sacred to their own tradition used trivially by others. But on the other, it is hard to draw a firm line, as if to say: learn, but do not empathize; understand, but keep your distance; study texts that have spiritual value, but keep away from the spiritual practice.

"What about praying like the other?" Here too, I agree that prayer is not a matter for casual borrowing, but I also do not think it bad if there happens to be some people of another religion who pray somewhat as we do, somewhat near to us, yet differently enough. I would not mind a Hindu coming to Sunday Mass or saying the rosary, even if they did so clearly from an enduring Hindu perspective. But Mr. Manohar, what do you think? Is the problem that too much interreligious learning is Christian-initiated, with too much of a bad history of colonialism in the background? Mr. Manohar will respond in the next entry.

A Hindu-Christian Conversation IV:
Some Final Exchanges

October 20, 2009

Cambridge, MA. Here is Mr. Manohar's latest entry to our conversation, following upon my recent reply to him, with my reply to parts of it:

MANOHAR: *In this post, I wish to consider two difficult issues—dialogue and the proselytizing imperative, and a Hindu understanding of "mediation through Christ." A few of you have already alluded to the proselytizing imperative of Christianity in your comments; this argument has its adherents and it has its detractors even within Christianity. It predisposes dialogue to familiar arguments and responses, it disturbingly evokes the past, and in the mundane grunge of the present, it creates stereotypes along with the attendant inhumanity, sentimentality, and unintelligent characterization of the other's theology and scholastic traditions. These are important issues.*

However, I seek to also understand the nature of dialogue when this proselytizing imperative and the response to it are explicitly not the defining motives. Behind this proselytizing imperative is the Christian understanding and expression of salvation, in particular when one is not explicitly united with the "body of Christ." Fr. Clooney referred to the fact that here "salvation is mysteriously mediated through Jesus Christ." In this post, I seek to understand this a little, in Christian terms but informed by my Hindu pluralism.

There are many articles and scholarly works on the effects of proselytizing—including during colonial India. And since. Fr. Clooney asks, "Is the problem that too much interreligious learning is Christian-initiated, with too much of a bad history of colonialism in the background?" there is this, but there is also the fact that much of dialogue, when it occurs in routine daily life, is dominated by the undercurrent of conversion. Ultimately, such dialogue where the argument and response is predetermined is boring and perhaps counterproductive. One of the persistent effects of such proselytizing appears to be progressive secularization and abandonment of religious traditions.

CLOONEY: As you know, Mr. Manohar, I live and work here in the United States, where the situation is different from that in India. Although I visit frequently, I cannot comment on how dialogue is carried out in particular places in India. But here, where I am stressing interreligious learning of a deeper sort, I do not see that the effort to convert is dominant; nor, if the learning is real, is the result predictable.

MANOHAR: *We know the motives of this kind of dialogue, but what are the meaningful motives for a dialogue where conversion is definitely not the motive? I can think of a few: Our children routinely encounter other religious traditions; how are we to educate them in respectful ways, without reducing the traditions of the other to literature or culture bereft of piety? When children question us about conflicting practices (cremation versus burial), how should we answer intelligently regarding the other? How are we to recognize equivalent symbolism? These are important reasons for interreligious learning, and Catholic documents too have stressed the value of learning about our neighbors and learning to better live as neighbors. As believers, how are we to understand together the validity of particular doctrines, and learn how to discern the essential aspects from the accidental ones? Such an encounter calls for the revival and appreciation of scholastic traditions of both religions.*

CLOONEY: Yes! This deeper learning, which requires study, is very important. But it takes work, on both sides, and does not lead to any predictable conclusions. Even as we engage in this study, however, our ideas are subtly changed, because we are learning to think in new ways.

MANOHAR: *Many Hindus are tentative about such dialogue, in part because of how they see the Christian understanding of salvation. Fr. Clooney mentioned that "in recent decades the church has made it clear that God's salvation is available to all and does not teach hell or damnation for non-Christians. Yes, that salvation is mysteriously mediated through Jesus*

Christ." (While this may be true, the 1953 excommunication of Leonard Feeney still appears to see this salvation in a limited way—available only because of the other's "invincible ignorance.") As a Hindu, how am I to understand this mediation?

CLOONEY: This was an important period in Catholic thinking about other religions, and indeed the time when we rejected the idea that non-Catholics all go to hell. Damnation for all non-Christians is not a Catholic doctrine. But the church has also learned a great deal in the fifty-plus years since then; I grew up in a post-Feeney church where interreligious respect was becoming an ordinary part of the Catholic way of life.

MANOHAR: *But I next turn my attention to the April 1, 2005, lecture in Subiaco by then Cardinal Ratzinger, where he explains things this way:*

> *Christianity must always remember that it is the religion of the "Logos." It is faith in the "Creator Spiritus," in the Creator Spirit, from which proceeds everything that exists. Today, this should be precisely its philosophical strength, in so far as the problem is whether the world comes from the irrational, and reason is not, therefore, other than a "sub-product," on occasion even harmful of its development or whether the world comes from reason, and is, as a consequence, its criterion and goal. The Christian faith inclines toward this second thesis [over against a first thesis, earlier in the Cardinal's document, favoring reliance on reason separated from faith], thus having, from the purely philosophical point of view, really good cards to play, despite the fact that many today consider only the first thesis as the only modern and rational one par excellence. However, a reason that springs from the irrational, and that is, in the final analysis, itself irrational, does not constitute a solution for our problems. Only creative reason, which in the crucified God is manifested as love, can really show us the way. In the so necessary dialogue between secularists and Catholics, we Christians must be very careful to remain faithful to this fundamental line: to live a faith that comes from the "Logos," from creative reason, and that, because of this, is also open to all that is truly rational.*

Thus Cardinal Ratzinger.

CLOONEY: This is vastly important, and I am glad you have picked up on the pope's remarks. There is no radical opposition between faith and reason. We do no service to the faith by refusing to be open to learning, and we do no favor to learning by disconnecting reason and Logos. But this is a venerable Indian teaching too—study, learning, and asking honest questions are all religious activities. I see no reason to do this only within the bounds of my own religious tradition.

MANOHAR: *We can also refer to Saint Augustine: "the very thing that is now called the Christian religion was not wanting amongst the ancients from the beginning of the human race, until Christ came in flesh, after which the true religion, which already existed, began to be called 'Christian.'"*

CLOONEY: This is representative of a long Christian tradition, that the truth of Christ is as old as the world, and it should open our minds. But I do not see a necessary dichotomy, as if the arrival of the true religion is also a declaration that all other religions are false religions. By the way, see the recent volume *Augustine and World Religions*, edited by Brian Brown, John Doody, and Kim Paffenroth.

MANOHAR: *To me, in light of these two positions, mediation through Christ is not about the historical accidents but of the eternal essence of Christ as Logos, as when he says in John 8:58, "Before Abraham was, I am." This is something that resonates with me as a Hindu, as a refrain heard several times in many Hindu texts. Fr. Clooney, am I reading these texts too conveniently so as to find a pluralism in them?*

CLOONEY: To be honest, I do not think the Catholic tradition separates history and the eternal; in Christ they have come together. But you are right, the Christian tradition does not reduce the work of God to what has happened at certain moments in history. There is an eternal truth and wisdom to God's work in the world, and no one can say that God does not work elsewhere, among other peoples.

Such is our Hindu–Christian conversation for now, unless you, the reader, pose some burning questions we cannot resist. But we will surely return to conversation after some time. I would like to thank Mr. Manohar for his willingness to take the time to write so thoughtfully in this way.

Archbishop Nichols at the Hindu Temple: Idol Worship?

December 18, 2009

Cambridge, MA. In November, Vincent Nichols, the archbishop of Westminster and president of the Catholic Bishops' Conference of England and Wales, visited the great Hindu temple in the Neasden section of London. As the Westminster website explains, "the visit took place on Saturday 21 November 2009 during Interfaith Week and on the birth anniversary of the worldwide spiritual leader of the Hindus who pray at the Mandir (Hindu Temple) at Neasden, His Holiness Pramukh Swami Maharaj." The archbishop toured the temple, prayed with those present for peace and understanding, and offered flowers at the central shrines in the temple.

As he left, he and the swami exchanged gifts: "Archbishop Nichols presented Yogvivek Swami with a special candle, 'a sign of the lovely light of God in our lives and a sign of the prayer which, in return, we offer to God.' Yogvivek Swami also presented Archbishop Nichols with a memento of his visit to the Mandir."

It is a very fine temple, which I had the opportunity to visit just once, when teaching at Oxford earlier in this decade. (For a full explanation of the concept of "temple"—or better, "*mandir*," see the temple's own explanation.) The founder of the Hindu community with which the temple is associated, the Swaminarayan Community, traces itself back to the eighteenth or nineteenth century in Gujarat, North India, and is inspired by the life and example of a holy man known most familiarly as Swaminarayan.

All this seems very fine, and so it was, until I received from a Hindu friend in India a link to a blog at *The Telegraph* site by Damian

Thompson, "Archbishop Nichols 'Offered Flowers at the Altar of Hindu Deities.'" Thompson was highly critical of the visit. According to Thompson, the archbishop could not have thought through the visit carefully, since when he placed flowers at the altar, he was in fact reverencing Hindu deities. As Thompson puts it,

> This is a blunder, however well-intentioned. Inter-faith dialogue is a minefield for Christian leaders, as Pope John Paul II discovered when he prayed alongside non-Christians at Assisi in 1986. This visit sounds ill-conceived from start to finish. The offer of the candle and the words accompanying it imply that Hindus worship the same God as Christians, which I would have thought even a primary-school textbook would make clear is not the case. And there's the clue, right in Westminster diocese's own press release—offering flowers at the altar of "the deities." Yes, there's a distinction between offering flowers at an altar and offering them to the gods themselves, but I think the general public and the average Catholic can be forgiven if they fail to appreciate it at once. Of course, Archbishop Vincent Nichols doesn't believe in these pagan gods (which is what they are, from a Christian perspective). But, as we saw when he allowed a chapel in Birmingham to be used for a celebration of Mohammed's birthday, his famous common sense deserts him when he is in the hands of his "inter-faith" advisers.

I am writing about this small controversy for two reasons. First, it raises some interesting questions about the limits of interfaith courtesy and respect. Second, it compels us to ask how our strongest faith beliefs affect how we relate to our religious neighbors. On the first, it seems to me that the archbishop did exactly the right thing, and rather courageously. We do better in interfaith relations when we are willing to visit each other's holy places, with an attitude of prayer and reverence; and if we visit, we must observe at least the basics of respect: removing one's shoes, for instance, or, as did the archbishop, paying our respects at the holy altars by gesture and tokens of esteem, such as flowers. I would hope that a Hindu swami visiting a Catholic Church would also come with a sense of respect, bowing or genuflecting as is appropriate, perhaps even lighting a vigil light. Words and theories are not enough; we have to be able to show, by how we act, that we really do respect one another's religions. And this is what the archbishop did.

The second question is more complex, since Thompson legitimately asks whether the archbishop was seeming to worship, or at least recognize, idols, false gods that have no place in Christianity. My understanding is this, as I have expressed many times in this space: yes, we must adhere deeply to our Christian faith, in its fullness; yes, we must avoid watering things down, and must steer clear of relativism. But it is also true that our deep faith commitment to Christ need not translate into disrespect for the beliefs and practices of others, and not visiting and not paying respect can end up being a deficiency, too. There is nothing to be gained if true believing Catholics avoid the holy places of other religious traditions and, by our body language, seem unable to respond to what is good and beautiful and holy in these other places. If we believe that there is one God who made heaven and earth, there is not, I suggest, any reason to think that our God cannot be present in the Neasden Temple, and there is no reason why we would feel compelled to stay away or to refuse to offer signs of respect upon entering the holy space. If a Hindu might conversely still feel that the Christian who comes with this attitude of reverence is too narrow and cautious, and trapped in a limited view of the divine, so be it. I cannot live by my faith while expecting others to refrain from judgments in accord with theirs.

If this makes it seem as if there is a gap between our faith in Jesus Christ and our intuitively generous respect for the deities and worship of others, it may be so. Our beliefs and our theology do not easily translate into exactly right practice; in our bewilderingly complex twenty-first century, we need not demand that the certainties of faith be acted out in a rigid, entirely logical attitude toward what is holy to our neighbors. Better to say, "I have received the gift of faith, and live by it. As I enter this temple, the God who has given me that faith walks with me. May I be as reverent and gracious as possible, for God is everywhere here too, and may God show me how to make sense of this deeply Christian reverence for our neighbors' faith." If my experience goes beyond what I can explain, that is probably for the better.

Obama, Gandhi, Jesus:
Realism and Nonviolence

December 12, 2009

Cambridge, MA. As you know, President Obama gave his Nobel Prize speech the other day in Oslo. It is a fine and thoughtful speech, well worth our meditation, so be sure to read it. It should make us proud that we have this very intelligent and insightful man as our president.

I worry, though, that his intelligent words, quite appropriate for a man who strove very hard to become president of the United States, might seem to count as universal common sense of the sort that sidelines radical nonviolence. Yes, he returns several times over to the heritage of Mahatma Gandhi (who was never awarded the prize) and the Reverend Martin Luther King Jr. (who did receive it) with great respect. But in the heart of his speech, he also looks beyond their wisdom, as if he is the greater realist:

> We must begin by acknowledging the hard truth that we will not eradicate violent conflict in our lifetimes. There will be times when nations—acting individually or in concert—will find the use of force not only necessary but morally justified. I make this statement mindful of what Martin Luther King said in this same ceremony years ago: "Violence never brings permanent peace. It solves no social problem: It merely creates new and more complicated ones." As someone who stands here as a direct consequence of Dr. King's life's work, I am living testimony to the moral force of nonviolence. I know there is nothing weak, nothing passive, nothing naive in the creed and lives of Gandhi and King. But as a head of state sworn to protect and defend my nation, I cannot be guided by their examples alone. I face the world as it is, and

cannot stand idle in the face of threats to the American people. For make no mistake: Evil does exist in the world. A nonviolent movement could not have halted Hitler's armies.

Negotiations cannot convince al-Qaida's leaders to lay down their arms. To say that force is sometimes necessary is not a call to cynicism—it is a recognition of history, the imperfections of man and the limits of reason.

To a large extent, Gandhi would have agreed with this sentiment, and the president is quite honest about his respect for proponents of nonviolence. Gandhi knew about realism; he had, after all, helped the British (albeit in nonviolent ways) in World War I, and favored the Allies in World War II. Yet, he was also clearly skeptical about well-intentioned realists who do use violence, even reluctantly, to fight evil. Sensitized to the Indian doctrine of karma, perhaps, he knew that violence leads to more violence in the long run.

My guess—since I am not a Gandhi expert either—is that he would admire President Obama's thoughtful position but also argue that those of us who have not chosen to be politicians and political leaders can do better. We are the ones who can and will not stand idle in the face of evil, letting others fight in our place. We, who are not politicians, can dare to be more radically nonviolent, drawing on a greater realism and deeper truth (in *satya-agraha*), to face down the lies, cowardice, and concealed systemic oppressions that are the perfect breeding ground for the overt violence that gains headlines only once in a while.

The inconvenience with Gandhi's position, of course, is that it is radical not merely at the moment when violence erupts but long before that. If we wish to be nonviolent, we need to find ways to live radically truthfully, without security, rejecting the comfortable ways in which societies such as ours hide injustice and oppression. We have to be bolder in refusing to live in peace while others fight wars on our behalf. As if to say: if you can do only so much, then be a political leader; if you are capable of more, leave aside political and military power and practice nonviolence as a way of life.

I think Gandhi, whose views I have merely sketched vaguely here, is more right than President Obama. Yet I close with two other comments. First, my own position is contradictory, since I do not practice what I preach (or blog). I live in a very nice section of Cambridge, Massachusetts, and I would be shocked if someone broke into my Jesuit house or my office and started taking things or threatening me—and it would be a great shock too if the police did not come, guns in hand, to protect me and save my body and my books. It is easy to imagine being personally nonviolent when others carry the guns. So the harder issue is, if I agree with Gandhi (or the Reverend King or Dorothy Day) more than the president, what are the implications for the life of the Jesuit scholar? How does a Jesuit and Harvard professor live out radical nonviolence while still a professor? How do you, my reader, live out radical nonviolence at work, at home?

Second, it is interesting to note that the president, while mentioning Reverend King, Gandhi, and others, never refers to Jesus. This is understandable, I suppose, given the audiences that presidents have to address; the president is not, thankfully, chief preacher of the United States. But we here at the *America* blog cannot get off the hook so easily. I think I am right in saying the following: Jesus, the ultimate realist, would not drop bombs on al-Qaeda hideouts, would not have gone to war against Hitler, would not shoot someone breaking into his house, would not, did not, fight even to save his own life. He would, however, keep confronting violence closeup, letting the truth be known and secret systems of wickedness be uncovered; he would keep turning the other cheek and when necessary die again, in vulnerable love, in the face of violence. Such is life: *imitatio Christi*.

While we may be secretly glad that Jesus is not president or in charge of security in the towns where we live, and while we may honestly thank God for our very good young president, if we are serious about our faith, we know deep down that it is not one government or another, whatever its philosophy, that will save the world, but rather this Jesus who refused to take up arms, who died at the hands of his oppressors.

Isn't this the truth that sets us free?

From Rome, in Tibet:
Interreligious Learning

November 6, 2010

Cambridge, MA. I spent a bit of time on this quiet Saturday rearranging books in the vain hope that by moving them around and to hitherto unnoticed corners and bookcase bottoms, I might find more space. For the rule is sure: if the graduate student spends a lot of time accumulating books with an eye toward a long scholarly career (any book gotten now might serve well in the decades to come), it is equally true that the professor accumulates books more than she or he wants: books kept from grad school, bought for this or that writing project or course, gifts from friends, and a good number of books that arrive unsolicited, sent by publishers who hope we will notice them, use them in courses, write about them.

One good result: in the midst of my reorganization, I did give due attention to two recent books deserving notice—by way of academic review, of course, but also here, in this blog, simply by way of special mention: *Catholic Engagement with World Religions: A Comprehensive Study*, edited by Karl J. Becker, SJ, and Ilaria Morali (Maryknoll, NY: Orbis, 2010), and *Jesuit on the Roof of the World: Ippolito Desideri's Mission to Tibet*, by Trent Pomplun (Oxford: Oxford University Press, 2010). Both are fine books that instruct the reader profitably, and while they are largely unrelated in theme and focus, they nicely converge to raise an important issue of interreligious import: how does fidelity to the church and Catholic tradition affect learning from other religious traditions? Or, more directly, how far can a "conservative" Catholic go in interreligious learning? How do we keep the faith and actually learn something at the same time?

The book by Becker and Morali (both professors at the Gregorian University in Rome) is a massive work of six hundred pages, with many distinguished contributors. It deals from a variety of angles with how Christianity and other religions are alike and different, focusing on the post-Vatican II period. Not claiming to be a work of global theology, it is also notably Eurocentric, not dealing much at all with what's happening in North America. In this instance, this is probably a good thing; over here we do not give sufficient notice to what European theologians are saying, and it is fair enough that this book has its center of gravity in Europe, offering a nice balance to our sense here that we are on the cutting edge of thinking about religions. *Catholic Engagement* makes a good effort to include information on religions other than Christianity, to give at least some depth to the subsequent assessment of what Christians are to think of those religions. It also has some good survey chapters on the history of encounters over the past four hundred years.

It was only when I turned to the second book, *Jesuit on the Roof of the World*, that I figured out a key element that might be added to the Becker/Morali book—namely, a still deeper, more intense, and more intellectually and existentially complex engagement with other traditions: "going there" and "learning *from* there." This very fine book by Trent Pomplun (professor at Loyola University, Baltimore) tells us the story of Ippolito Desideri (1684–1733), one of those intrepid and amazing early Jesuits who traveled to a far-off part of the world, witnessed to Christ and the Gospel, and—without any of the easy resources available today—learned deeply from Tibet's rich and deep traditions. Desideri spent the better part of a decade in Lhasa and thereabouts, when that Himalayan land was barely known at all to Westerners. He was a pioneer in describing the geography and social customs, studying the Buddhist practices and beliefs of the lamas close-up and working out, with full attention to cultural and political issues, an engagement between Tibetan Buddhism and Western Christianity. His works are invaluable even today for understanding Tibetan history and the East-West encounter, and his *Notizie istorische del Thibet* (perhaps, "Historical Narrative of Tibet") is an erudite work of scholarship that finally, with Pomplun's book, receives due attention in English. The back-cover comments by distinguished scholars of Tibetan culture and religion testify to Professor Pomplun's erudition and likewise to his commendable grasp of how theological encounter worked itself out in the eighteenth century. Father Desideri was no more a liberal (in our terms) than was Matteo Ricci in China, Roberto de Nobili in India, or Joseph Lafitau in French Canada. For him, too, missionary zeal and firm Christian commitments seem to have served as both a counterweight and energizer for deep cross-cultural learning. Pomplun studies the rhetoric of Desideri's letters and reports and notes how a certain stylized zealousness—overcome the pagan!—did not stop him from living respectfully and learning deeply during his years in Tibet.

My own instincts lead me more in the direction of Desideri's work, and not just because my first exposure to Hinduism was in the Himalayas, in nearby Kathmandu. The survey and theological reflections offered by the many contributors to the Becker/Morali volume are valuable and necessary; yet I cannot help noticing that the essays seem far more sensitive to the cultural, political, and theological complexities of Catholic thinking in Europe than to the comparable complexities of other religious traditions and cultures, which never fit neatly into the patterns the traditional theologian might wish. Desideri's life and work were a bit untidy, more questions raised than answered by his life and writing; he trod a dangerous path—icy, cold, unhealthy, way up there in the mountains, and full of insights that no one in the West can fully digest, then or now. It is right that volumes such as *Catholic Engagement* try to make good Catholic sense of that messy learning of and from other religions, in both its historical and contemporary versions. But reading Pomplun's book alongside that of Becker and Morali is a necessary help, forcing us to notice the concrete and even sacramental details of the world's religious history—a stubborn concreteness that endures beyond our control and gives life and deeper purpose to theological reflection.

It is notable, finally, that both volumes put forms of traditional, even conservative Catholicism before us: the Becker/Morali volume is, as I have said, carefully, cautiously Catholic; Desideri did not treat his Jesuit and Catholic beliefs loosely, no matter what he learned. Together, these volumes remind all of us that neither being liberal nor being conservative predictably facilitates or bars interreligious learning. However we frame our faith commitment, we still have to learn, and we have to keep the faith and make sense of it in our church and our experience; neither faith nor learning is an excuse to be lazy about the other.

But both books deserve real reviews—best left to the reviewers!

The Pope and Other Religions—
Once Again . . .

December 23, 2010

Cambridge, MA. Taking a deep breath at semester's end—a semester that has in some ways seemed an eternity—I had the opportunity to look into Pope Benedict's new book, *Light of the World*, conversations with journalist Peter Seewald that, for various reasons, have attracted a good bit of attention. Naturally, as I do with almost any book I read (excepting novels), I looked around in the book for things that were more likely to be of interest to me: So what does the pope now think about Hinduism and Buddhism? Are there warnings against meditation, yoga, and Zen? Teachings on religious diversity? But unless I've missed them, such things are not in the book, which is rather populated with more in-church issues, ranging from sex abuse by clergy to rules about condoms, to reflections on Catholic-Orthodox relations and more intimate thoughts about becoming pope. All of this is fine, of course, and the book will sell quite well. (I had to try several bookstores before finding it, and Amazon seems to be bereft of copies at the moment.) That the great religions of the East or issues of dialogue are not present needn't be an issue. We need not look to the pope to speak about everything that is of importance to Catholics today.

But in any case, one section did jump out at me, and for now (I may return to the book later, after Christmas) I will simply highlight a few pages. In the chapter entitled "Ecumenism and the Dialogue with Islam" (many chapters seem to have double topics, as if pasted together), the pope is asked to reflect on the unfortunate circumstances surrounding his 2006 Regensburg address, in which he quoted the Byzantine emperor Manuel II Palaeologus rather calmly and even neutrally, and thus seems to have no problem with the emperor reducing Islam to violence: "Show me just what Mohammed brought that was new, and there you will find things only evil and inhuman, such as his command to spread by the sword the faith he preached." The pope admits that he was not prepared for the negative reactions that occurred everywhere, as people found the words inflammatory. He had thought of the address as a "strictly academic address" but found it was not to be received as such. Of course, even academics are better off when we find ourselves among colleagues who, as our intellectual peers, give us a hard time. I suppose that at Regensburg, German good manners let the pope just say what he wanted to say, without serious debate—even if he would have been better off if some other German professor had then and there questioned him on the motive for that particular quotation.

But more interestingly, in his interview with Seewald the pope goes on to talk about the good things that came out of that unfortunate, even awful Regensburg moment. He saw himself as sticking to his position, challenging Muslims to talk more about their attitudes toward violence and their view of how reason functions with respect to their faith. He makes a link to the well-received *Common Word* statement signed by 138 Muslim scholars (that ultimately drew the Vatican into dialogue) and a series of other conversations he had—and had to have—to make peace after Regensburg.

But what is most interesting to me is that he then adds, regarding himself and Muslims, "today we are on the same side of a common battle. There are two things we have in common: we both defend major religious values—faith in God and obedience to God—and we both need to situate ourselves correctly in modernity." He willingly admits that both Catholics and Muslims face the same challenges and have much in common. It is a collegial model that he thus puts forth: we—Catholics, Muslims—have the most important things in common as we battle secularism, mindless violence, and widespread stupidity on matters religious.

In response to yet another question, he insists that old stereotypes of Christianity versus Islam are simply outmoded, since today we live "in a completely different world" than that of the Middle Ages and early modernity. No more crusades or jihads. Secularism, not another faith tradition, is today's problem: "In this world, radical secularism stands on one side, and the question of God, in its various forms, stands on the other." Accordingly, people of various religions—and here it makes no sense, in my view, to exclude Hindus or Buddhists or people of smaller faith traditions, as if the reality of faith and experience of God is just a Jewish-Christian-Muslim property—must respect the distinctive differences among religions. Even while not confusing one religion with another, we must "try to understand one another. . . . We must try to live the grandeur of our faith and to embody it in a vital way, while, on the other hand, trying to understand the heritage of others." Studying other religions is something we must do! And all this is practical: "The important thing is to discover what we have in common and, wherever possible, to perform a common service in this world."

As I have said a number of times on this blog, it is absolutely clear by now that Joseph Ratzinger, as pope, is committed to dialogue and cooperation. There is no comfort in this papacy for the closed-minded, at least on these issues. No matter how spirited his articulation of Christian truth may be, he does *not* want our apprehension of truth to be distorted into a platform from which to look down on people of other faiths; he does *not* want us to pat ourselves on the back and congratulate ourselves about how much better our religion is than other religions; and he *does* want to us to work together with people of other faith traditions on issues that concern all of us. And for that, I add, we must learn about those other traditions from their believing members.

I stress this single passage—pages 97–100 in the book—because while there is hardly anything about dialogue or meditation or the many world religions in the book, beneath the surface there is a wider sense of our duties to the whole. If we take these pages—right in the middle of the book—seriously, they become the vantage point from which to review the inside-the-church and inside-the-West issues that make up the bulk of the rest of the book and capture the news headlines.

Open our mind, think, study, learn across religious boundaries: what better thought for Christmas as we read by a pope a book entitled *Light of the World?*

Could Matteo Ricci Have Done It Today?

July 7, 2010

Cambridge, MA. As always, I am way behind on current events (insofar as I ever catch up), due to a very busy June and most recently my retreat near Dublin. Much that I would have written can be allowed to pass without observable loss. However, I did want to return to the item noted in the press back in May, "Pope praises Father Matteo Ricci, sixteenth-century missionary to China," on the four hundredth anniversary of his death. See also *America*'s fine May 4 cover story, by Jeremy Clarke, SJ, a China expert.

The pope spoke to visitors from Fr. Ricci's hometown of Macerata in Italy. His brief remarks, which can be found at the Vatican website, serve well to honor the occasion but—since I always expect greater insights from this pope in particular (whether he actually composed his comments or not)—there is more we can learn from what we read. Here I will just highlight a few points, by way of gentle arguments, with respect to the possibility of ventures such as Ricci's in today's church; don't trust this as a summary of the pope's speech, be sure to read his comments for yourself at the Vatican website.

The pope observes, "Fr Ricci is a unique case of a felicitous synthesis between the proclamation of the Gospel and the dialogue with the culture of the people to whom he brought it; he is an example of balance between doctrinal clarity and prudent pastoral action." This is easy to say in retrospect, but in that day and age, Fr. Ricci and other early Jesuits in China had to find their way experimentally, taking risks that others disapproved of, often going too far, in the judgments of their more cautious Catholic contemporaries, in making the gospel at home in China. Clarity and prudence were easier to see with hindsight.

Second, the pope notes that Fr. Ricci's perspective "consisted of a humanism that viewed the person as part of his context, cultivated his moral and spiritual values, retaining everything positive that is found in the Chinese tradition and offering to enrich it with the contribution of Western culture and, above all, with the wisdom and truth of Christ." This too is a wonderful insight, and very true, but it is, I would guess—since I am not a China expert—hard to prove in practice. How, for instance, does the foreigner, living for but a few years in China, decide what is "positive" in Chinese culture? Surely there must have been positive elements—in Chinese Buddhism, or in the more arcane parts of the Tao, or in popular religion—that Fr. Ricci missed. So too, it is tricky to distinguish where "the contribution of Western culture" ends and "the wisdom and truth of Christ" takes over. Even today, Asian theologians struggle to decide which parts of the heritage of the West can be left behind as not essential to the gospel.

Third, the pope nicely quotes Fr. Ricci, "For more than 20 years, every morning and every evening I have prayed with tears to Heaven. I know that the Lord of Heaven takes pity on living creatures and pardons them. . . . The truth about the Lord of Heaven is already in human hearts. But human beings do not immediately understand it and are not inclined to reflect on such a matter." The pope adds that in this way Ricci was making the gospel known, which is to say, making God known. My guess again is that things are a bit more complicated, since the reading of the human heart is not an easy thing to do, particularly far from one's native culture, and since the move from the "Lord of heaven"—a term with rich resonances in Chinese culture—to Jesus Christ and the gospel really requires a wisdom that discovers or makes connections in a way that is not heavy-handed or pompous, a facile identification of "their" best values with "our" best values. I mention this neither to criticize Fr. Ricci nor to disagree with the pope, but to point out how breathtaking a move it was, and is, to make such connections in a noncolonizing or patronizing way. Do we give our theologians room for these adventures today, when Rome is not a year's sea journey away but a quick phone call or email?

Fourth, the pope points out that in Fr. Ricci's ministry, "the encounter motivated by faith also became an intercultural dialogue." Here I am a little puzzled. Wouldn't the intercultural dialogue, with all the patience that requires, come first and then become, open the way to, a subsequent encounter in faith? This is not a major issue, of course, but has to do with intentions and cultural skills: how do we begin to make Christ known when we are strangers in a strange land?

Fifth and finally, the pope rightly recollects Fr. Ricci's Chinese companions, particularly Xu Guangqi, "a native of Shanghai, a literary man and a scientist, mathematician, astronomer and agricultural expert who reached the highest ranks in the imperial bureaucracy, an integral man of great faith and Christian life, who was dedicated to serving his country and occupied an important place in the history of Chinese culture," and Li Zhizao, who "helped Fr Ricci in completing the last and most developed editions of the world map that were to give the Chinese a new image of the world." This is a wonderful corrective to missionary narratives that give all the credit to the Western missionary and see natives as passive recipients of our wisdom. I would just add that Fr. Ricci surely learned a great deal from Chinese intellectuals who did not become Christian, who resisted the logic of Fr. Ricci's cultural and religious arguments, and who, in their resistance, taught him something of the difference of China, how he could never quite understand it or make it fit perfectly with his expectations. Every missionary should have room to thank those who take him or her seriously but still do not convert.

Think about it. The real point, I am suggesting, is that the very fact that we honor Fr. Ricci four hundred years after his death—just as in 2005 we honored Fr. Roberto de Nobili four hundred years after his arrival in India—is no safe thing. They were pioneers who took risks, put together things that never had been put together before, and hoped and prayed that all the religious and cultural pieces would hold together, so as to convince both the people they visited and church officials back in Europe. We honor Fr. Ricci and Fr. de Nobili most honestly, I think, by creating spaces for similar experiments today, letting novel efforts bear fruit, or not, over a longer rather than shorter period of time—being patient enough to wait, assessing their work only after a good period of time has passed.

Can we honor Fr. Ricci, then, by celebrating today the fact that right now all kinds of new and uncharted interreligious encounters are coming to birth, such as require us to figure out how to connect the gospel to our culture(s)? (This needn't be taken merely as a rhetorical question, implying a negative answer. Perhaps we do leave open this space for the interreligious imagination. But in that happy circumstance, the point is to make sure that we keep the space open, lest we kill our prophets and then later on honor their graves.)

Meeting the Divine Mother:
Amritanandamayi and Me

July 14, 2010

Marlborough, MA. I was invited to speak last evening at an appearance in one of the Boston suburbs by the famous modern Indian teacher Mata Amritanandamayi (literally, "the mother," "the one entirely composed of bliss in the imperishable")—Amma—who tours the world regularly and has been widely honored for her charitable works for the poor in many places. She is also famous for embracing those who come to see her. For she is also "the hugging guru" and is known to receive for hours at a time whoever comes to her, embracing them warmly and with a loving smile. She is also considered by many of her disciples to simply be a divine person come down to earth.

So I had the opportunity to speak a few words in introduction to her own lecture (in Malayalam, her native South Indian language, with a subsequent translation read by a disciple) and subsequent devotional hymns and a long evening of embraces. I was invited partly as a specialist in Hindu-Christian relations and partly, I suspect, as a Harvard professor. But what to do, speaking a few words before nearly one thousand people (mostly Western, most "converted" to being her devotees) gathered to see this person they know to be divine? One might turn down such a request, of course, but if one does accept it, how to speak in a way that honors the occasion, respects her loving presence and good works, while yet also communicating something of Christian love too? It is quite a challenge to weave everything together in the right balance, definitely a Catholic and definitely standing before so large a group of very sincere devotees of Amma. So I pondered this for days, finally accepted the invitation, and eventually came up with the speech below. I showed up in my Roman collar, gave my talk, garlanded her, was embraced by her, spoke with her in Tamil for a brief moment, and enjoyed it all. But see what you think of my little speech. Did I say too much? Too little? Would you agree to speak on such an occasion? Here are my remarks (and you can find online a summary and video excerpt posted by Amma's organization):

Namaste, *vanakkam*, good evening. It is a grace to be here tonight with you. I know that we all travel by so many personal paths, yet by a singular invitation we are here together for a time, and that is good that it is so. I offer you this ancient Jewish blessing as we collect ourselves:

> May the Lord bless us and keep us;
> may the Lord make his face to shine upon us,
> and be gracious to us;
> may the Lord lift up his face upon us,
> and give us peace. Amen.

(Numbers 6)

We are here tonight, gathered together with Amritanandamayi Amma. When we speak this name—*Amritanandamayi*, "perfect, complete in the bliss of the imperishable"—the Sanskrit scholars among us may think first on a philosophical level, perhaps turning to the Upanishads to probe the meaning of "bliss" and "the imperishable." We may eventually think of the undying spark within all beings and of a bliss grounded in the highest immortal Reality.

But we also know that this name—Amritanandamayi—tells us something simpler and more immediate. We are invited to see how our guest—our host—is open to the undying Spirit that blows where it will—in, through, and around each of us. With her tonight, we learn again to stop covering our light with a bushel basket and to share the bliss that is within us.

I am told that Amma does not teach by many words, that she offers no elaborate instructions. When she speaks to you, I have been told, it is a living word that exists not as an idea or lesson but as the intimate dialogue that happens when two people meet one another, face to face, and receive at some deeper level the gift of words so simple that they have more to do with receiving than giving information, listening than talking. This is the way it should be. Far better, tonight, is a true word that helps us as we need it right now, perhaps even before we know what that need is.

I think you know that my guru, the only guru I know as my own, is Jesus. He spoke many memorable words as the teacher, living words that surprised and awakened and guided his listeners, but most often he spoke just the word or two needed to change a person's life: get up and walk; you are forgiven, go in peace; do not be afraid, I am with you always; come, follow me; go forth and preach the good news, I am with you always. Think too of Lord Krishna, who said many things to Arjuna, but in the end said a simple word that was enough: "*ma sucah*, grieve no more" (*Bhagavad Gita* 18.66).

And so tonight we listen carefully, we listen in stillness and by song, as we once again become witnesses to God promising to be with us always.

We also know very well that Amma's words blossom into the doing of good deeds, acts of compassion. This is what Saint Francis meant when he said, "Preach the Good News always; use words only when necessary." Amma's concrete and real works of mercy are known everywhere, hers is a faith lived out in compassion, love realized in feeding the hungry, giving shelter to the homeless.

And so it should be. As Saint John puts it, "God is love, and those who abide in love abide in God, and God abides in them. . . . There is no fear in love, but perfect love casts out fear. . . . We love because God first loved us. But those who do not love the brother or sister they see, cannot love God whom they have not seen. The commandment we have from Jesus is this: those who love God must love their brothers and sisters as well" (1 John 4). True wisdom is not separate from compassion; this core insight gives life once and again, and it emerges with the greatest force when the message and messenger are one.

From the first time I heard about Amma I, like many of you, have known how she hugs people, envelopes all who come to her in her embrace. This too speaks more than words, showing us in visible form that no one is untouchable, no one is to be kept at a distance, and no one need be the alien or exile, shunned by others. Such compassion flows around us, like a river that recognizes no stopping point. As Jesus said, "The water that I give will become in you a spring of water welling up to eternal life" (John 4).

When Jesus came, he lay his hand upon the leper and the outcaste, he called the little children unto himself. He was kissed, embraced, touched by those who simply wanted to be where he was. He ate with the sinner and the prostitute, he dined in the house of the tax collector and the Pharisee. In love, the scorned woman washed his feet with her tears. He stretched forth his hands, that he might be nailed to the cross of our suffering and despair. Or think of Rama, who came into the home of Sabari the outcaste woman, accepted her gift, and embraced her.

It seems right then that Amma, a mother indeed, should open herself to all who will come near to her and by a hug offer so intimate a pathway to bliss: a smile, just a word, a deed that is good news for the lonely and the brokenhearted today—and still more simply, the loving embrace that welcomes us home. Such is the great gift we share tonight.

I close by sharing with you the very first Indian prayer that touched my heart, Rabindranath Tagore's words of recognition of God who is wondrously near to us:

You have made me known to friends whom I knew not.
You have given me seats in homes not my own.
You have brought the distant near
and made a sister of the stranger.
. . . .
Through birth and death,
in this world or in others,
wherever you lead me
it is you, the same,
the one companion of my endless life
who ever links my heart
with bonds of joy to the unfamiliar.
When one knows you,
then alien there is none,
then no door is shut.
Oh, grant me my prayer
that I may never lose
the bliss of the touch of the one
in the play of the many.

(from *Gitanjali*, adapted)

Amen.

A Hindu America?

July 24, 2010

Cambridge, MA. I recently came across a column by Loriliai Biernacki in the On Faith section of the *Washington Post*. A friend of mine, she is a professor of Indian religions at the University of Colorado, Boulder, and a specialist in the study of Hinduism. Her piece is entitled "A Rich and Strange Metamorphosis: Glocal Hinduism." She suggests that Hinduism today is becoming much more widely established in different parts of the world, and it is flourishing in many parts of the United States among Americans of Indian ancestry, but also among many converts to Hinduism.

In her piece, Biernacki recollects Lisa Miller's essay in *Newsweek* a few months ago on how Americans are becoming Hindus ideologically: "[Lisa Miller] tells us that an astounding number of Americans now believe in reincarnation. This conceptual, indeed cosmological, importation from Hinduism is seeping indelibly into the American psyche. Even a percentage of self-identified Christians have little difficulty incorporating this Hindu notion. Similarly, the word and concept of 'karma' is so commonly parlayed in everyday conversation that its Hindu origins no longer even register, as the concept finds its way across wide ranges of socio-economic circles and in all sorts of milieus." Biernacki speculates that Hinduism is uniquely able to be "glocal"—present across the globe, yet still local in a multitude of particular identities. Alas, before our present era of over-centralization, the Catholic Church too excelled at being glocal.

This Hinduism meets our needs, Biernacki goes on to say, offering "a kind of proliferation of particularities, particular Gods, particular practices among communities that might have not ever had any access to these new, imported Hindu perceptions—and at least for the

West, beckoning a rich and strange metamorphosis." She concludes by suggesting that Hinduism may help us by showing us where we are going:

> Our own increasingly plural world might take some solace, find a steady ease in the Hindu comfort with the multiple—multiple Gods, multiple practices, and simultaneous multiple ontological structures of monotheisms, monisms, polytheisms, and panentheisms. In this sense, the future of Hinduism suggests a kind of opening to a global world in a way that sidesteps the vision of a one-world government or one-world ideology. It proposes instead a world model without hegemonic center, linked by a thread of cosmology, multiplicity instanced as network, a seamless interconnectivity that echoes a conceptual cosmology from Hinduism's past into our own global and glocal future.

It is an interesting essay that deepens Lisa Miller's *Newsweek* piece, and I recommend reading all of it. I am tempted to confirm her insights out of my own experiences—including my recent brief encounter with Amritanandamayi Amma. But my thought now goes in a different direction: if there is truth in Biernacki's insights, and there is, then what does this say about Christian identity in the United States now? Catholic identity?

It is probably right that we are most concerned most of the time about issues in the church, ranging from social ministries to ongoing debates about the ordination of women, and are rightly horrified by the individual and systemic aspects of the clergy sex abuse crisis; but we can overdo it, suffering too much introspection with our good and our bad when the culture around us is going through deep changes. (One could add many others to Biernacki's particular focus, since Buddhism is influential, Pentecostal Christian Churches are multiplying, and of course Islam will become more and not less of an important presence in this country; but Hinduism is enough for this blog.) Just think of the example Biernacki and Miller dwell on, the growing comfort of a wide range of Americans—surely including churchgoing Catholics—who accept reincarnation as a good spiritual possibility. This is no small change in the way people think, and it challenges us to speak more powerfully, more simply, about Jesus as one who dies and rises, even today.

The danger then is that we Catholics—to stick with us for a moment—will endlessly build and rebuild our church in order to improve it and correct its failings, while yet forgetting that many,

many people are no longer interested, are not waiting for us to discover spiritual depths, and care so little about us that even being "anti-Catholic" is no longer all that important. If our neighbors are practicing yoga (even Christian yoga), meditating, visiting gurus, and enjoying the prospect of multiple deities and multiple births, then we have to bear down and think more deeply about who we are and how we speak, act, and live.

Yes, we need ever to return to the message of Jesus, as given in the Bible and as celebrated in the liturgical life of the church; yes, we need to really believe that "loving our neighbor" is indeed what Jesus would do, does do. But no, it is not enough to broadcast our faith without listening or to insist with open mouths and closed ears that Jesus is the way and that Christian faith is superior to religions such as Hinduism, when we—the church—seem not to understand Hinduism except in a most superficial way, and have no clue why Americans might embrace reincarnation. (Education is lacking: as far as I can see, neither CCD programs nor major seminaries spend much time exploring the religions of India, and few deacons, priests, and bishops have done a single yogic stretch or quiet breathing exercise.) If we commend ourselves for proclaiming the gospel while not getting Professor Biernacki's point, we may rather ironically find that for many, the Jesus of the church will remain a distant and institutional figure, while Jesus seen through Hindu eyes may be the more powerful spiritual figure.

So, to turn on its head the old notion that yoga is navel-gazing, we would do well to be more yogic, more Hindu, less into Catholic navel-gazing, more attentive to the very interesting spiritual cultures flourishing around us, and unafraid at a diversity that we cannot control yet that does nothing to harm the uniqueness of Jesus. Attentiveness will help us to see better what it means to be a follower of Jesus in the world we actually have, in the one life given to us.

Raimon Panikkar, Rest in Peace

August 31, 2010

Cambridge, MA. I heard just yesterday that Raimon (Raimundo) Panikkar died on August 26 at his home in Tavertet, Spain. He was ninety-one. Many will surely write in celebration of Fr. Panikkar's long and very productive ministry as a scholar and spiritual master, and this brief blog is simply my own initial recognition of his passing. His biography can be read in many places, including his own site and at Wikipedia, but in all these accounts we find mention of his Indian Hindu father and Spanish Catholic mother, a double belonging that in some way helped symbolize his lifelong intellectual and spiritual journey. From his early *Unknown Christ of Hinduism* to his recently published *The Rhythm of Being*—his 1989–90 Gifford Lectures—Panikkar wove together his knowledge of many religions, Hinduism and Catholicism in particular, with sensitivity to language, image, and subtle philosophical concepts. For beginners wishing to learn of his thought, his 2006 *The Experience of God: Icons of the Mystery* would be a good place to begin. I met him three times and will never forget his aliveness, his good humor, and his sparkle of intellectual acuity.

In my 2010 *Comparative Theology*, in the section discussing comparative theologians, I had occasion to refer to Fr. Panikkar's work:

Panikkar's decision to entangle his Christian faith and theology inside the Hinduism which he inhabits demonstrates a version of the intense, engaged learning that in my view is essential to comparative theology. His preferred "mutual inhabitation" seems to me a worthy goal, the price of the engaged model of comparative theological practice. . . . Intense particularity, becoming a part of that other tradition in some way, is the goal, rather than elegance in explanation. While we do well to avoid the wise persona he assumes in works such as *The Intrareligious Dialogue*—as if the comparativist, the wise man, sees what no one else sees, rising beyond each of the religions compared—I am sympathetic with his insight into how each religion is necessarily chastened and humbled by the truths of other religions. Even his idiosyncratic vocabulary suggests that his mode of intense reflection cannot be easily explained in the settled vocabulary of one or another tradition. It is nearly impossible to read Panikkar without paying special attention to the author as someone who, ever the poet, crafts his own wise speech. Panikkar wants to inspire his readers likewise to reflect on their personal location and personal choices, as they encounter the mystery of God, in person, in their embodied reality. All of this attests to what may be a shared Catholic and Hindu sacramentality. . . . It may be that [a Catholic study of] *Hinduism* [always has to do] with personal engagement, loss of independence in the presence of the other, and a rediscovery of ourselves again in the home where we began.

He was, is, a kind of personal mirror in which I ponder my own meditations on Hinduism and Catholicism.

Or, more eloquently, let me close with the ancient Upanishadic words that preface *The Rhythm of Being*: "That is Wholeness, this is Wholeness, / From Wholeness comes Wholeness, / If Wholeness is taken from Wholeness / Wholeness will remain." To this divine Wholeness Fr. Panikkar was an eloquent witness, and his wisdom will remain. Amen.

Dominus Iesus Ten Years Later I

August 28, 2010

Cambridge, MA. It is ten years since the Congregation for the Doctrine of the Faith (CDF) released the declaration entitled *Dominus Iesus*, with the theme of "the unicity and salvific universality of Jesus Christ and the Church." (The "release date" was September 5, 2000, although the document itself indicates that it was approved by John Paul II on June 16, while it is officially dated August 6.) It seems appropriate—in the "light manner" of a blog, at least—to reflect on its meaning and impact after a decade, and so I will do in several entries on this site. First, we might recall its basic teaching—and for this, forgive me for a very quick sketch of subtle points that have been debated extensively over the past decade. I do not speak authoritatively here. And, of course, reread it for yourself.

Dominus Iesus showed its major thrust right in the first paragraph: "The Lord Jesus, before ascending into heaven, commanded his disciples to proclaim the Gospel to the whole world and to baptize all nations: 'Go into the whole world and proclaim the Gospel to every creature. He who believes and is baptized will be saved; he who does not believe will be condemned'" (Mark 16:15–16), and "All power in heaven and on earth has been given to me. Go therefore and teach all nations, baptizing them in the name of the Father, and of the Son, and of the Holy Spirit, teaching them to observe all that I have commanded you. And behold, I am with you always, until the end of the world" (Matt 28:18–20). It was clearly intended to undergird and defend this missionary nature of the church.

It placed Christ in the center of the Christian faith, reaffirmed mission, insisted on the unity of Jesus and the Christ, the human Jesus and the transcendent primordial Word of God; it sought to make it clear that the mystery of Jesus Christ is intrinsically connected with the mystery of the kingdom of God, and the kingdom with the Roman Catholic Church. From its opening meditation on the Creed through its web of biblical and ecclesial documents, including Vatican II's "*Nostra Aetate*" and the teachings of John Paul II, the point of the declaration was to keep straight, authoritatively, the wholeness of what the church teaches on its basic truths. Its overall teaching also sought to put dialogue in its proper place, as a movement within the larger work of proclamation. In all of these assertions, it stands up comparatively well alongside the robust faith statements one finds in other religious traditions. This is what religious leaders do.

It is also true that the declaration came across as rather rigid and chilly, as a turn away from the warmer pastoral tone of "*Nostra Aetate*," and even from John Paul II's warmer initiatives, as when he gathered religious leaders of many faith traditions for prayer at Assisi in 1986. The declaration, in fact, offended a wide range of Christians and members of other faith traditions, who were not willing to treat it as a Catholic "in-house" document, instead taking personally its insistence that other Christian communities are defective embodiments of the church fully present in the Roman Church, and that even in dialogue, the Christian is not to allow their faith to be treated as equal to that of those with whom one is in dialogue. It was recognized as critical even of middle-of-the-road theologians such as Jacques Dupuis, who was at that time under investigation by the CDF for his 1997 book, *Toward a Christian Theology of Religious Pluralism*, a book that was exonerated in 1991—chastised mainly for subtleties that might be misunderstood by some readers. (But that would be the topic of a different blog: our immeasurable and enduring debt to Fr. Dupuis, the leading Catholic theologian of his generation on Christ and religious pluralism.)

Like many other theologians, I wrote about the declaration when it came out, first in the pages of *America* itself, and then as a contributor of *Sic et Non* (2001, edited by Charles Hefling Jr. and Stephen Pope). As I look back on the document ten years later, though, my thinking has evolved a bit. First, *Dominus Iesus* was and is definitely an important document that has served, in many a discussion since 2000, as a fundamental reminder of our basic beliefs on the issues it treats. Thus, it is good for us to remember that Jesus + Christ + word + kingdom + church + mission + dialogue go together, without any option for selective choice of a few of these elements to the exclusion of others. The Catholic faith, like that of other faith traditions, has its integrity, and certainly the CDF is not alone in pointing to a necessary integrity in what we believe.

Second, some of its distinctions still seem unhelpful and hard to maintain neatly in practice—for example, our theological *faith* versus the lesser *beliefs* of other religions, our *sacraments* versus their *rituals*. It is still hard to understand how the proposed superstitions and errors of other religions' rituals are explained by reference to 1 Corinthians 10:20–21, "No, I imply that what pagans sacrifice, they sacrifice to demons and not to God. I do not want you to be partners with demons. You cannot drink the cup of the Lord and the cup of demons. You cannot partake of the table of the Lord and the table of demons." Even the important and basic claim about dialogue late in the document seems nearly impossibly distant from a normal vision of how dialogue might actually happen: "Inter-religious dialogue, therefore, as part of her evangelizing mission, is just one of the actions of the Church in her mission ad gentes. Equality, which is a presupposition of inter-religious dialogue, refers to the equal personal dignity of the parties in dialogue, not to doctrinal content, nor even less to the position of Jesus Christ—who is God himself made man—in relation to the founders of the other religions." And again, as I mentioned above, many religious intellectuals in other traditions equally hold to the superiority of their own faiths and are not outdone in such assertions by the CDF. Consequently, after *Dominus Iesus*, they see little point in dialogue, particularly with Roman Catholics. But perhaps cooling the enthusiasm for interreligious dialogue was part of the point of *Dominus Iesus*?

Other documents since 2000 are actually more helpful—for example, the 2007 "Doctrinal Note on Some Aspects of Evangelization," but that too builds on *Dominus Iesus*, which remains the benchmark document. But on this tenth anniversary, several other questions strike me as still important: What is the purpose of interreligious dialogue after *Dominus Iesus*? What is the work of theologians with respect to religious diversity if the declaration sets forth the "straight truth" that is never going to change?

Dominus Iesus Ten Years Later II

August 31, 2010

Cambridge, MA. In part 1 of this three-part blog, I reflected simply on the September 5, 2000, Vatican declaration *Dominus Iesus*. I suggested that this influential document, despite its flaws and annoying tone, is an important marker of the unity and boundaries of Catholic teaching with respect to mission and dialogue. In this second blog, I ask simply what kind of theologizing is possible after *Dominus Iesus*: how do we think usefully about our faith in a diverse world, if it seems that the answer to or against religious diversity has already been given?

Theology seems in some way to be possible, even to the authors of the declaration. Even as it stresses the integrity of Catholic teaching and gives the impression that there is nothing more to be said, it also insists that there is room for theological reflection: "The expository language of the Declaration corresponds to its purpose, which is not to treat in a systematic manner the question of the unicity and salvific universality of the mystery of Jesus Christ and the Church, nor to propose solutions to questions that are matters of free theological debate, but rather to set forth again the doctrine of the Catholic faith in these areas, pointing out some fundamental questions that remain open to further development, and refuting specific positions that are erroneous or ambiguous." The subsequent and rather candid "Commentary on the Notification of the CDF Regarding the Book *Toward a Christian Theology of Religious Pluralism* by Jacques Dupuis" admits again the importance of theology:

> Theology is proving even more important in times of great cultural and spiritual change like ours which, in raising new problems and questions

concerning the Church's consciousness of her faith, require new answers and solutions, even daring ones. One cannot deny that today the presence of religious pluralism obliges Christians to look with a renewed awareness at the place of other religions in the saving plan of the Triune God.

So this is good news, in theory, but the practical import is less clear. What value is there in learning of other religions and thinking about our faith in light of them if *Dominus Iesus* rules out most answers? We can ask ourselves whether there is room for theology—not just for professional theologians doing their work, but for intelligent and reflective believers exploring their faith—after *Dominus Iesus*'s many answers to questions we've asked or not even thought of. We need, of course, to avoid easy alternatives: on the one hand, a dismissal of the declaration due to a rejection of its authority or an insistence that no doctrine is fixed and true over time (history keeps changing everything, all the time) or on the other, a surrender of intelligence by simply insisting, out of a political loyalty, that *Dominus Iesus* is the last word, the silencing of opposition. In fact, for the Catholic, it was neither merely one more opinion nor merely a superior truth.

Better, we might agree that it was and is a guide, a set of limits that leave much room for debate, even more than its authors would allow. We who read the document and who also pay attention to the world in which we live, we are not fixed, settled, determined, and passive in asking only questions to which the answers are already given. *Dominus Iesus* answers some questions very clearly, but it seems not even to imagine how true interreligious learning might change not the Creed but how we hear and profess the Creed, which we are likely to keep reciting, in the same words, into the far future. Thinking may upset us but does not diminish our faith. The declaration seems not to consider how a clear and honest affirmation of Christ is not less vigorous and firm, even if we have noticed religious diversity as a fact of life that is not about to go away any time soon, even as we live in a world where claims about truth do not substitute for the work of actually showing to seekers what is true. Even if we suppose, in faith, that Jesus is Lord, we who live among people of many faiths are the ones who need to show what that Lordship means, among people who respect each other's religions deeply. *Dominus Iesus* is a help, a boundary marker, but not itself the meaning of Christ amid diversity.

Since we keep changing in a changing world, then questions about our faith will keep arising, even after *Dominus Iesus*. Even with great respect for its teaching, we have questions that did not motivate its authors, questions that need answers ten years later. Yes to Jesus the Christ, the Word of God, revealed in the church in a magnificent way—but what about thinking through seriously how Muslims and Hindus have thought about Jesus? (Or even learning from Protestants?) What about being deeply moved by a Jewish Sabbath prayer or Buddhist chanting and unable to be satisfied simply by seeing these as "rites" and not "sacraments"? And what about being deeply impressed by Lord Krishna or the Buddha and, while not ranking them as equal to Jesus, deciding instead that it is actually a bad idea to rank superiors and inferiors? Such questions, and many others, are hard and stubborn; even if they do not threaten to change the Creed, neither does *Dominus Iesus* silence such questions. So people of faith who are also intelligent still have a lot to think about.

But even if we can keep thinking after *Dominus Iesus*, we can still ask, Is interreligious dialogue possible when the declaration seems to indicate that we have all the answers before the dialogue starts? Is dialogue possible when people of other faith traditions too have already read *Dominus Iesus* before they come to our dialogue meetings? Why should we, and they, learn across religious boundaries? Isn't the declaration on the side of those who say, Let's talk about politics and culture, but not about what we believe?

Dominus Iesus Ten Years Later III

September 3, 2010

Cambridge, MA. This is the third and last of my blogs on *Dominus Iesus* as the September 5 anniversary of its release approaches. My first was a general comment, the second focused on theology after the declaration, and this one is about dialogue after *Dominus Iesus*. First, though, I wish particularly to recommend readers review the comments on my previous entry, on dialogue, the experience of life in interreligious marriage and social contexts, and even on theology as the domain of the 1 percent, while the 99 percent of Catholics have to deal with these issues in other ways. This last comment is actually very apt, since the declaration in its technicalities was indeed aimed primarily at theologians. In any case, I recommend reading all the comments.

As for dialogue, in this brief space I will make a series of brief observations, again written at blog speed, and then welcome your further comments. First, we do well to distinguish "institutional dialogue"—carried on by religious leaders and their delegates as official events, much like acts of diplomacy—from "lived dialogue," experienced in various degrees of informality as part of people's lives. "Institutional dialogue" proceeds at its own glacial pace, dependent on numerous factors. How Catholics dialogue officially with people of other faith traditions is often mirrored in how the church imagines its conversations with Christians of other denominations and even how the Vatican contemplates its ability and willingness to dialogue with Catholics in the church. All of these dialogues have been dampened, it seems to me, by *Dominus Iesus*, which signals a church leadership less interested than in previous decades in exchanges across all these boundaries. Reaffirming boundaries comes across as the priority, and when dialogues of sorts occur, they are driven by cultural and political factors, as when we might read of a meeting with Muslim leaders.

When it comes to "lived dialogue," however, it seems to me that the role of *Dominus Iesus* is more limited. We all live in religiously diverse societies, our individual lives and social networks have permeable boundaries, and for the most part, we are "works in progress," simultaneously rethinking who we are, how we relate to others. If we are Catholic, we are also all negotiating how we are going to be Catholic—with what mix of beliefs, practices, experiments, border crossings—and thus too, how we learn from our religious others and where we draw the line on that learning and its implications. We may be practicing yoga, but not submitting to a Hindu guru; we may learn from reading the *Bhagavad Gita*, but not worship Krishna; we may find Hindu insights helpful in rethinking gender and the divine, but not actually pray to a Goddess. Similarly, many of us are learning from Islam or Buddhism or Native American traditions. On one level, *Dominus Iesus* is simply not the kind of document, and simply does not have the spiritual or moral effectiveness, to get us to stop being religiously interactive all the time.

All of these personal experiments, of course, involve both introspective and social elements. Much goes on inside each of us, but increasingly it is the case that we are also talking to neighbors, colleagues at work or school, perhaps also spouses or partners or children who are committed to other religions. This is dialogue, and it happens largely in atmospheres of equality and with varying degrees of openness, attentiveness. This fact of dialogue can also be writ large, since issues of public import—for example, the proposal to build an Islamic Center in lower Manhattan—necessarily get us into conversations with our religious neighbors. For the most part, *Dominus Iesus* has little influence on the course of such conversations. Dialogue is not going to stop, and no one is going to be able to stipulate what gets dialogued about or what is learned in the dialogue. The sun rises whether I think it should or not.

However, in keeping with what I said in the first of these blogs, once we start reflecting—as we should—on the meaning of what we are doing in our inevitable interreligious exchanges, *Dominus Iesus* can be a very important and instructive reminder of who we are when we say we are Catholics who, even in our very diversity, still accept the wholeness of the faith, keeping together Jesus + Christ +

word + kingdom + church + mission + dialogue. We need to live experimental lives, and we have a right to our personal successes and failures in dialogue; we also need to correct ourselves along the way, seeing what we've forgotten or left out. While it is very easy today to shut out the Vatican entirely and close our ears to words from Rome, I think it would be a mistake to stop remembering *Dominus Iesus* and the cautions it put in place. It is possible to go too far in learning from another religion; it is possible to become merely confused in our openness. And while it may be good for some of us to convert to the other religion, this should not be done casually. The declaration reminds us how much is at stake if we go to the mosque on Friday instead of Mass on Sunday, or pray to Siva instead of Jesus. And when a whole community is touched by the "living dialogue," *Dominus Iesus* becomes all the more relevant as a reference point for the discernment that must still take place in that local church community.

Finally, it is still important after *Dominus Iesus*, even if to some extent despite it, to keep trying to foster local dialogues among people of faith, dialogues that are planned and grassroots efforts, even if they are not the "institutional dialogues" indicated above. Ours is not the only tradition with firm and fundamental beliefs, condescending attitudes toward outsiders, rigid leadership, and sad histories of unhappy relations with the other, steps forward and backward mixed together. All of us, whichever religion we belong to, need to engage in the spiritual practice of talking to—and listening to—our religious neighbors. Much of this can be spontaneous and part of everyday life, but there is also an urgent need for study groups, shared scripture study, days and festivals of interreligious harmony among the religious sites in a town, interfaith boards in cities, and so on. We ought neither hide nor glorify *Dominus Iesus* when we work for such happenings. We might even ask our neighbors, "If your community was to write a document like this, what would be the foundations, guidelines, and uncrossable borders that shape your talking to us?" (Of course, some documents like this already exist—think of the Muslim scholars who wrote *A Common Word* and opened a powerful Muslim-Christian dialogue, or the Jewish-Hindu declarations of common understanding that came out of 2007 and 2008 meetings in Jerusalem and New Delhi.)

Anyway, let us think of taking time on September 5 to reread *Dominus Iesus*, start to finish. We might learn from it even now, even if we still doubt parts of it. And let's pray for deeper spiritual open-mindedness in us the readers, and in those who wrote *Dominus Iesus* too.

Gandhi at 141

October 2, 2010

Cambridge, MA. Today is the birthday of Mohandas K. Gandhi. It is true that his particular programs and positions have faded with age—Indians do not live in the past and have moved on, for better or worse. And it is true that now, as in the past, there are thoughtful Indians of Hindu and other communities who dispute his politics, his compromises, and his personal eccentricities. All this is true. So why remember him on the day he would have turned 141? I suggest three reasons (which certainly do not form the exhaustive list).

First, Gandhi is still, after all this time, a very interesting thinker who wrote very well (and not just voluminously). Everyone knows about him, but few read him. And if you read him, you will like him less, then you will like him more. Of course, his *Autobiography* remains a spiritual classic and vividly recounts key personal moments in which he worked out his basic principles of nonviolence and truth seeking (in nonviolence as *satyagraha*). But there is also his *Satyagraha in South Africa*, in which he recounts in more thorough detail his efforts to defend the Indian community in South African against biased and oppressive laws, and how his realization of nonviolence and self-purification—by suffering—became such a potent liberative force in India and throughout the world. His commentary on the *Bhagavad Gita*, while not a scholarly work, is a vivid and lively exposition of detached action, that spiritual indifference that, as in the spirituality of Ignatius Loyola, opens the way for free and liberative action in the world. And there is the less well known but still powerful 1910 treatise, *Hind Swaraj*, his "manifesto" setting forth the principles that he thought had to underlie a truthful and effective Indian independence movement; real history, he says there, is primarily a story of nonviolent-resistance living, but unfortunately the history books mistakenly count as history the wars of rulers, their weaponry and violence. If we change our perspective, we can see that nonviolence works most of the time for most people—and can change the world if we start thinking for ourselves, take our lives into our own hands, and resist the thoughtless flow of ordinary, somewhat violent life.

Second, core issues that occupied him so powerfully have not gone away. Examples abound where Gandhi might well matter. Jonathan Chait of *The New Republic* just posted a provocative piece, "Why Don't Palestinians Adopt Nonviolence?" which, in light of today's remembrance of Gandhi's birthday, seems a useful prompt—despite skepticism—to ask again if Gandhi (not mentioned by Chait) was in fact offering, the better part of a century ago, a more practical path of nonviolence—one that fails today not because it is impractical in politics but because communities have not found ways to inculcate among their members the necessary detachment and spiritual discipline. Or, just the other day, the Allahabad High Court issued its decision on the hotly contested issue of the Babri Masjid (mosque) in Ayodhya in North India, where, in 1992, by an act that led to terrible communal violence, a Hindu group tore down the mosque claimed to have been built on the site of an ancient temple marking the place of Lord Rama's birth. The court decided to divide the site three ways, among one Muslim and two Hindu communities. For the moment, as the decision is appealed, further unrest seems to have been avoided. But while this may be a wise and thoughtful solution to a very difficult situation, it seems to me that Gandhi would have imagined a different dynamic: not several communities contesting the site, so as to demand it for their own, but rather each community—Hindu or Muslim—insisting that the other take the entire site. Neither community needs the site, and both would be better off with a bit more detachment in the matter. Gandhi himself did not cling tightly to Hindu identity, even as he refused conversion to Christianity or other religions; rather, he sought a spiritual/moral ground that would make communication possible even as established communities protected their vested interests.

Or, closer to home, the push and pull over an Islamic Center in lower Manhattan is surely vexed and depressing enough that it at least calls for the consideration of a Gandhian solution—some public act of solidarity with Muslims by Christians and Jews in the area—perhaps for instance a Jewish-Christian declaration that unless the Center can be opened, the nearby churches and synagogues will close in solidarity until minds are changed. (Would Gandhi have suggested this? I invite experts on Gandhi to add their views.)

Third, he is a saint, and we should honor the saints. Our Catholic observance of saints' birth and death anniversaries need not be entirely limited to Catholic saints. Without undue harm to anyone's theological sensitivities, we might very well join other Christian communities in adding figures like Gandhi to our calendar, mentioning him at Mass, and praying in his memory for peace and nonviolence. We can do this because, from a moderate Catholic perspective, he is obviously a figure radiant with the grace of God, grace that loses nothing of its splendor because it radiates in the life, work, and personality of this man who deeply respected Jesus yet chose not to become a Christian. Recall what Dorothy Day wrote in *The Catholic Worker* when Gandhi was assassinated by a Hindu extremist in January 1948:

> "Greater love than this no man hath—that a man lay down his life for his friends." There is no public figure who has more conformed his life to the life of Jesus Christ than Gandhi, there is no man who has carried about him more consistently the aura of divinized humanity, who has added his sacrifice to the sacrifice of Christ, whose life has had a more fitting end than that of Gandhi. "A prophet is not without honor save in his own country . . . he came into his own and his own did not receive him."
>
> The folly of Gandhi's life, the failure of Gandhi's life—it is the folly and failure of the Cross. The failure of the supernatural in the world. The failure of those who would teach love and non-violence in a world which has apostatized, which accepts no absolutes, has no standards other than utilitarian, is devoid of hope, persecutes the prophets, murders the saints, exhibits God to the people—torn, bleeding, dead. . . .
>
> It was because he went the full way, because he adhered to an Absolute, because he insisted that there be no hatred, that Hindu and Moslem live together in peace—it was for these things he was murdered. It was because he believed in a Revolution that went beyond the social and ended in personal regeneration, because it was pacifist that he has now attained to that failure that leads to ultimate glory.
>
> Truly he is one of those who has added his own sufferings to those of Christ, whose sacrifice and martyrdom will forever be offered to the Eternal Father as compensating for those things lacking in the Passion of

Christ. In him we have a new intercessor with Christ; a modern Francis, a pacifist martyr.

Think too of these words when we mark Francis of Assisi's feast Monday, October 4.

The Pope, the Jews—and the Pagans

March 6, 2011

Cambridge, MA. Recently Pope Benedict published *Holy Week: From the Entrance into Jerusalem to the Resurrection*. Though I have not read the whole book, my attention was caught by the pope's comment that in the passion narratives, the evangelists did not mean the Jewish people in general when referring to the Jews who killed Jesus, and did not mean all the Jewish people when referring to the crowd who called down the blood of Jesus on their heads. Rather, the pope writes, "the Jews" refers to the "Temple aristocracy," and the crowd calling for the death of Jesus was by no means the whole people, but rather a small group, perhaps a "rabble," brought in for this deadly purpose. Yes, indeed, and reading the narratives with sensitivity can be of great help in getting at what the evangelists truly meant. I appreciate this reminder, even if it is not novel, as we look forward to Lent and Holy Week and the question of how to proclaim and interpret the passion narratives without lapsing, by our silence, into old anti-Semitic accusations and stereotypes.

But as our relationship to the Jewish people changes, so too should change our relationship to the wider array of religious people through the world, in history and now. Once we start noticing the literary style and rhetoric of biblical texts and learn to narrow down the scope of what at first seem to be sweeping claims about Jews, then the pope's insights can be extended further, to other groups that were stereotyped in the Hebrew Bible and New Testament—namely, the nations, gentiles, the Egyptians, the Moabites, and also those who worshipped their deities on high places, who worshipped the Baal, who made idols and worshipped them. Surely there were people in all these groups who were the enemies of Israel, who were blinded by worldly desires, who hated truth or who in their pride thought they could evade the will of God. Surely there were some who worshipped things thoughtlessly and in a demeaning fashion, and perhaps even people who really thought of carved wooden and stone objects as their deities. Surely there were some pagans—Athenians for example—who balked before the evident truth, refusing to recognize the evidence of the creator God's presence and action in creation.

And yet we can say, following the pope's generous insight, that it would be a very great mistake to imagine that the Biblical authors were seriously attempting to characterize all non-Jews (and later all non-Christians), all Egyptians or Canaanites or Moabites or Greeks, or seriously claiming that all Baal worshipers were blind and foolish, obsessed with blood sacrifices, and so on. Just as "the Jews" did not mean all Jews, it seems appropriate to extend this generous insight to those who did (and do) venerate images carved of wood and stone: the idolaters who are dangerous and on a downward path are few, and no generalization can be made, rhetoric aside, about the much larger number of people in all the nations referred to in the Bible who lived good religious lives, in Canaan, among the Moabites, with their Baals and the like. Let us not speak ill of idol worshipers, even if you do not know any personally. Even the larger New Testament claims about the nations who do not know Christ seem, in the spirit of the pope's remarks, to be claims that need to be deciphered, but do not, at the start, offer reliable information about people outside of Israel and the church. As we learn to rethink—and state in different words—our relation to Israel and the Jewish people, this opens the door to a less heated, more productive relation to the peoples we used to call heathens, pagans, idolaters, and the like. It is not just about dropping offensive language, but of reinterpreting, as the pope does, the Biblical claims themselves.

This matters today because we still, and rightly so, turn to the Bible for guidance in thinking about our relations with people of other religious traditions. We are given the shorthand by which Biblical authors spoke of "others" near and far. Once we know that the New Testament did not give us the full reality of the Jewish people by talking about "the Jews" who sought the death of Jesus, we do well also to realize that neither does the New Testament give us the full reality of any religious group, anywhere in the world, simply by this or that biblical label or shorthand reference. If we see this, we can become freer in refusing to stereotype Hindus and Buddhists and others, even the West's atheists and humanists, merely by applying to them labels lifted from the Bible.

While the pope's insights are not new, it is good that he has reminded us not to underestimate the wisdom of the Bible—or the real-life complexity of the peoples about whom it speaks.

Easter and Our (Inter)Religious Imaginations

April 23, 2011

Cambridge, MA. All week, while mixing the business of school with the solemn events of Holy Week, I have been pondering the existential question, "What shall I blog for Holy Week/Easter?" Given my interreligious commitments, the question has become, "How does the resurrection affect how we relate to people of other religions?" At the moment, at least, it is a question without an easy answer. Christmas manifests God's embrace of being human, so that nothing human is alien to Christ and our faith; the crucifixion manifests the depth of God's love for the world, even as it has often occasioned hard questions about how God saves the world and how we are to see the diversity of God's people in light of the cross. The cross is shocking, an upset to settled ideas we might have previously had about what God is like—guided by it, we learn to be less confident that we already know how God acts in the wider world, amid all God's children.

The resurrection is harder. It is hard to preach on Easter Sunday, and not just because of the influx of unfamiliar faces, parishioners who find their way back on just one or two Sundays a year. We know what it is like to be born and to struggle and to die, but we do not know what it means to rise from the dead. The many Gospel stories of the postresurrection period show us a world we are still, after two thousand years, unfamiliar with. Even longtime disciples are surprised again and again to discover the Risen Christ in their midst. When we ponder Easter, we should remain aware that in a good sense, we have no idea what we are talking about.

Still, if this core fact of our faith—Christ is risen!—is relevant to our lives today, and if our lives are inevitably interreligiously connected, then the resurrection does shed some light on how to be, see, act in this world of many religions. Allow me to suggest four ways, among many more, in which the event and experience of the resurrection (as told at the end of each Gospel) does guide us interreligiously.

First, there is the fact of the empty tomb. Things are not as we expected them to be. It is empty, the dead one is not there; Jesus is not even predictably, securely deceased. No one sees him arise from the grave, either. But that emptiness and absence set the tone for all that follows; a bit of emptiness and not-finding is good for us.

Second, Jesus is alive and active in our midst, but not like before, in the ways familiar while he preached in the towns and villages. If the cross shatters preconceptions about how far God will go, the resurrection surprises us even more, because the Christ we knew previously and alongside us now goes ahead of us, in the body but no longer bound by the narrow expectations we have about what is possible in the world of time and space. God may be impossibly present, even on religious and spiritual paths we had discounted.

Third, it was not the apostles (only eleven of them by then) who encountered the risen Christ first. Rather, it was those who were secondary by the standard account: Mary, the sister of Lazarus, who grieved by the tomb until the "gardener" surprised her, calling her by name; the other women, first encountered by the angel and then by Jesus himself on the road, and sent with a message for those apostles who were waiting in their room for something to happen; and the two disciples (male or female, it does not say) who walked with the stranger on the road to Emmaus and recognized him in the sharing of a meal. We ought not make too much of this point, I suppose, but it seems fair to say that the leaders of the church find it harder to recognize God's presence and work in the midst of other religions. It is ordinary people, rubbing shoulders with people of other faiths all the time, who become the messengers to those in charge: Christ has already been elsewhere, as we always belatedly find out.

Fourth, the disciples form a group of women and men who, transformed by the risen Christ, are empowered to go forth and make him known throughout the world. But how are they empowered? It is not simply that these first Christians were encouraged by the fact that Jesus seemed to be back, or that they took the resurrection to a proof of the truth of his words and deeds. Rather, filled with his spirit, the Spirit, they were the people who had faced up to the emptiness of the tomb, who found him in unexpected places and learned to listen to the marginal and even unnamed people were met the Risen Christ first. As such, those disciples became able to use their imaginations, to be at home in strange places, unafraid of the unexpected.

All of this teaches us how to behave in today's interreligious world. If we are like those first disciples who lost the familiar Jesus and were found by him in new ways, then we too can be children of the resurrection—able to meet Christ along the religious and spiritual paths of our near and far brothers and sisters. If we share the faith of the very earliest church, we find ourselves no longer needing to cling to a God entirely familiar, known in just the right ways and by just the right people. He is risen, he is elsewhere too.

Of course, there is more to be said. We must also read the letters of Saint Paul and the Acts of the Apostles, which have a lot to teach us about the resurrection. But it is good to stop for a moment, at Easter and early in the Easter season, lingering with the endings of the four Gospels and the amazing freshness and inventiveness we find there—and then learning again to find God in all things, even amid the many religious possibilities that surround us.

Death of a God-Man:
Sai Baba Dies at Eighty-Five

April 25, 2011

Cambridge, MA. On Easter Sunday, Sri Sathya Sai Baba (1926–2011) died in India at aged eighty-five. The accounts of his death are many in the Indian press, and will increase as the day of his funeral, a state affair, approaches. (Just Google "Death of Sai Baba" and you will see.) Professor Tulasi Srinivas of Emerson College here in Boston just published a fine scholarly study of the movement surrounding Sai Baba, *Winged Faith: Rethinking Globalization and Religious Pluralism through the Sathya Sai Movement* (New York: Columbia University Press, 2010). And today, she sent us all an email about his life and death, and has kindly given me permission to quote from it here:

Shri Sathya Sai Baba's life was extraordinary by any description. Born Sathya Narayana Raju to a poor peasant family on November 2, 1926, he became a nationally recognized guru and mystic who counted leading Indian politicians, sports figures, and media celebrities as well as the poorest among his devotees. In 1940, he declared himself an "avatar," or reincarnation, of another Hindu holy man called the Sai Baba of Shirdi, a town in the western Indian state of Maharashtra, who had died in 1918. In the 1960s and after, riding a wave of popularity in the West, he became a celebrated global guru, often providing solace through his twice daily darshan *(sacred sighting) to the tens of thousands of devotees, interacting with them, magically manifesting healing* vibhuti *(sacred ash) or talisman for those who sought his blessings.*

Devotees scrambled to get a good seat during darshan, *often waiting hours in long queues. . . . His devotional base grew to an estimated 20 million in 160 countries around the world, and they were predominantly middle class and professional. Sai Baba used his enormous influence to harness this human power to do* seva *(charitable works), including raising money for educational institutions, hospitals to treat the poor, and drinking water to parched rural districts in and around his home town. He grew the Sai Movement into a transnational phenomenon allowing people to remain in the faith they were born into yet offering them hope and solace as his devotees through a strategic set of embedded practices, multivalent symbols, and ambiguous performances.*

But he was also the eye of the storm as controversy swirled around him. Skeptics and non-believers accused him of being a "mere magician," using trinkets and conjuring acts to increase faith in him. He never denied the magic but rather claimed that the talismen produced were magical merely a pathway for his larger maya *(divine magic) of devotional transformation to occur. In the 1970s a commission to investigate miracles and other superstitions was set up by Dr. H Narasimaiah, the Vice Chancellor of Bangalore University to investigate Sathya Sai Baba. The BBC documentary* Sai Baba: Godman or Conman *detailed the so called "tricks," but this did not deter devotees and followers. More recently ex-devotees and former devotees have accused Sathya Sai Baba and the Sai Trust of more serious infractions including embezzlement, fraud, and sexual abuse of young boys, which they claimed culminated in the death of four young men within the ashram in 1996. A series of films and internet websites detail these allegations. But neither Sai Baba nor the Trust were ever convicted of any wrongdoing. Rather Sai Baba and his devotees, on his behalf, claimed that he was vilified in the public arena by disaffected devotees. The Anti Sai movement has been appropriately silent about the current happenings in the ashram.*

It is a real test of interreligious openness to move beyond respect for the scriptures of another religion to ponder a contemporary representative of another tradition. It is one thing to admire famous figures of the past, or to imitate a reformer like Mahatma Gandhi, but quite another to reflect on the meaning of a figure whose power lay primarily in himself, his claim to divine status; it was on that basis that millions have been devoted to him, and perhaps it is impossible for us to respond to Sai Baba in that way. (But read about Fr. Mario Mazzoleni, who left the priesthood after becoming a devotee of Sai

Baba—excommunicated, I believe; his book *A Catholic Priest Meets Sai Baba* is most unusual.)

My own contact with Sai Baba was minimal. In 1990, while at a conference in Bangalore, three of us drove up to Whitefield to visit his afternoon audience. By that time, he had taken a vow of public silence, and so for about forty-five minutes he just walked up and down in front to the crowd, giving blessings, touching the sick, receiving notes from especially devout people who were seeking an audience. Though it was not a singular moment, I've always remembered the occasion and have been glad that I did go to see him. A few years earlier, when studying here in Cambridge, I knew some students who were entirely dedicated to his message, even allowing him to guide them—by spiritual inspiration and dreams—in their choice of marriage partners. I was impressed, and a bit worried, by their total devotion. Even earlier, when I was in Kathmandu in 1973, someone gave me some of that divine ash he was wont to produce. I still have the little folder paper containing the ash even now; it was not something to misplace.

But I will leave to him the last words, gleaned from the Sathya Sai Baba website:

There is only one religion, the religion of Love;

There is only one language, the language of the Heart; There is only one caste, the caste of Humanity;

There is only one law, the law of Karma; There is only one God, He is Omnipresent. . . .

Nations are many, but Earth is one; Beings are many, but Breath is one; Stars are many, but Sky is one; Oceans are many, but Water is one; Religions are many, but God is one; Jewels are many, but Gold is one;

Appearances are many, but Reality is One.

Fr. Amorth's Yoga and the Devil

December 10, 2011

Cambridge, MA. A few weeks ago, there was a flurry of news around the rather sensational comments made by Fr. Gabriele Amorth on the diabolical influence of both the Harry Potter series and the practice of yoga. See, for instance, the version given at UCANews (a Catholic website in East Asia). I do not know Fr. Amorth and could not discover an exact transcript of his remarks, so I have been hesitant to comment. Many have, and there is no lack of comments about his comments on the web. Many are merely repetitive and seem singularly ill-informed. Some come from more educated Christians who refer to the church's record of suspicions about yoga—as in Cardinal Ratzinger's 1989 letter worrying about the indiscriminate borrowing of Asian spiritualities, or the Vatican document *Jesus Christ, the Bearer of the Water of Life*—while some come from thoughtful yoga practitioners who, whether Christian or not, fail to see what Satan has to do with yoga. Enough has been said, it seems.

But I have been asked both by friends and relatives, and by Hindus in India, about the meaning and significance of the attack on yoga. I think it simplest to make a short series of comments, sketched here and none fully developed (we are at the end of the semester, after all).

First, mere recriminations against the religion of another are hardly ever acceptable or useful. No Catholic likes it if the Eucharist is written off as merely "priestcraft" or "patriarchal machinations" or even the venerable "hocus pocus," and it is hard to imagine that it helps in any way to burden the millennia-old theory and practice of yoga with the deadly charge of being satanic. And it is a really bad idea to insult a nearly billion Hindus—who see Hinduism as having a special affinity to yoga—by charges of Satanism that echo centuries of heated Christian attacks on Hinduism. I hope church leaders in Rome have instructed Fr. Amorth not to make such sweeping charges.

Second, if one is a professional exorcist, one may indeed see everything in light of that profession, and so it is not surprising that Fr. Amorth sees the devil at work everywhere; perhaps it is his default explanation of the woes that afflict us. Others might appeal to literary or philosophical measures of worth, but the exorcist sees things in his own way. To others this will seem odd, exaggerated, and this is all the more reason to be careful when speaking to a wider audience who does not share one's profession or expertise but sees the world through other legitimate lenses.

Third, it is not as if only Fr. Amorth has intelligent cautions to offer against facile equations of yoga and Christianity, or only sources such as the ecclesial documents mentioned above. Others do it well and to the point, without harshness. For example, at the recent annual meeting of the American Academy of Religion in San Francisco, I attended a panel on yoga and Christianity. The tenor of the papers was intelligent and careful, a major theme being that it would be intellectually careless to equate Christian and yogic spiritual practices, or to claim loosely that "God"—Isvara—means the same thing in both traditions. Nor does it help, the panel and a host of scholarly sources suggest, to imagine that yoga is simply and only whatever it may happen to appear to be in this or that yoga studio, or in the eyes of one or another current or former practitioner. Scholars, often without any particular bias to protect, take it for granted that yoga cannot simply or without inevitable recalculations become a Christian practice. For yoga to be Christian or American or secular or new age does not happen of itself; it is something people choose to make happen, and like other things we do, sometimes our creativity works better than others. But there can be no blanket condemnation of yoga as essentially not Christian. (Nor, of course, is Christian meditative practice just one thing.)

Fourth, study helps. I am a professor and scholar, and turn very often—too often for the tastes of some readers, I suspect—to the study of the text. My tendency in this direction is really not the delusion that books and words are preferable to "real-world reality" but the idea that careful reading performs the admirable service of pinning us down to ascertain whether we know what we are talking about. Several years back, I posted a series of reflections on yoga and the *Spiri-*

tual Exercises—related to a course that I am thinking of offering again next year—and one of the salutary aspects of that study of Patanjali's ancient treatise on yoga was that while this study does not replace practice, which is something else, it does open up a reliable space for careful study and consideration of how yoga has been theorized, what worldview and anthropology often go with it, and what claims were made at the heart of the written tradition as to where it leads. My point then, and now (I won't repeat myself here), is that once we study the texts of yoga, we are in a position to make far more refined choices about what we like or not, what we think is compatible with Christian theology (of one or another tradition), and—because we remember what we read—how the study of yoga can usefully, deeply, and in a way open to ongoing assessment affect our Christian think-ing, practicing, praying, even if we do not become yogis. And still, in the end, yoga will not be right for some Christians. What we need are not prohibitions but Christian spiritual directors who know some-thing about yoga from the inside, as it were.

And so, as I mentioned, I have never met Fr. Amorth, and it is not right to criticize him for comments I have not been able to find and read in full. I am sorry if even here I have misjudged him. But what I can do is suggest that in an age when interreligious knowledge is increasing at an incredibly rapid rate, it is wise to avoid most of the heated information that pops up on the web, from Fr. Amorth as well as his critics, and instead go read a good book. On yoga, I recom-mend Christopher Chapple's *Yoga and the Luminous: Patañjali's Spir-itual Path to Freedom* (SUNY Press, 2009) and, if you can find it, Fr. JM Déchanet's *Christian Yoga* (Harper, 1960), in its day a rather dar-ing opening of the door to the Christian practice of yoga.

And then, if you do practice yoga as a Christian, do so with reflec-tive attention to see how your yoga and your Christian commitment interact, intensify, and at times possibly disturb one another. Then sit up straight, close your eyes, and take a deep breath before stop-ping—or going deeper—into yoga.

If the devil is anywhere in this, he surely finds to his liking careless words that sensationalize rather than shed light.

To Convert a Hindu . . .

March 16, 2012

Cambridge, MA. Many readers will think of me as a progressive on interfaith matters, one of those Jesuit liberals. You may not know, however, that I am also, with some regularity, pilloried in the conservative Hindu blogosphere by journalists concerned about Christian aggression against Hindus.

I have been described as a famed evangelist or, considering how positive my writings about Hinduism often seem to be, as a tricky Jesuit wolf in sheep's clothing, covertly dedicated to the conversion of Hindus by the strategy of saying nice things about them. Consider for example a January 2012 post by Ms. Sandhya Jain at the site Malayalee.com. You can still find the piece online. It sums me up in a brief statement: "Of course, [Clooney's] priority is the conversion of pagan Hindus to Catholicism. To this end, he has steeped himself in the process of inculturation and drawn many intellectual Hindus into his interfaith orbit."

While I think such comments are inaccurate, and wide of the mark, they do raise for me an inelegant question: after forty years of studying Hinduism, learning from wise Hindu teachers, becoming friends with many a Hindu in India and the West, do I intend to convert Hindus? Mr. Jain and others like him are good to raise the question, If you are a Christian and never preach the Gospel, what kind of Christian are you? So what have I done with the Christian imperative to evangelize? This is a large question, and this blog is fortunately not the place to answer it, particularly in the forty minutes or so I allot for any entry at this site.

But I raise the topic here and now, as I have been reflecting on this Sunday's Gospel—the fourth Sunday of Advent, year B—from the

Gospel according to John, where we hear the famous words, "For God so loved the world that he gave his only Son, so that everyone who believes in him may not perish but may have eternal life" (John 3:16), words that speak to the core of the Christian message and words often invoked in the course of inspired efforts to convert others.

But I have always thought that any such faith claim is likely to be misunderstood—a truth floating in space, a challenge unmoored from John's actual text—unless we take it in context.

Remember where we are in John 3: Jesus is speaking to Nicodemus, who has come to him in the night for fear that he might be seen by others. He came of his own will; he was not summoned. Jesus teaches him in riddles about being born once and again, here and above, even alluding to the bronze serpent that Moses held aloft in the desert, so that people might not die. After the teaching, which surely focuses on John 3:16, the chapter ends, and we hear no more of Nicodemus until after the death of Jesus, when all hope is lost and the wisest thing to do seems to be to join the apostles in running off and hiding, denying any knowledge of Jesus. But instead, Nicodemus suddenly reappears, facing the cold, naked light of failure. Joseph of Arimathea has asked Pilate for the body of Jesus, and then Nicodemus steps forward: "Nicodemus, who had at first come to Jesus by night, also came, bringing a mixture of myrrh and aloes, weighing about a hundred pounds" (John 19:38–39).

All of this seems to teach us something about conversion—not in the Clooney-as-wolf-in-sheep's-clothing mode, but otherwise. Think about it: Jesus did not go seeking after Nicodemus but waited until Nicodemus decided to come to him. Jesus talked to him, answered his questions, but also puzzled and confounded him. He gave no smooth answers to naïve questions, he packaged no convert-to-my-religion message. Jesus—or the narrator—indeed proposes a great truth that "God so loved the world . . ." but did not make this a test for Nicodemus. Jesus neither held onto him nor condemned him, nor even invited Nicodemus to follow him. He spoke to this man who had come to him, then let him go, perhaps never to return. And yet, in his own good time, when perhaps even Jesus might have thought him gone forever, Nicodemus risks everything by helping to claim and bury this criminal, loser, non-Messiah. He did convert, we might say today, but in his own good time, as he saw fit.

I don't know what Hindu journalists such as Mr. Jain think conversion means, but they often seem to reduce the process to street-corner preaching, imperial power applied to force people to change religions, or the intellectual sleight of hand by which people are robbed of their intellectual and spiritual dignity and tricked into changing religions. Perhaps there are some such evangelists, and if so, it is well that they fail in their mission.

But to be a missionary is first of all to be like Jesus, and Jesus was never just one thing. This Sunday, at least, I favor the Jesus of John 3 and pray to be like him: Don't go chasing after people, but talk to those who come to you. Answer questions and raise new ones, and never worry about the effects of the conversation, as if there are dead-lines to be met. Sometimes, like Jesus, we may have an effect on a Nicodemus, but only much later, even after we are gone. Or not. What happens is in God's hands, not ours.

And not only among Christians. The world is full of seekers; people travel the spiritual highway all the time now, everywhere in our world, visiting religious teachers, seeking wisdom but sometimes finding confusion, sometimes quickly changing their lives, other times delaying until everyone else thinks it is too late. Some disappear in the night, and some like Nicodemus decide only at the last minute to witness to the truth that others cannot see; they stick their necks out, risking everything for the sake of a wisdom they heard long ago.

Suspicions notwithstanding, I honestly do not think of myself as an evangelist, and anyone who reads my work will be hard put to find evidence of such plans and purposes. But since the question arose—Clooney out to convert the Hindus—I wouldn't mind being like Jesus, who lets Nicodemus come and go as he wishes, trusting him right to the end. For freedom is key, it is what the spirit is about; as Jesus puts it, "the wind blows where it chooses, and you hear the sound of it, but you do not know where it comes from or where it goes. So it is with everyone who is born of the spirit" (John 3:8).

Buddhist Christian Prayer(s)

May 6, 2012

Cambridge, MA. I recently was asked to offer a closing prayer at an event in my long-time parish—Our Lady of Sorrows in Sharon, Massachusetts—where the speaker was Paul F. Knitter, a distinguished Catholic theologian and the Tillich Professor of Theology, World Religions, and Culture at Union Theological Seminary in New York. Paul had given a fine presentation of his inviting and provocative book *Without Buddha I Could Not Be a Christian* (Oxford: One World, 2009), and my prayer was to be the conclusion of the event.

Given the interfaith and exploratory nature of the event, I thought that in the closing prayer for this ecumenical and interfaith gathering, I would bring together, in one utterance, the Christian and Buddhist streams of prayer. I did so by weaving together a famous prayer attributed to Saint Francis of Assisi—well known to readers of this blog, I am sure—with a version of the vow of the Bodhisattva (a kind of Buddhist saint who vows the protection of all beings and delays her or his own liberation until all beings have been liberated). There are many versions of this vow on the internet, and I found online the translation I use below.

For the sake of that evening's prayer, I edited both in small ways, but the editing/omissions do not, I think, detract from the overall benefit gained by weaving them together. The reaction at the parish was quite positive, so I thought I would share the results with you here. I will not offer any heavy-duty theology of the melding, nor express any views at the moment on praying in two traditions at once, but would rather let the text speak for itself. Try reading aloud the prayer of Saint Francis with the Bodhisattva Vow and see how far hearing them and meditating on them together can lead you:

> Lord, Make me an instrument of your peace. Where there is hatred, let me sow love. Where there is injury, pardon. Where there is doubt, faith. Where there is despair, hope. Where there is darkness, light. Where there is sadness, joy. May I be a safeguard for those who have no protection, A guide for those who journey along the way; For those who wish to go across the water, May I be a boat, a raft, a bridge. May I be a home port for those who yearn for landfall, And a lamp for those who long for the light; For those who are tired, may I be a resting place, For all who need help, their servant. O Divine Master, Grant that I may not so much seek To be consoled, as to console; To be understood, as to understand; To be loved, as to love.

> Like the great earth itself and other eternal things, Enduring as the sky itself endures, For the boundless multitude of living beings, May I be the ground and vessel of their lives. For every single thing that lives, In number like the boundless reaches of the sky, May I be their sustenance and nourishment Until they pass beyond the bounds of suffering. For it is in giving that we receive. It is in pardoning that we are pardoned. It is in dying that we are born to Eternal Life. Amen.

Margaret Farley on the *Kama Sutra*

June 21, 2012

Cambridge, MA. Another reason for reading Professor Margaret Farley's *Just Love*, the book recently censured by the Congregation for the Doctrine of the Faith, is a reason that might occur mainly to people like me, theologian-cum-Hinduism-scholar-and-comparatist: it talks about the *Kama Sutra*, India's famous classical treatise (ca. third century CE) on erotic love. Everyone knows that *Just Love* deals with issues central to Catholic sexual ethics today, but it is worth noting that it also, in an introductory way, looks more widely.

Professor Farley creates space in the center of the book for learning from non-Western cultures and other religions and, most remarkably, from the *Kama Sutra*. Chapter 3, "Difficult Crossings," considers first the reasons why the *Kama Sutra* has been taboo in Christian ethics—closedminded, lingering colonial condescension toward the rest of the world and an Orientalist mentality that uses the East simply to buttress our already-settled views about the world and what we want others to be, so that we can admire ourselves all the more confidently. It is obviously very hard for us to take others' views to heart; it is hard work to break open the circle of the conversation and learn from the wider world without being too judgmental or oblivious to real points of disagreement. It is particularly hard when a text like the *Kama Sutra* brings such new insights to bear.

Farley then goes on to take up four cases that potentially have a lot to teach about sexuality and how to think about it: the "premodern islands of the South Seas," "African cultures," the *Kama Sutra*, and "the world of Islam." She does not delve deeply into any of these cases but, as it were, opens the door to further reflection. She does not, in this third chapter, draw any normative conclusions; neither does she blandly approve of what she presents.

Let me say a bit more about the *Kama Sutra*, of which you can find the old (Victorian) Burton/Arbuthnot translation online (though now very much superseded by the Wendy Doniger/Sudhir Kakar translation). The *Kama Sutra* is one of a series of instructive Sanskrit texts, summaries, and condensations that appeared in medieval India. Some such texts covered the law and society's rules, or commerce and the best practices of kings; others condensed the true meaning of the scriptures, be it the ritual texts of the Vedic hymns or the more theological meditations of the Upanishads. Some, like the *Yoga Sutras*, distilled the practical and intellectual insights required for a true discipline of the bodily, psychological, and spiritual reality of human being. The *Kama Sutra* distills the overall meaning, physical practices, and social conventions of love, sexual and social, in premodern India. Farley is correct in pointing out, in her elegant few pages on the framing insights of the text, that it puts love and pleasure in the context of human life as a whole, and makes *kama*—desire, pleasure, yearning, delight—available to learned readers. (It notes that even if women, barred from learning Sanskrit, cannot pick up and study the text, they do nevertheless relate to the same human realities of which the sutras speak.) She makes a good case, albeit very briefly, for learning from India's tradition of erotic love.

What Farley does not do is give us a feel for the vivid teachings of the *Kama Sutra* on erotic love, the parts of the treatise that make it one of the world's most famous books. Nor will I do so here, but some of the *Kama Sutra*'s section themes are wonderfully suggestive, again according to the Doniger/Kakar translation: in book 2, we hear about the lifestyle of the man-about-town; reasons for taking another man's wife; ways of embracing and procedures of kissing; types of scratching with the nails; ways of biting and slapping; varieties of sexual positions; the woman playing the man's part; a man's sexual strokes; oral sex; and how intercourse is to begin and end. Great detail, indeed. But the rest of the text expands our thinking about love and desire still more widely. Book 3 is about courtship, ways of winning over a bride, and how to manage a wedding, while book 4 talks about homelife after marriage, particularly in the situation where the man, as was allowed in some parts of India, had multiple wives. Book 5 is about extramarital sex, and the remarkable book 6 is advice to courtesans on what do with the men that come as customers. Book 7 is full of detailed, nearly pharmaceutical advice on stimulants, potions, things to sprinkle and things to rub, and all manner of ways of enhancing pleasure and potency.

Farley gives none of this detail—which would be enough to keep Christian ethicists, right and left, busy for quite a while—but nonetheless closes her section on the *Kama Sutra* wisely, helping us to begin to figure out what to do with all that detail, which we can and perhaps should read for ourselves. She cites an instruction near the end of the *Kama Sutra*, on its overall purpose: "A man who knows [*Kama Sutra's*] real meaning sees religion, power, and pleasure, his own convictions, and the ways of the world for what they are, and he is not driven by passion. The unusual techniques employed to increase passion, which have been described as this particular book required, are strongly restricted right here in this verse, right after it" (trans. Doniger/Kakar). The quote goes on, somewhat paradoxically, to observe that a clinically precise description of body parts, arousals, ointments and procedures, and manifold forms of union does not merely encourage one to do such things but also—perhaps primarily for the author, Vatsyayana, if we take him at his word—instills awareness and then dispassion: this is sex, this is pleasure; it is nothing more or less.

Farley's own book, in its careful considerations of today's sexual values and practices in light of tradition and divergence from it, might serve not to encourage such practices—as if anything goes—but perhaps to banish all kinds of false views—vague, naïve, disembodied—regarding what sex is about. As she says in concluding the section, the effect of studying a text like the *Kama Sutra* may be that "our eyes [are] turned forward and backward," are "sharpened," and our thoughts "both concentrated and provoked." Love is itself; it is just; it is just love, when the world is full of other things too.

As a comparative theologian, I wish to commend *Just Love* for where it points us, even if it does not quite take us there: the wisdom, lofty and exceedingly mundane, that other traditions—the *Kama Sutra*, and Farley's other examples too—have regarding the meaning and flesh-and-blood reality of human love. Today the uproar is about the rest of the book, about Margaret Farley, and about the CDF's insight into the fact that her book does not represent official church teaching. Perhaps, though, twenty or fifty or one hundred years from now, it may also be remembered as taking a cautious first step into that wider world, where we do well to learn from many cultures and religions and their classic texts—without necessarily approving of *everything* we learn—before finalizing our thoughts on the meaning of human reality and our deepest passions.

The Interreligious Mary of Colm Tóibín

January 20, 2013

Cambridge, MA. I spent a little time this week reading *The Testament of Mary* by the Irish novelist Colm Tóibín. It is a meditation in the voice of Mary, the mother of Jesus, in her old age, as she looks back on her life. I needn't summarize it here, since *America* has already printed a fine review by Diane Scharper, which you can find online.

The *Testament of Mary* draws on the Gospel according to John and not the other Gospels, and thus is directly limited to the wedding feast at Cana and the terrible, climactic scene where Mary stands by the cross of her crucified son. The wedding and crucifixion scenes are connected in Tóibín's telling, since Mary goes to the wedding primarily to try to get her son's attention and warn him about the danger his "signs" are bringing upon himself. That he changes water into wine—without her prompting—is a marvelous thing that she, too, is not prepared for, but which is also out of proportion with ordinary reality, a warping of the world most people can comfortably tolerate, just as the raising of Lazarus (recounted here as before Cana) is an upset to the expected, inevitable pattern of life followed by death. Eventually the signs of Jesus become too much, and the established powers become determined to kill him. Unable to stop the inevitable and sway her son to play it safe, she leaves the wedding before he does and returns home. (I was reading the book, by the way, in hopes of using it for my homily today, on the wedding feast at Cana, but decided it would have been too complicated to do so. For the same reason, I also omitted reflections on the "Cana of Galilee" chapter of

The Brothers Karamazov, since high school my favorite chapter in any literary work. If you've never read it, you can find it online.)

In reading the book, my interreligious radar turned on as well, for at the beginning and end of her testament, Mary confesses her "secret," lowkey but real connection to Artemis, the great Goddess whose great temple stood in Ephesus, where Mary lives out her last years. As Tóibín recounts Mary's visit to the temple, she recollects:

> And then I remember turning and seeing the statue of Artemis for the first time; in that second, as I stared at it, the statue was radiating abundance and bounty, fertility and grace, and beauty maybe, even beauty. And it inspired me for a moment; my own shadows fled to talk to the lovely shadows of the Temple.
>
> They left me for some minutes as though in light. The poison was not in my heart. I gazed at the statue of the old goddess, she who has seen more than I have and suffered more because she has lived more.

Later, still struggling with memories of her son who died so horrible a death, she not so much prays to Artemis as shares memories with her, mindful of her presence, telling "the story of what happened and how I came here." On the last page of her testament, Mary admits how sometimes alone in the morning she goes to the temple of Artemis, "when I awake or later when there are shadows coming over the world, presaging night. I move quietly. I speak to her in whispers, the great goddess Artemis, bountiful with her arms outstretched and her many breasts waiting to nurture those who come towards her. I tell her how much I long now to sleep in the dry earth, to go to dust peacefully with my eyes shut in a place near here where there are trees."

This is a fictional account, of course, and Tóibín is unlikely to win any awards from the church or find his book for sale in the Vatican bookshop. He is, to be sure, not a Catholic theologian.

But in the whole of the book, and in these brief moments where Artemis is mentioned, he perhaps catches something of an experience we need not entirely rule out in our own meditations on Mary. Even if today we for the most part accept the slow growth of Christian consciousness in the earliest church, and even if we recognize, in theory at least, how it took a long time for the Gospels to be composed and finalized, perhaps we are still too confident about what this early period must have been like for those closest to Jesus, those who loved him most. Mary, who pondered "all these things in her heart," as Saint Luke says, is shown by Tóibín to be slow in settling the meaning of her son, slow in accepting the growing sureness of the church about who Jesus was, what happened, and what her own role was at Cana and at the cross. We might say that even for her, Jesus truly was God, and that in part means that he was even to the end, and after it, a mystery to her. When the boundaries were not yet fixed, Tóibín is suggesting, it is not inconceivable that Mary, like her son, was open to things later foreclosed. And so, in a way that the church could not receive and record, because such things had no room in a world focused on Jesus and his Blessed Mother, Tóibín's Mary finds a connection to Artemis and talks to her.

I recount all of this here not to suggest that what Tóibín imagines was the truth of Mary or that his images give us reason to do the same as did his Mary. But in our world, a world where many religions flourish and it is nearly impossible to exclude the images, words, shadows of other faiths from our own meditations and prayers, we might take to heart this gentle, albeit sad account of Mary, who loved Jesus more palpably and concretely than anyone else, and who also found in Artemis, that Mother Goddess in Ephesus, a kindred spirit. We might welcome, quietly, into our meditation the images and words and shadows of other religions, so hard to welcome by way of good theology.

So Mary is now the patron of interreligious humility and learning? Perhaps too much of a claim to make. But read *The Testament* and see what you think about Mary there, in the beginning, and Cana and Artemis, when the mystery of Jesus was still stark and raw and the church had not yet found its language about its boundaries. At least imagine the possibilities before saying no.

9/11—1893: A Day of Interreligious Hope

September 11, 2013

Cape Cod, MA. A colleague has reminded me that 9/11, now seared into our memories as a day of tragedy and the clash of civilizations, is also, by a longer perspective, a day of hope for those committed to interreligious understanding.

For it was on this day in 1893, 120 years ago, that Swami Vivekananda created a sensation by his address to the World Parliament of Religions in Chicago. Other Hindus and Buddhists had come to the West before the Swami, to be sure, and he was not the only such representative at the parliament, but his words and rhetoric captured the imagination of those who were there that day.

In retrospect, it seems to have been one of those pivotal moments that brought a possible hope vividly before the eyes of people in that era of a slowly dawning global society. We have still not done with striving for true mutual understanding and deep religious exchange, but events like the Swami's speech are positive milestones along the way. Noting this does not take away from the sorrow of 9/11/2001, but it does remind us that violence is neither the beginning or end of our human destiny.

You can read more and hear the audio of his address online. Here is the written text of the relatively short speech:

Sisters and Brothers of America,

It fills my heart with joy unspeakable to rise in response to the warm and cordial welcome which you have given us. I thank you in the name of the most ancient order of monks in the world; I thank you in the name of the mother of religions, and I thank you in the name of millions and millions of Hindu people of all classes and sects.

My thanks, also, to some of the speakers on this platform who, referring to the delegates from the Orient, have told you that these men from far-off nations may well claim the honor of bearing to different lands the idea of toleration. I am proud to belong to a religion which has taught the world both tolerance and universal acceptance. We believe not only in universal toleration, but we accept all religions as true. I am proud to belong to a nation which has sheltered the persecuted and the refugees of all religions and all nations of the earth. I am proud to tell you that we have gathered in our bosom the purest remnant of the Israelites, who came to Southern India and took refuge with us in the very year in which their holy temple was shattered to pieces by Roman tyranny. I am proud to belong to the religion which has sheltered and is still fostering the remnant of the grand Zoroastrian nation. I will quote to you, brethren, a few lines from a hymn which I remember to have repeated from my earliest boyhood, which is every day repeated by millions of human beings: "As the different streams having their sources in different paths which men take through different tendencies, various though they appear, crooked or straight, all lead to Thee."

The present convention, which is one of the most august assemblies ever held, is in itself a vindication, a declaration to the world of the wonderful doctrine preached in the Gita: "Whosoever comes to Me, through whatsoever form, I reach him; all men are struggling through paths which in the end lead to me." Sectarianism, bigotry, and its horrible descendant, fanaticism, have long possessed this beautiful earth. They have filled the earth with violence, drenched it often with human blood, destroyed civilization and sent whole nations to despair. Had it not been for these horrible demons, human society would be far more advanced than it is now. But their time is come; and I fervently hope that the bell that tolled this morning in honor of this convention may be the death-knell of all fanaticism, of all persecutions with the sword or with the pen, and of all uncharitable feelings between persons wending their way to the same goal.

Is Allah Not Our God?

October 14, 2013

Cape Cod, MA. If you Google "Allah" and "Christian" and "Malaysia" together today, you will come up with a number of websites, including the BBC and *Wall Street Journal*, reporting the news today that the Malaysian Court of Appeals has ruled that Christians in that country will no longer be allowed to use the word "Allah" to refer to God. As the BBC reports it, "Upholding the appeal on Monday, chief judge Mohamed Apandi Ali said: 'The usage of the word Allah is not an integral part of the faith in Christianity. The usage of the word will cause confusion in the community.'" By implication, this Arab word is a Muslim word, not to be used by Christians (or Jews)—as if the Deity of each was a different person. The Christian protests to the contrary, supported by a lower court, were to no avail even if, as Ester Moiji, a Christian, put it, "If we are prohibited from using the word Allah then we have to retranslate the whole Bible, if it comes to that."

I am no expert on Malaysia, its political and religious tensions, and the history of Christianity there, and do not know the languages involved, so I cannot comment further on this particular case. But it does raise the question about the "ownership" of religious language. When does a term become so deeply connected with just one religion that it becomes impossible, or politically unacceptable, for other religions to use the same? In early modernity, Christian missionaries in Asia struggled with this problem, looking into Chinese, Japanese, Sanskrit, and other languages to see if there were words in use locally that could properly communicate the mysteries of the Christian faith. Some efforts were successful, but in India, for instance, straightforward and relatively safe translations—"deva" for "God"—often communicated the wrong meaning and reduced the meaning of "God" to something more like a "demigod." Conversely, too robust translations—"God" as "Ishwara" or "Bhagavan"—either seemed to be identifying the Christian God with Shiva or Vishnu (which was, to be sure, more than most missionaries intended) or to be co-opting Hindu terminology for a colonial deity arrived from the West. In some cases, missionaries despaired and opted for transliterations, as when the Holy Spirit remained, even in Asian languages, "*Spiritus Sanctus.*"

I am guessing that despite the political dimensions of the case in Malaysia, where religious tensions have grown in recent years, there is something of the same difficulty at stake as Muslims and Christians try once again to sort out what they have in common and what divides them. If "Allah" and "God" share the same perfections, superlatives, and uniqueness, how could they not be the same Person? Yet, if "Allah" has a lineage of revered usage reaching back in Arabic to the holy Qur'an, how could it not seem to pious Muslims that Christians are borrowing/taking over the name of "Islam's Deity"? Such choices are unfortunate: on the one hand, to use the same word, but without the educational processes in place to explain to the wider public how such a word as "Allah," properly understood with intellectual as well as religious reverence, cannot be a sectarian private property, or on the other, to refrain from using a common name, as if to communicate that the supreme compassionate and loving Being of Islam and the supreme compassionate and loving Being of Christianity (and the supreme compassionate and loving Being of Hinduism as well) are not necessarily one and the same? All of this is another reason for vigorous religious and interreligious education, to help us to avoid bad choices in theology and in politics.

Of course, I concede in closing, the Catholic Church is not immune to this kind of privatization of a popular and more inclusive religious language. It was only a few years ago that *Dominus Iesus* instructed the world that words such as "faith," "revelation," and "sacrament" are to be reserved for Christian usage alone, and that even "church" is a word that most Christian communities should not use regarding themselves. While the document had its own deep logic for such claims, the danger, evident to many Christian readers and readers of other faiths, was that the authors of the document missed the reality of the softer boundaries and vital bonds among religions that cannot be made secure by making them harder and fixed, by stipulating that words be used only the way "we" want them to be used.

Or even more generally, how many Christians in the United States today assume that "God," with that capitalized G, intends only the God of Christianity and take this to be such an obvious fact that "God" is simply a synonym for "the Christian God"? Now it is true that one can argue that in English, "God" has such a Christian heritage that, in fact, it serves as a proper name and not so smoothly as the designation of a Being who could similarly be called on by others as well. But there is a great deal to be lost by an interfaith stinginess, ours or the Court of Appeals in Malaysia, that would seem to say, "Your God is not God, your God is not Allah," ours alone is. Imprecise language too often gets us into trouble, but there are occasions, as this one, when the unruliness of language can be the saving grace.

"Is Allah not our God?" Together we need to ask and answer such questions, neither insiders nor outsiders getting to decide it on their own.

Finding God in Uluru

July 12, 2014

Uluru, Australia. The waning days of my sabbatical have seen me in Australia again, and again at Australian Catholic University (ACU) in Melbourne (and more briefly in Sydney and Brisbane), where I have served for the past month as a visiting research fellow. It has been a privilege once more to interact with the ACU faculty, particularly those engaged in interreligious dialogue and comparative theological studies, and it may turn out that I visit again next year. But at this moment I am somewhere quite different: in a motel a few miles from Uluru, that amazing, great rock right in the middle of Australia's outback. Formerly known as Ayer's Rock, Uluru is an amazing natural phenomenon with a complicated geological story reaching back over four hundred million years. It is an awesome spiritual site for the Anangu, that is, the indigenous peoples of Central Australia, who have been continuously resident on this land for forty to sixty thousand years. The land around Uluru is not quite desert, since there is some rain each year (twelve inches or more), but the terrain is dry and sandy with a range of trees, shrubs, and flowers I've not seen elsewhere. I saw some birds today, but not the kangaroo or emu or other animals that live around here. It is winter below the equator, and so at night the temperature drops to the thirties, even if during the day it can reach close to seventy. But all of this is the environment for the great rock itself.

Hardly anyone climbs Uluru any more, as tourists had done for decades, in deference to the strong views of the native peoples against climbing the Rock merely to see the view. (My impression is that after a sad history and long neglect, Australia, people and government as a whole, has in the past thirty years been sincerely making amends and respecting the original Australians, including their reverence for the land. Much remains to be done, but progress is being made, it seems to me.) But people do walk around the Rock, as I did this morning. The path is about six miles long, perhaps closer to seven if one adds in the necessary added trek back to the bus stop at the Cultural Centre. It is true that six miles on level terrain, on a cool morning (the forties rising to the sixties by noon) with refreshing breezes, is no great hardship. Yet the walk goes quite a bit slower than one might expect.

I slowed down to read the many informative signs along the way, some of which remind the walker that the cracks and colorations of the Rock, its ripples and strata (vertical, not the usual horizontal, since apparently some hundreds of millions of years ago the Rock was upended; what we see is actually the one end of a rock now reaching perhaps miles deep into the earth), and also the caves and rare, precious pools of water all have great power and significance for the people of the land. As several signs said, "the rock details are equivalent to a sacred scripture," a vivid and perhaps (to us) unexpected text for the reading. Living near the Rock for millennia, the Anangu people have been reading it over and over again, have learned to live with reference to it, and have woven a texture of stories, natural and supernatural, around it. For them, it is everywhere rich in deep meanings, which can only be shared in a minimal way with the visitor.

Certainly, I cannot read this language in stone, even when those "pages" tower over me, right in my face. But today at least, the Rock spoke to the newcomer and outsider. Every few minutes, I would see it in a new light, its supple and rippling surface casting new shadows and offering concise, sharp contrasts to the very blue and cloudless sky behind it. No vista was merely the same. I kept stopping, as did the few other walkers out today, at every turn in the road, now shown something new yet again. The Rock teaches even the one-day visitor, as if speaking in the elemental language of natural beauty that is a kind of universal language. (And, I may dare to add, it also reminds us that no one owns the sacred, so as to keep it entirely incommunicable to others.)

I also realized, as I trekked the final mile away from the Rock to the Cultural Centre, that its presence charges the atmosphere and terrain around it as well. I ended up noticing in very fine detail all those plants and shrubs and trees that I still cannot name, the little rocks that protrude from the ground like miniature Ulurus (and of course they are part of it), and the interplay of sun and shadow in even the most ordinary section of the path. Perhaps this is how the sacred radiant in nature works: by proximity and touch, in hot open spaces and cool shadows, with gusts and interruptions of the wind, through shifting colors in sunlight and (tonight) in the full moon, the Sacred makes everything around it sacred too, in circles emanating out from its center.

I'd better stop here, lest my professorial mind start to raise questions about "the sacred," "the natural sacred," the continuities and novelties one can expect in traditions passed down for thousands of years. I'd better stop before I am tempted to explain how this Uluru Rock, though seemingly silent over its millions of years, can truly be said to lay a hand upon even those who visit it for just a day. What does all this mean to the Christian? These are interesting questions for the academic and the theologian, and important ones too, not to be dismissed as irrelevant. But for now (particularly with my tired legs and palpable sunburn making themselves known a little more forcefully as the sun sets), I do better to add my voice of reverent appreciation to those of the very many others who have visited here, walked and seen and imbibed this special place—like the innumerable pilgrims who have walked through, around, across, up, and down other sacred places in every part of the world where natural and human powers, meanings wordless and worded, invest certain sites with an aura of holiness.

But finding it hard to deny the ever-present Jesuit instinct to affirm that here too—today at Uluru—we verify the fundamental truth of "finding God in all things—and places," I close by citing words from near the beginning of "*Nostra Aetate*": "From ancient times down to the present, there is found among various peoples a certain perception of that hidden power which hovers over the course of things and over the events of human history; at times some indeed have come to the recognition of a Supreme Being, or even of a Father. This perception and recognition penetrates their lives with a profound religious sense." It is not just the Hindu and Buddhist, the Jew and the Christian and the Muslim, who know of God's presence everywhere. And we need not be merely spectators; fifty years after the council, we can tweak these famous words, to admit that not just *they*, *some*, and *various peoples* before us come to recognize the hidden power of the Mother/Father in such holy places—but *ourselves* as well.

BKS Iyengar: Rest in Peace

August 20, 2014

Cambridge, MA. As many of you will know by now, BKS Iyengar, the distinguished and venerable master of yoga, died today at age ninety-five. A student of the renowned T. Krishnamacharya (1888–1989), who renewed yoga traditions for the modern era, Mr. Iyengar became a globally known and revered teacher himself. His disciples are found all over the world; many would come from afar for regular visits to his yoga center in Pune, India. His focus, I think, was on yoga for health, with an emphasis on physical practice such as would be available to people of all ages and conditions, even those who needed physical props to aid them in holding positions. When I visited his center in Pune in February, there was a special workshop under way for those seriously ill; many of those I saw seemed to be suffering from cancer and other debilitating diseases. He did not neglect the value of study, and seemed even in his old age increasingly intent on learning the wisdom of Patanjali's *Yoga Sutras*, often taken to be the first and classic text of the traditions of yoga. Mr. Iyengar was a writer, and his books, such as *Light on Yoga* and *Light on the Yoga Sutras*, have sold very widely, ever helpful to his students around the world.

But all of the preceding you can read in the obituaries for him, of which there are already many. And his disciples, some who have studied with him for four or five decades or more, will speak far more eloquently to his impact on their lives. All I can add are two things. First, there is always controversy in some Christian communities about yoga, whether it is good and salutary for Christians, a complement and support for Christian faith, or rather a distraction or a subtle temptation that draws people away from the Christian faith entirely. Indeed, though even among experts this is debated, it can be taken to be a religion unto itself, a powerful reappropriation of body and thus too mind and soul for an integral awareness that needs no other refuge. Certainly, I know a good number of people for whom yoga, often enough in the tradition of Mr. Iyengar, offers a spiritual way they had not found in the religion of their youth: Catholics practicing yoga; Catholic yoga; yoga.

But this brief remembrance at the time of his death is not the place to repeat lengthy considerations of what yoga is or how Christians should respond to the possibilities. I think rather more directly of the Gospel text that I would use, were there to be a Catholic memorial service for this master:

> John said to him, "Teacher, we saw someone casting out demons in your name, and we tried to stop him, because he was not following us." But Jesus said, "Do not stop him; for no one who does a deed of power in my name will be able soon afterwards to speak evil of me. Whoever is not against us is for us."

(Mark 9:38–40)

Now of course, Mr. Iyengar did not teach yoga in the name of Jesus; we need not exaggerate here. But neither need we resent a teacher who so clearly helped his disciples beyond their crippling disabilities of mind and body, who by attention to the inner secrets of the body cast out demons of the heart and intellect. He opened a path of well-being and healing for so many, including followers of Christ. He was not against us; he was therefore, Jesus seems to be saying, for us. We who are Christian can see his "deeds of power," in a deep sense, as "for Christ" and not "against Christ." (He told me, the time we talked last February, that when he met John Paul II in Rome, the pope told him that he would have loved to have Mr. Iyengar as his regular yoga teacher. But it was not to be.)

My second contribution is simply to draw your attention to his last book, *Core of the Yoga Sutras* (London: HarperThorsons, 2012). This late-in-life writing brings together in a simple way much of his life's work in teaching. To my newcomer's eyes, it seems to be one of the simplest and most unencumbered of his writings, wherein he sought out "the hidden links" inside the sutras in order to "unveil the core meaning, or heart," of Patanjali's wisdom on yoga. So I give Mr.

Iyengar the last word, by quoting from page xxxv of his prologue. His words are grounded in his spiritual autobiography, the journey of his soul, and they radiate his discernment, his own spiritual exercises:

> I began practicing with reverence, to study my own body and mind in those rare moments when they were co-operating; usually there was a tug-of-war between them. Despite many restless and negative thoughts, I persisted and pursued my sadhana, and this began to transform my physical and mental framework, bringing positive thoughts and hopes. I began to observe the deep reflexes of my practices, and penetrate my inner self, which enthused me and brought me further understanding.
>
> My practice roused my instinctive reflex actions, which remain sharp even now in spite of my advanced age. They are innate responses to natural tendencies. I began correlating and transforming these natural tendencies that occurred in my sadhana with my own reflexive, intuitive thoughts, to achieve right and ever-lasting experiential feelings.

And on page xxxvii,

> Each day, the moment I begin my sadhana, my entire being is transformed into a fresh state of mind. My mind extends and expands to the vastness. It is in that inner limitless space that I begin to work, trying various ways and means.

May he now rest in the way he found, dwelling in the light, in the vastness of the everlasting bliss.

High Holy Days, Twice Over: When Jewish and Hindu Feasts Coincide

September 25, 2014

Cambridge, MA. It is more than enough of an opportunity for those of us who are Christian to be mindful during the next days that Jews are observing a series of most intense and varied holy days—from last night (September 24, Rosh Hashanah year 5775) to Yom Kippur (October 3), the Day of Atonement. We ordinarily do not note or notice the holy days of another religion, but the deep connections of Jewish and Christian traditions should give us pause and slow us down in the next days, so that we see our ordinary lives differently, with a renewed sense of what God promises us and a deepened sense of repentance for the possibilities we have missed. Certainly, our Jewish neighbors are reminding us that starting over and repenting for our sins are not once-a-year events but right-now possibilities for us.

But there is more. Today (September 25) also marks the beginning of Navaratri, the nine days of the fall harvest festival marked by many Hindus with a mix of celebration and fasting that culminates in special worship of the Goddess Durga (October 3) as she triumphs over a great demon who in myth takes the form of a buffalo. It is a festival of the harvest and a time to worship the Goddess. For us who are Christian, it is an early reminder of harvest as a time of thanksgiving and an opportunity, in our bloody and violent, violated world, to recognize how God turns evil back into good.

That so many of our neighbors—Jews and Hindus—are right now in the midst of a holy season invites us to recognize and glimpse again the holiness of days that seem to us so ordinary. We can with Jews mark the freshness of the year and regret our straying and errors; with Hindus, we can give thanks for the bountifulness of divine gifts year after year, and the eventual, sure divine triumph over evil.

But most basically, by this convergence of Jewish and Hindu holy days, we are invited and challenged to put aside a purely secular notion of time in favor of a richer sense of multiple calendars and multiple markings of the divine. Time is uneven, varied, and never quite what suits our own calendar of events. So in the end, our time too—even if it is not Jewish, not Hindu—is made holy, holier, by the sacred days upon which we have now embarked. In our own way, our own ordinary days too are holy, thanks in part to the piety and celebrations of our Jewish and Hindu sisters and brothers.

The Pope and the Hugging Guru

December 2, 2014

Cambridge, MA. The Vatican today (International Day for the Abolition of Slavery) was the site for an unprecedented gathering of religious leaders, signing together a Declaration of Religious Leaders against Slavery. You can find the pope's speech online. It includes these important words of justice and interreligious witness:

> Let us call to action all persons of faith and their leaders, Governments, businesses, all men and women of good will, to lend their unwavering support and to join the movement against modern slavery, in all its forms. Supported by the ideals of our confessions of faith and our shared human values, we all can and must raise the standard of spiritual values, our joint efforts, our liberatory vision, to eradicate slavery from our planet. I pray that the Lord will grant us the grace to become a neighbour to all persons, without exception, and to provide active support whenever we encounter on our way an elderly person abandoned by all; an unjustly enslaved and mistreated worker; a refugee caught in the snares of crime; a young person walking the streets of the world, a victim of the sex trade; a man or a woman tricked into prostitution by people with no fear of God; a child mutilated for his or her organs, all of whom call out to our consciences, echoing the voice of the Lord: I assure you that whatever you did for one of the least of these brothers and sisters of mine, you did for me.

I can add here only a more specific, even personal connection. The photo with this post shows Pope Francis with Amritanandamayi Amma—Amma, Mother—one of the most well known of the globe-trotting Hindu gurus of the modern era. (See my earlier piece, reporting on my encounter with her.) She is known most popularly as "the hugging guru" because, speaking only a few words of English, she simply embraces those who come to her. To her devotees, she is a physical, concrete presence of the divine, a kind of living sacrament. As I reported here several years ago, I met her once when I offered a word of welcome at one of her American functions. I remember the brief encounter, and her personal warmth, fondly.

I also had occasion this semester to give a lecture on her, sharing the presentation with a student, a disciple of Amma, who reflected on the identity of Amma for her disciples as a divine-human teacher. The productive comparison—resemblance and contrast—was with Mary, mother of Jesus, as the single human being, other than Jesus, who in Catholic piety verges on a human-divine identity. While Amma, the Hindu Mother, is in many ways different from Mary, mother of Jesus, meditating on Amma and the Blessed Mother together was instructive.

It was interesting, then, today—the last class day of the semester—to see her with the pope, not merely for a photo op, but to make a shared public claim, along with other religious leaders, again the evils of traffic in humans, subjected to degradation and slavery. Faith in action, faith across boundaries.

Caste and Christianity:
Old, New, Old Insights

February 2, 2015

Cambridge, MA. Given today's new snowstorm—it may be February 2, but no chance of even seeing the groundhog here, at least—it seems hard to believe that two weeks ago I was still in India. Time flies, climates change quickly. But today's storm, which has almost closed Harvard, has given me time to sort out a few more things from my trip, including some of the books I brought back with me and that have been piled up on my desk.

A very small but fierce book given to me on the last day of my trip by a pastor in New Delhi is *Slavery* (New Delhi: Critical Quest, 2008) by Jotirao Phuley (1827–1890). It caught my attention since there is a lot of debate in India today about being Indian, being Hindu, being Christian—and how these identities relate to caste identity, embraced or imposed. Phuley was a reformer and social critic, sensitive to the plight of women in India, the need for education for the poor, and above all, the dignity and rights of tribals and people of the lowest castes—who, in perhaps coining the term, he called the crushed (*dalits*). His pages vividly portray the plight of the poorest and most oppressed members of society; ahead of his times, he believed firmly that society could change if people no longer accepted inequality merely because they had no hope for changing it. Phuley and a host of others after him have struggled to rethink the social and religious structures of India, for the benefit of all.

A second book—which I had bought even before my trip but had in mind throughout it—is David Mosse's *The Saint in the Banyan Tree: Christianity and Caste Society in India* (Berkeley: University of California Press, 2012). This book was recently honored by the Society for Hindu-Christian Studies as the Best Book in Hindu-Christian Studies (History/Ethnography) 2009–13. It traces back long before even Phuley the problems of caste in India (especially in South India) and, in particular, the complicated, sometimes unfortunate history of Christianity and caste. From the time of the first Western missionaries in India, and particularly with figures such as Roberto de Nobili (1579–1656), Christians—perhaps most notably Catholic Christians—have sought ways to accommodate caste rather than reject it entirely (and thus require of converts a total disowning of caste status). Often very well intended and without any intent to abandon those of lower and untouchable castes, this policy was forever traversing mine fields of politics, de facto but also oppressive hierarchies, and the complications of compromises with power. As a result, Mosse shows in great detail, all kinds of distortions became part of Christian/Catholic life for the sake of building the Christian community but also, to ill effect, gave that community a deeply caste-inscribed identity. As the Dalit movement has grown, particularly in South India, the controversies over caste have grown, as Dalit Christians—or Christian Dalits—have become more outspoken and critical, arguing vehemently not only against the dominant religious hierarchies and structures but also against caste consciousness within the church. Much of this controversy is being even now lived out in Indian communities; Mosse's great service is to offer a long perspective on it and, by careful attentiveness to the complexities of caste and Catholicism, to disabuse us of any expectations that a simple solution is at hand, justice dealt out in stark contexts where good and evil are sharply contrasted. Like the banyan tree of the title, Catholicism has become deeply part of the cultures of India—not indistinct, but no longer easily separable.

The third book of note given to me shows how much the struggle continues, and yet how far it has come: the *One Volume Dalit Bible Commentary: New Testament*, edited by T. K. John, SJ (New Delhi: Centre for Dalit Studies/Subaltern Studies, 2010). Each book of the New Testament is expounded and commented on from a Dalit perspective by some of the most prominent scholars writing on the Bible today from a Dalit perspective (including James Massey, Monodeep Daniel, A. Maria Arul Raja, SJ, Philip Peacock, Sunil Caleb, and other distinguished scholars). Eventually, I am told, the volume will appear also in various regional languages in India. T. K. John's introduction

("Why a Dalit Bible Commentary Now?") and a series of short introductory essays come first, then a set of longer essays on the relevance of the various New Testament books to the Dalit community, and then full commentaries on each book of the New Testament.

Here I can give just one example, pertinent to the Gospel of Mark, which we are using at Sunday Mass during this cycle "B." After a preface to the Gospel, "A Society Caste-Free with Jesus Culture," the passage-by-passage commentary begins. Take for example Mark 1:21–28 NRSV:

> They went to Capernaum; and when the Sabbath came, he entered the synagogue and taught. They were astounded at his teaching, for he taught them as one having authority, and not as the scribes. Just then there was in their synagogue a man with an unclean spirit, and he cried out, "What have you to do with us, Jesus of Nazareth? Have you come to destroy us? I know who you are, the Holy One of God." But Jesus rebuked him, saying, "Be silent, and come out of him!" And the unclean spirit, throwing him into convulsions and crying with a loud voice, came out of him. They were all amazed, and they kept on asking one another, "What is this? A new teaching—with authority! He commands even the unclean spirits, and they obey him." At once his fame began to spread throughout the surrounding region of Galilee.

Here is the *Dalit Bible Commentary* comment, in full:

> Jesus did not undergo any formal training in any of the Jewish schools, nor did he belong to any of the Jewish sects. But with his divine assertion through his words and deeds he healed the sick while mercilessly dealing with the evil forces that oppressed them (v. 25). What amazed the people was the irresistible authority (vv. 22, 27) with which the untrained young man was teaching with charismatic assertion. The newness of Jesus' teaching was his direct encounter with evil forces while restoring people with good health and honor. Giving a death blow to social wickedness too is part of his mission. The arrogance of the caste-minded people, like the evil spirits, would be decimated when the Dalits are awakened to God-given human dignity. The mention of places like Nazareth, Capernaum, and Galilee indicates the nature of Jesus' ministry amid those who were relegated to be dirty people by those counting themselves as holy and hence privileged.

Every New Testament passage receives a similar succinct, sharp-edged treatment. My sense of the volume is largely very positive, though I do have some hesitations. On the one hand, I am very impressed and grateful that these scholars have done the work of putting together so singular and forceful a reading of the New Testament. The problems historically traced by Mosse, and exposed so prophetically by Phuley, are now receiving a systematic treatment in light of the word of God. Particularly when the volume appears in the vernaculars, it will be an indispensable tool for preaching and catechesis and should have a long life in the churches of India. My hesitation comes when, as in the passage quoted, the hard edge of criticism is so pronounced. It portrays a Jesus entirely against the establishment, perhaps more extremely so than the passage being interpreted warrants. Jesus read in the synagogue; however trained or not, Jesus was a Jew; the demons cast out are not simply a stand-in for the religious establishment. More nuance on who Jesus was and how he related to his own Jewish people at all levels would complicate matters, to be sure, and perhaps diffuse some of the anger. In other words, this reading of the Gospel passage exemplifies one long strand of Dalit criticism of Hinduism and Brahmanical structures: the fierce and unrelenting voice of protest. Anger is justified, and I, not a Dalit, have no grounds casually to say otherwise. But stark oppositions can be too dialectical, too stark a dichotomy, too oppositional a relationship to the Jewish people as a whole, or the Hindu communities as a whole. These seem not conducive to the healing that must occur across the whole of any socially and religiously riven society. Caste is a universal problem and fact of life; but not all Hindus or all Brahmins are arrogant, evil, or demonic. As an outsider but one with many years of experience in India and many Christian and Hindu friends (from Dalit to Brahmin), I worry that skipping over complexity for the sake of stark polarities will not in the long run work very well either. Jesus too saw complexity in the world around him, and we might end up simply extending the old history of Christianity and caste in a new guise, and echoing again the strong words of Jotirao Phuley, in yet another century.

Compassion and Dialogue Shall Embrace

November 27, 2015

Cambridge, MA. Most of my posts for *America* have to do with interreligious dialogue and the deeper learning that occurs when we take each other's religious traditions seriously. You will also know that I've insisted, again and again, that interreligious cooperation and commitment are distinctive features of the church today. Good Catholics embrace dialogue; it is only our latter-day cafeteria Catholics who think they can omit dialogue from their theology, piety, and practice.

In any case, in the past few days I've been struck once again by how Pope Francis is giving his own interpretation to the importance of dialogue. Consider what many of us read in the *New York Times* on November 27, the day after Thanksgiving, about the visit of Pope Francis to the Kangemi neighborhood—community, slum—of Nairobi in Kenya, as part of his first visit to Africa. During this poignant and perfectly wonderful visit to the poorest and most vulnerable, Francis made starkly clear the concern of the church and the responsibility of Christians in Kenya and globally:

> I wish to call all Christians, and their pastors in particular, to renew their missionary zeal, to take initiative in the face of so many situations of injustice, to be involved in their neighbors' problems, to accompany them in their struggles, to protect the fruits of their communitarian labor and to celebrate together each victory, large or small. I realize that you are already doing much, but I ask to remember this is not just another task; it may instead be the most important task of all, because "the Gospel is addressed in a special way to the poor."

In this context we can discern and notice Francis's particular slant on interreligious dialogue. Certainly, he remains steadfast in affirming Vatican II's commitment to dialogue as an indispensable and irreversible dimension of the church's work in the world. So too, as in the interfaith service at Ground Zero during his American visit in September, Francis remains firm in showing, in word and practice, that people of different faiths need to work together and pray together, in powerful witness and strong rebuke to those who cloak violence and selfishness in religious language. He states this clearly in an interfaith gathering in Nairobi:

> Ecumenical and interreligious dialogue is not a luxury. It is not something extra or optional, but essential, something which our world, wounded by conflict and division, increasingly needs. Indeed, religious beliefs and practice condition who we are and how we understand the world around us. They are for us a source of enlightenment, wisdom and solidarity, and thus enrich the societies in which we live. By caring for the spiritual growth of our communities, by forming minds and hearts in the truths and values taught by our religious traditions, we become a blessing to the communities in which our people live. In democratic and pluralistic societies like Kenya, cooperation between religious leaders and communities becomes an important service to the common good. In this light, and in an increasingly interdependent world, we see ever more clearly the need for interreligious understanding, friendship and collaboration in defending the God-given dignity of individuals and peoples, and their right to live in freedom and happiness.

Francis's habitual slant on dialogue is becoming familiar. In *Laudato Si'*, for instance, he insists that there are many dialogues that are now part of the work of the church, and interreligious dialogue is one of those undeniable dialogues:

> The majority of people living on our planet profess to be believers. This should spur religions to dialogue among themselves for the sake of protecting nature, defending the poor, and building networks of respect and fraternity. Dialogue among the various sciences is likewise needed, since each can tend to become enclosed in its own language, while specialization leads to a certain isolation and the absolutization of its own field of knowledge. This prevents us from confronting environmental problems effectively. An open and respectful dialogue is also needed between the various ecological movements, among which ideological conflicts are not infrequently encountered. The gravity of the ecological crisis demands that we all look to the common good, embarking on a

path of dialogue which demands patience, self-discipline and generosity, always keeping in mind that "realities are greater than ideas." (n. 201)

Authentic Catholicism cannot neglect dialogue, even when this does not silence the necessary and distinctive voice of Christians, as the same encyclical shows:

> Furthermore, although this Encyclical welcomes dialogue with everyone so that together we can seek paths of liberation, I would like from the outset to show how faith convictions can offer Christians, and some other believers as well, ample motivation to care for nature and for the most vulnerable of their brothers and sisters. If the simple fact of being human moves people to care for the environment of which they are a part. . . . It is good for humanity and the world at large when we believers better recognize the ecological commitments which stem from our convictions. (n. 64)

In the following pages of the encyclical, Francis sensitively finds his way through key biblical texts to discern the Christian starting points for our care for the environment and our protection of all living being. Dialogue, compassion, and justice form the substance of Christian witness today and make clear, rather than obscure, what the good news of Jesus Christ means in today's world.

Francis thus is beginning to show us that he has as distinctive a stance on interreligious dialogue as did his predecessor Joseph Ratzinger, Benedict XVI. He is no less an intellectual; he is just a different sort of thinker. If Benedict was concerned primarily about doctrinal purity and the danger of relativism, Francis is concerned primarily about charity, love, and service, including a direct religious and Christian response to the most urgent needs of our world today. He has not shown any hesitation or timidity regarding doctrine and truth; neither has he equated doctrinal correctness with the mission of the church. He has not dwelt on the nature of the relationship among religions, but simply insisted, over and again, that religious people must work together, learn from one another, and pray together. We are all, as it were, in the Kangemi slums, and we shall be judged by our compassion, our charity, and our refusal to turn away from those in direct need. Those of us who are scholars ought not to leave our desks or stop writing our books, but we need to recognize very vividly and urgently the greater whole of which our writing is just a part. If our research, writing, and teaching do not directly help the poor, we had better make sure that what we do is part of the compassionate, merciful, and just work of the church. But what the scholar, in the disciplined and quiet work of mind and heart, is to *do* is the topic for another post.

In this light, we can turn finally to Francis's announcement of the Jubilee Year of Mercy, which begins on December 8. It includes a turn to dialogue, as one of its ordinary, expected features:

> I trust that this Jubilee year celebrating the mercy of God will foster an encounter with these religions and with other noble religious traditions; may it open us to even more fervent dialogue so that we might know and understand one another better; may it eliminate every form of closedmindedness and disrespect, and drive out every form of violence and discrimination. (n. 23)
>
> The opening of the Doors of Mercy tolerates no miserly controls of entrance: there are no border patrols keeping people away from God's mercy, regardless of religious differences.

But let me end by hearkening to a different voice. This Sunday, the first Sunday of Advent, is November 29, and so it marks exactly thirty-five years since the death of Dorothy Day in 1980. Who better than her to sum up what Francis has been saying again in our era:

> What we would like to do is change the world—make it a little simpler for people to feed, clothe and shelter themselves as God intended them to do. And to a certain extent, by fighting for better conditions, by crying out unceasingly for the rights of the workers, of the poor, of the destitute—the rights of the worthy and the unworthy poor in other words, we can to a certain extent change the world; we can work for the oasis, the little cell of joy and peace in a harried world.

(*The Catholic Worker*, June 1946)

Jews and Christians Together:
On the Deep, Too-Brief Wisdom
of Joseph Redfield Palmisano, SJ

January 1, 2016

Cambridge, MA. On Christmas Day, Joseph Redfield Palmisano, SJ, died at Campion Center, the Jesuit health facility in Weston, MA, brought down finally by a brain tumor. Joe, a Boston College (BC) graduate, had worked as a Jesuit in Jamaica, given retreats at Eastern Point Retreat House (Gloucester), and studied for his degree at Trinity College in Dublin, at the Irish School of Ecumenics. But slowly, in the past few years, he had slowed down. He had just turned forty-one when he died.

His funeral on December 30 was a moving—sad, reflective, joyful—event that brought together his parents and brother, family and friends, at least one hundred Jesuit concelebrants, and a standing-room only congregation in the Jesuit chapel at Campion. Robert Levens, SJ, the rector at Campion and presider at the Eucharist; Anthony Soohoo, SJ, the homilist; and many of us in conversation before and after the Mass testified to how Joe radiated warmth and graciousness, simplicity and openness, a natural ability to get along with everyone and readiness to help others, a deep faith and companionship with Jesus and his fellow Jesuits, and, in his final illness, an edifying patience and surrender of his life into God's hands, just after turning forty-one.

I knew Joe since he was an undergraduate at BC, but many knew him deeper and better than I over the years. The last time we had lunch together was two years ago. So all I can add here is a testimony to his contribution to interreligious dialogue, and specifically to building on the Second Vatican Council's great heritage of closer and deeper relationships between Christians and Jews. His impressive book, *Beyond the Walls: Abraham Joshua Heschel and Edith Stein on the Significance of Empathy for Jewish-Christian Dialogue* (Oxford University Press, 2012), explored the vital movements that have and must underlie Jewish-Christian encounters in our era. Throughout, Joe reminds us, the dialogue must be nourished by empathy—a deepening communion with our others, an intuitive connection that allows us to glimpse respectfully how they see themselves, a coming to be of friendships that change us and create for us a new home together. This is where the Jewish-Christian conversation can lead if we understand what is possible and at stake.

Joe spells out the dynamics of this empathy in a sensitive and expertly researched portrayal of Edith Stein (1891–1942), a convert to Catholicism and nun who died in Auschwitz. As he puts it, drawing on her wisdom:

> One may draw the analogy from Stein's experience to the interreligious dialogue for "dialogues and conversations with people of other faith traditions usually begin with the familiar" and move towards "a progressive encounter with the unfamiliar . . . a movement—literal as much as metaphorical—over the threshold into a world where one's sense of identity is questioned." Hence, through the hermeneutic of Stein's phenomenological theory and praxis we may enter the ebb and flow of the dialectic of giving and receiving that widens memory for us through Stein's interreligiously important narrative. Stein incarnates a way of loving in both her writings and her praxis that responds to the givenness of another. Norris Clarke argues that any "particular action, if done consciously and responsibly, is inescapably my action." By these repeated actions "the whole person behind the act" will "gradually construct an abiding moral portrait" of oneself, "like an artist's self-portrait." Stein's narrative portrait is one of *empathy*. (3)

In turn, he brings her vision of human and humane connectedness into conversation with that of Rabbi Abraham Joshua Heschel (1907–1972), a Polish-born American rabbi and one of the leading Jewish thinkers of the twentieth century:

> In a fashion corresponding to Stein's thesis on empathy, Heschel refines his categories in speaking of prayer as "an act of empathy" where "our

reading and feeling the words of the prayers" is accomplished through "an imaginative projection of our consciousness into the meaning of the words." In this way we may con-primordially *feel* "the ideas with which the words are pregnant." Heschel argues, "at first, the words and their meaning seem to lie beyond the horizon of the mind . . . we must, there-fore, remember that the experience of prayer does not come all at once. It grows in the face of the word that comes ever more to light."

Joe observes, "Notice the correspondence between Heschel's and Stein's perspectives. 'I' imaginatively project 'myself' towards the Other in prayer. And just as one rises to the 'greatness' of the words in the prayer of empathy, we rise to the greatness of the other when our prayer becomes the deed of a *living* empathy" (71).

The book was well noticed and received very favorable reviews. Certainly, Joe might have influenced several generations of students on campus, opening for them the way of dialogue. And where might Joe's deep study and humane, spiritual learning have led him, in a next book or books on the Jewish-Christian encounter and com-munion? For one thing, he would have kept reminding us who are Christian to be courageous and humble in rediscovering ourselves in giving thanks for the Jewish roots of our Christian faith, that we might all the more deeply discover in Jews our neighbors and friends, our elder sisters and brothers. Near the book's end, he voices an insight that bears study in the overheated political arena of 2016:

A Catholic ecclesio-theological *rapprochement* towards a concept of God who is *always, already* in dialogue with otherness respectfully recognizes, and engages with (and is not threatened by), Catholicism's own Jewish otherness. This frank and mature affirmation allows for Jews to be our partners in dialogue *as Jews*, without any expectation, as Vatican II argues, for conversion. And yet, this basic affirmation has the power today of being subversive in the sense that our sharing of narratives with one another creates a richness in diversity that subtly challenges the postmodern isolationism of a life fragmented by fear of the other. Jewish and Christian stakeholders have been engaging with one another, espe-cially since Vatican II, through a narrative exchange. The personal nar-ratives and faith narratives, stories about self and community, have built up the bonds over the years. (145)

And so, there can be no demonization or exclusion of the other, as if the borders might be closed: "If a person is an end in him/herself, then the goal of every stakeholder regarding an interdependently minded way of proceeding will only be realized insofar as the different dialogue partners become vulnerable for one another through the drama of embrace" (146). But deep and demanding virtues are then needed, since at times it will not be easy:

> Our desire for empathy with the other will also mean simply waiting for, not forcing, the other to dialogue. And *waiting* is itself an empathic stance, an approach rooted and grounded in the silent and humble solidarity with "the powerless." It is a *teshuva* of listening where a return to a shared future becomes possible only "when we become the victims' ally."

And so the work lies before us who continue:

> The real-time work of reestablishing ethical relationships between oneself and many more others is our future, hope-filled work in Jewish-Christian dialogue. The theory and praxis of Abraham Joshua Heschel and Edith Stein, against the horizon of the *Shoah*, have given us an action-transforming principle for this project: our dwelling together in empathy. Our con-primordial presence with one another in the world may only assist us in hastening slowly towards a deeper presence in the world, a way of being with one another and with the powerless from within the twenty-first century. (148)

Presence to one another, an empathy that is also listening, waiting, solidarity with the powerless—all brings us full circle back to Joe himself, the person and Jesuit. In his short life he exemplified the very ideal of the scholar whose thinking and writing stand in harmony with his praying, living, being. The book leads to the man, the man to the book.

Scholars like Joe are rare indeed, and the church needs more such women and men if we are to live up to the invitations and challenges of Vatican II and our ongoing dialogue with Jewish people. For this reason, too, among so many others, we will sorely, sadly, miss the voice and writing of this promising thinker, scholar, teacher, so deeply committed to the building of twenty-first-century Jewish-Christian understanding and friendship. Perhaps right now, though, might he not be sitting with Edith Stein and Abraham Heschel in the communion that does not end?

Should Christians Fast This Ramadan?

June 18, 2016

Cambridge, MA. The murderous event that occurred in Orlando early Sunday morning has, of course, captured the attention of us all, and it has been interpreted, rightly I think, from many angles. Omar Mateen was a disturbed young man, struggling with his own sexuality and disastrously lashing out; he was a terrorist dedicating himself to ISIS and its war on America. The event, as terrible as it was, is but a moment in the much larger scandal of our government—the Senate, the House, and we who elect them—and its abysmal failure to put even reasonable controls on guns. It was a hate crime once more victimizing the LGBTQ community, within the Latino/Latina community, a crime made worse by the leaders who cannot bear to mention the targeting of lesbian, gay, bisexual, transgender, and queer people when they lament the crime in general terms. All of this raises questions about how we are to act when our brothers and sisters have been killed and wounded, when Congress fails to fulfill its duties, when the violence rampant in our society seems to get ever worse; what ought you and I do? And does prayer do any good, prayer with or without urgent action?

What did come to mind during the week, as we think about the still larger picture, is that this is the month of Ramadan (June 5–July 5), this holy and rigorous month where nothing can be taken by mouth—even water—between sunrise and sunset. The observance of the Ramadan fast has over the centuries become one of the five pillars of Islam, and right now approximately a billion people worldwide are observing this fast, so very hard in the heat of summer and its very long days. The supports for this practice are deeply rooted in tradition, custom, traditional sayings (hadith), and the Qur'an itself. My study Qur'an highlights this passage:

> O you who believe! Fasting is prescribed for you as it was prescribed for those before you, that haply you may be reverent, for days numbered. But if any one of you be ill or on a journey, it is a number of other days, and for those who can bear it, the ransom of feeding an indigent person. Whosoever volunteers good, that is better for him, and to fast is better for you, if you knew. The month of Ramadan is that wherein the Qur'an was sent down as guidance to mankind, as clear proofs of guidance, and as the Criterion. Let him among you who is present fast during that month. And whosoever is ill or on a journey, it is a number of other days. God desires ease for you, and He does not desire hardship for you. It is so that you may complete the number and magnify God for having guided you, that haply you may give thanks. (2:183–85)

Fasting, with exceptions for those who are ill or on journeys; having less, and sharing it with the indigent; giving thanks to God the Protector, who protects us and does not test us beyond what we can do; marking the coming down of the Qur'an to earth, the criterion for separating the true from the false (2.53).

There are many hadith on this practice, including this beautiful one:

> The Messenger of Allah (saw) addressed his companions on the last day of Sha'ban, saying, "Oh people! A great month has come over you; a blessed month; a month in which is a night better than a thousand months; month in which Allah has made it compulsory upon you to fast by day, and voluntary to pray by night. Whoever draws nearer (to Allah) by performing any of the (optional) good deeds in (this month) shall receive the same reward as performing an obligatory deed at any other time, and whoever discharges an obligatory deed in (this month) shall receive the reward of performing seventy obligations at any other time. It is the month of patience, and the reward of patience is Heaven. It is the month of charity, and a month in which a believer's sustenance is increased. Whoever gives food to a fasting person to break his fast, shall have his sins forgiven, and he will be saved from the Fire of Hell, and he shall have the same reward as the fasting person, without his reward being diminished at all."

Multiplied a billion times over, this faith and this fast become a very powerful force indeed, greater than the violence, the hatred, the wall building and immigration banning that capture the headlines. Surely many readers will have noticed yogis who every once in a while call for worldwide days of meditation and mind focusing for peace; Ramadan is a much older, much more deeply rooted global practice for the better.

Really for the better? The *New York Times* has a front-page story today on the ambivalence and distress of young Muslims in this particular Ramadan season, amid the election politics and after Orlando. Worse, it has been reported that Mateen chose to carry out his murderous attack in Ramadan because it was Ramadan, to do his duty as a believer. Some politicians, in Europe at least, have claimed that Ramadan is a dangerous time because it drives Muslims to excessive fervor and some to erupt in violence. I cannot deny the possibility of sad exceptions, but such complaints surely miss the point, what Ramadan means for nearly all the Muslims on earth. It is a time of prayer and fasting, purification, charity, self-humbling before God, who alone metes out justice.

In 2001, when I was still teaching at Boston College, Ramadan fell in the month of December. To mark the three months commemoration of the 9/11 attacks, at Boston College we promoted a day of shared fasting for students, staff, and faculty of all faiths. At sunset (early, in December), we shared a simple meal. It was a very good thing to do.

One thing we can do—the billion-plus Christians in the world, with people of all faiths and spiritualities—is join with our Muslims neighbors and friends in some fasting and, when possible, in the sharing of the post-sunset meal (*iftar*) that breaks the fast.

Now I admit that it would be hard, very hard, for most of us, to undertake a fast as radical as that of Muslims: nothing to eat or drink between sunrise and sunset. Even for experienced Muslims, it takes days to adjust to the new rhythm. I could not right now undertake a serious Ramadan fast on my own, not if I want to keep doing all the things I need to do each day. (For Jesuits, food is fuel, no working on an empty tank.) But something is better than nothing, and if, let's say, we Catholics can undertake some acts of fasting of the modest, small Catholic kind (skip a snack, skip a meal, don't take that drink) during the rest of Ramadan, either by ourselves or right with our Muslim sisters and brothers, then we will be pushing back, spiritually and in solidarity, against the violence, against the irresponsible production and sale of weapons of mass murder, against the splintering of communities, against fanatics who think they own faith and own devotion, against the would-be wall builders, who only claim to be brave against the cowardice of our elected representatives and our own stupidity in electing the wrong people again and again.

Check around; I am sure some people you know are thinking of fasting in a time like this, even if they are not Muslims.

But will small tokens of solidarity between now and July 5, make a difference? Throughout history, as Mahatma Gandhi showed us so clearly—and also Dorothy Day and Cesar Chavez and Buddhist monks during the Vietnam war—fasting can become a powerful tool, resistance to evil great and small and a force for unity and community. Or as Jesus says: some demons can be driven out only by prayer and fasting (Mark 9:29).

Hindus and Catholics Together in Washington, DC

July 12, 2016

Cambridge, MA. Religion is much in the news these days, with the bad and the tragic gaining most of the attention. Much more is happening that is good and constructive and hopeful, even if rarely capturing the headlines, as most people of most religions do live together in harmony and mutual support, living out their faith in our complicated world.

One of the important conversations that does not capture much attention these days is that between Hindus and Catholics here in the United States. Catholics, we know, have been here a long time and constitute a major portion of the nation's population. The Hindu population of the United States is growing, now reaching about 2.5 million, or 0.5 percent of our nation's population. While at various times over the centuries there have been Hindu-Catholic tensions in India, here the relationships have been largely very friendly and positive. The Hindus who have come here, like other Indians, have been largely of the professional classes, doctors, educators, and engineers, committed to settling down, and interested in good schools, stable community life, and civic leadership. Many American cities now have Hindu temples built by the local community, and larger cities, such as New York, Chicago, and Los Angeles, have numerous temples.

Perhaps because no real problems have arisen, and because of the very diverse nature of Hindu religious structures, Hindu-Catholic conversations have been mainly local and low-key, rarely if ever reaching the level of official dialogues. In Los Angeles, for example, a Hindu–Christian dialogue group has been meeting for a number of years, with annual forums at Loyola-Marymount University. I have participated several times in the Hindu–Christian dialogue meetings that have been occurring annually in the Washington, DC, area for over twenty years. In May 2015, I was privileged to be part of a dialogue at the Durga Temple in Fairfax Station, Virginia, in which Cardinal Jean-Louis Tauran, president of the Pontifical Council for Interreligious Dialogue of the Vatican, was a leading participant.

Just the other day, on July 7—hence this post—there was another very valuable Hindu-Catholic dialogue, hosted by the US Conference of Catholic Bishops, in Washington, DC, near the Catholic University of America campus. This exploratory meeting, a follow-up to the May 2015 meeting, brought together about thirty Hindus and Catholics, leaders in their communities who are actively involved in the work of insuring that the two religions work together on issues of shared concern. We were particularly glad to have members of the Indian Catholic community in attendance too. Naturally, the long-settled and large American Catholic community has its own history and place in American society; it was exciting to hear from the Hindus present of their efforts to make sure that the Hindu religious traditions are better understood in American society. I have always thought that despite significant differences in theology and in some practices, Hindus and Catholics are meant for one another, possessed of consonant philosophical, theological, spiritual, and devotional traditions, and I was glad to be invited to participate in the day-long meeting.

While much was accomplished by the time together (including a fine Indian lunch), three substantive topics were discussed during the day, with speakers from the two traditions:

- Session 1: theological presentations on exclusivity and pluralism in Hindu and Catholic traditions, led by Shri Anuttama Dasa, with supplementary commentary by Dr. Abhaya Asthana and Dr. Francis X. Clooney, SJ

- Session 2: topics in Catholic-Hindu education, including curricula development and editorial review of religious texts in Catholic schools with special attention on Hinduism, led by Dr. Murali Balaji, with supplementary commentary by Dr. D. C. Rao, Dr. Carlos Taja, and Dr. Harry Dudley

- Session 3: a conversation on Hindu and Catholic approaches to environmental justice, led by Mr. Dileep Thatte, with supplementary commentary by Mr. Hemant Wadhwani and Rev. Charles Cortinovis

These topics were, I would say, wisely chosen, since they are diverse and of importance in various ways. The first deals with a fundamental theological topic, deep faith stances, and dispositions toward the other; the second with the practical essential matter of education, both the learning of the other tradition and the self-presentation of one's own tradition in textbooks used in private and public schools; the third with a matter of monumental urgency facing all people of all faith traditions today. It was good to hear from both communities on each topic, since this highlighted both common concerns and differences distinctively of import to each. The discussions following each were lively, perceptive questions were raised, and new angles were brought forward. It was a good sign that each discussion could have gone on much longer. While much more is required on these topics, both theoretically and in practice, we were thinking them through together, and that in itself is a valuable step forward.

The meeting was given a spiritual tone right from the start, with prayers offered by members of each community and a blessing (in Sanskrit) before lunch.

The organizers, including John Crossin, OSFS, executive director of the Secretariat for Ecumenical and Interreligious Affairs of the USCCB; Dr. Anthony Cirelli, associate director of the Secretariat for Ecumenical and Interreligious Affairs of the USCCB; and Mr. Sant Gupta, director of Interreligious Affairs at the Durga Temple, prepared for this meeting over the past year, with abundant consultation in the two communities. That the meeting ended with everyone asking when the next meeting will occur was a good sign that their meticulous work paid off.

At one point I was asked what the point of such meetings is. I said that I thought the meetings are valuable on several levels: first, there are many theological issues and matters of historical importance that we need to face together; second, every community today needs to build relations with other communities for the sake of good relations and friendships, all of which are of value especially before any crisis occurs; and third, as I mentioned above, Catholics and Hindus have much in common spiritually and in the presence of God, and can learn, in companionship, to be better Hindus and Catholics, wiser and more dedicated while advancing on the path to God.

We Can't All Be Mother Teresa

September 2, 2016

Cambridge, MA. I have been graced to meet a number of saints in my life—God's holy people, living lives of faith and hope and love, going beyond the bounds where most of us stop. And these have been fellow Catholics and Christians, and people in other faith traditions as well; if we have eyes to see, we are meeting them every day.

But I have never met and spoken with a canonized saint, though I have been in the presence of two. Saint John Paul II visited Chicago in 1979 when I was a doctoral student there, and I was in the assembly of priests and religious that he addressed one evening. And in December 1973, I worked for a few days at the Home for the Dying in Calcutta (now Kolkata). One morning I was mopping the floor when Mother Teresa came into the home with some foreign visitors, possibly benefactors. I was about twenty feet away from her, mop in hand; I probably could easily have gone up to her to say hello, but I couldn't at the moment think of anything to say. ("Mother Teresa, thank you! Keep up the good work! You inspire us!" Such words, sincere enough, seem to fall short. So I just watched, from a distance.) In any case, I was in the room with Mother Teresa—who, as you all know, will be canonized in Rome this Sunday.

I never really met her, then, and I think have never written about her, but Mother Teresa has played a role in my life. I have been studying Hinduism for over forty years. In 1973, I was already living in Kathmandu and teaching at St. Xavier's; the trip to Calcutta was part of that stay, a memorable drive down through the foothills of the Himalayas and across the plains of North India to the city, where I spent a few days, including my days volunteering at the Home for the Dying. When people ask me how I became interested in

Hinduism and why I went to India after college in 1973, I tend to say it was something unexpected, a kind of miracle, for a young man from New York who until 1972 or so had shown no interest whatsoever in Asia, India, or Hinduism. Some Hindu friends (half-jokingly) say that I was destined to visit India by the good karma of a previous life there, or that I am indeed Francis Xavier—one of the first Jesuits, and the first to visit India—returned once more.

But the reason I end up with is usually, "I was inspired by Mahatma Gandhi and Mother Teresa, and in stepping out into the wider world, I wanted to go where they did their wonderful, amazing works of mercy and love and peace, so as to be like them." Regarding Mother Teresa (more on Gandhi, another day), I was particularly enchanted by the fact that she not only went to India as a member of the Sisters of Loreto to dedicate herself to work in the schools but, most famously, discovered that such a vocation, as challenging and worthwhile as it was, was not enough, was not what God wanted of her. So as we all know, after some twenty years, she left the convent and went out into the streets to serve the poorest of the poor. She invented a new way of religious life by the instincts of faith. She was on her own. She had simply experienced, one day riding a train, her "call within a call": "I was to leave the convent and help the poor while living among them. It was an order. To fail would have been to break the faith."

Like other idealistic young persons, I wondered in 1973, and at other times, too, if the life I chose—being a Jesuit (I had entered the order in 1968, five years before going to Kathmandu)—was enough. Wasn't it too comfortable, too predictable, too safe? It was riveting to think of Mother Teresa, after decades of service, leaving behind a respected ministry to risk everything in faith. Like that merchant in the Gospel—"The kingdom of heaven is like a merchant in search of fine pearls; on finding one pearl of great value, he went and sold all that he had and bought it" (Matt 13:45–46)—I thought that the least I could do for "regency," the interim part of my Jesuit training between philosophy study and theology study, was to go far away, to a new place, among the poor, to see what God had in mind for me. To be, in a little way, like Mother Teresa.

I think of this today not only because of Sunday's canonization but because of the radical words of Sunday's Gospel. Jesus surprises the large crowd following him with words that must have stunned many of them:

Now large crowds were travelling with him; and he turned and said to them, "Whoever comes to me and does not hate father and mother, wife and children, brothers and sisters, yes, and even life itself, cannot be my disciple.

Whoever does not carry the cross and follow me cannot be my disciple. For which of you, intending to build a tower, does not first sit down and estimate the cost, to see whether he has enough to complete it? Otherwise, when he has laid a foundation and is not able to finish, all who see it will begin to ridicule him, saying, 'This fellow began to build and was not able to finish.' . . . So therefore, none of you can become my disciple if you do not give up all your possessions."

(Luke 14:25–33)

Mother Teresa, I am sure, would have been happy to know of this Gospel on the Sunday of her canonization (whether or not she would have wanted such an honor from Rome): to leave home, then to leave the convent, to seek God in the streets among the poorest. (I haven't quite yet figured out how to preach on this Gospel on Sunday, to the gathered congregation in my parish, but it will be hard to soften the challenge of such words: following Jesus is not for the fainthearted—it is not about moderate measures; it is all or nothing. How to speak of such a high ideal when it is so hard even to be moderately Christlike in our daily lives?)

Much more can be said about Mother Teresa and her work—there have always been critics, and we must listen carefully to their complaints about her and about how India often gets portrayed poorly in stories about her—but I will not take up such themes. Rather, I close by noting that, as you might have noticed, I did not end up acting just like Mother Teresa: I have remained a Jesuit. Over the decades, I have returned to India many times, but only as a visitor. I did not dedicate myself to the poorest of the poor but got a PhD in Indian studies. I did not find a way to live among the poorest, living rather in Chestnut Hill at Boston College, and now in Cambridge, Massachusetts, as a professor at Harvard. I spend my time not on the streets among the needy but in my office. I teach and I write books, not mop floors.

But I think, in my own way and by God's grace, Mother Teresa's good example set me on my course. Learning from the saints is rarely about literal imitation. We are not meant to be exactly like her or Francis of Assisi or Gandhi or Dorothy Day or Thomas Merton, or even exactly like Jesus but rather, in a similar way to take up "our" cross—not their crosses—and live out our own calling in the most compelling, wholehearted way each of us can. We all have a "call with a call" waiting for us. Mother Teresa, by her life and witness, is really reminding us to answer that personal call in the radical way that only you and I can. To be a (canonized) saint is not to be on a pedestal or to be a blueprint for others to follow but rather to be a kind of light, to show us how to walk our own ways of holiness.

The Clash of Religions Is Overstated:
The Coming of Interfaith Awareness
Is Irreversible

September 27, 2016

Edinburgh, UK—I spent only one day here and so will be content with a brief post. The city is lovely, much larger than St. Andrews and not quite so old. It was laid out in the nineteenth century, I think, and in most directions there are great vistas, avenues leading to imposing buildings. It is a city of imposing government buildings, including several great castles, but it is proud of its intellectual heritage. There are statues of the economist Adam Smith and the philosopher David Hume, and of John Knox, the fierce Reformer (who might well be dismayed at the progressive learning occurring in Edinburgh today), and a very large and imposing monument to Sir Walter Scott, that prolific and popular novelist of the nineteenth century.

My destination was New College, which is several hundred years old and to be distinguished from Old College, which is several centuries older. New College, which looks out onto the Firth of Forth, is home to the School of Divinity and its distinguished faculty. I had been invited to give a lecture to a gathering of about seventy-five faculty and students on interreligious learning after Vatican II and how my study of Hinduism is a genuinely theological discipline with serious implications for Christian and Catholic theology. I think it went well, judging from the many good and hard questions that were asked.

My host was Joshua Ralston, a young American professor who has recently become lecturer in Muslim-Christian relations in the divinity faculty here and who works with the faculty in the Centre for the Study of World Christianity. In attendance at the lecture was Alex Chow, lecturer in world Christianity, who also came to dinner afterwards.

There were also scholars and students from a number of different countries, including some working in the fields of Judaism, Hinduism, and Buddhism, and even a student scholar of the indigenous peoples of northern Scandinavia. I was honored to meet the well-known and now very senior scholar Robin Boyd, former director of the Irish School of Ecumenics and known for more than five decades for his work on Christianity in India. And so on—an incredible diversity of people and interests in old Edinburgh.

At dinner, Joshua and Alex discussed their work, and I was particularly impressed with the scope of their connections with scholars across the United Kingdom and the European Union, and more widely in the Middle East and across Asia and other parts of the globe. Global Christianity is exactly that, a new comprehension of Christianity as not merely Western, nor merely the West plus its former missions and colonies, but rather a truly global phenomenon— East and West, North and South—that is impossible to understand from any single vantage point. There is much in history and doctrine and practice that links Christians back to Jesus himself, but no single instance of how that works out is sufficient to predict how Christians will be elsewhere. The study of Muslim-Christian relations is part of a worldwide living network of scholars and practitioners, Muslim and Christian, who work together to improve understanding between these two great communities. We are inundated with reports of Muslim-Christian friction and enmity. Yet deeper, more widespread, and more enduring is a great global web of old and new connections linking Muslims and Christians as never before, in study and work and prayer.

I mention all this detail because it made clear to me—and I hope now to you as well—that interreligious violence and hatred, suspicion, the building of walls and the exclusion of the stranger are truly *not* the main forces of our time; ignorance is *not* growing stronger all the time; differences are *not* becoming insurmountable. Yes, there are terrible problems in our world, and no one should minimize the violence and threats to minorities in certain places; we ought not merely pretend that all is well.

But centuries from now, what I could see happening in Edinburgh—just as in Cambridge and myriad other cities and towns globally—will stand out as a monument to our times. Generations to come will remember our era as a time of an ever-increasing interreligious connectedness. The emergence of a world Christianity is part of this, as Christians of every kind find ourselves deeply and irrevocably drawn into new bonds with each other, now as equals, and with people of other faith communities, large and small. In like manner, differences aside, every other tradition too is redefining itself—event by event, conversation by conversation, classroom by classroom—in relation to religious others who are now becoming religious collaborators, dialogue partners, and friends. The clash of civilizations captures the headlines, but the actual reality is that of a growing harmony and understanding that surpasses anything seen on earth up to now.

What Catholics Can Learn from a Hindu Saint on His Thousandth Birth Anniversary

December 13, 2016

Cambridge, MA. I am the kind of person who remembers anniversaries, and 2016 and 2017 offer a few worth remembering. This academic year marks the two hundredth anniversary of Harvard Divinity School. And, in 2017, it is the five hundredth anniversary of the Reformation, culminating on October 31, 2017, the date when by tradition Martin Luther posted his Ninety-Five Theses on the door of All Saints' Church in Germany. And one even greater number is before us: the one thousandth anniversary of the great theistic Hindu theologian Ramanuja (1017–1137). His anniversary year is 2017, but since this blog series itself will be ending this month, I want to call him to your attention now.

The remarkable Ramanuja was born in Sriperumbudur, a town not far from today's great city of Chennai (Madras). He was a Sri Vaishnava Hindu, for whom Vishnu is the supreme Deity, ever accompanied by his eternal consort, the Goddess Shri Lakshmi. All other deities lead to him alone.

Ramanuja is respected even today in the small but vital Sri Vaishnava community as a reformer of temple ritual at the great Srirangam temple in deep South India (where his body is preserved in iconic form), as a proponent of the study of the Tamil devotional tradition of the Alvars (saint poets immersed in the reality of God), and as a leader in showing that this Tamil tradition is not at odds with the great Sanskrit tradition of the Vedas, Upanishads, and *Bhagavad Gita*.

Though a leader and codifier of a very orthodox set of traditions, he was also something of a radical.

By one famous story, having received from his guru, after much penance and repeated requests, the holy mantra (Tiru Mantra) sacred to his faith, he risked his own spiritual well-being by ignoring his teacher's command that he share the mantra with no one. Instead, he went up onto the temple balcony and proclaimed it to one and all, saying that he could not bear to withhold so great a gift from all people: *om namo Narayanaya* (OM, obeisance to Narayana). This mantra is said to express simply the truth that we exist entirely and only for God—Narayana, the ground (*ayana*) of all beings (*nara*). By reciting it, one confesses that fact as one's own truth.

Ramanuja by tradition wrote nine works, including two great commentaries on the *Bhagavad Gita* and on the *Brahma Sutras* (which was, in turn, a systematic organization of the teachings of the Upanishads). In both cases, he argued that the true meaning of the scriptures was an affirmation of the view of the world as real and dependent on God but not the same as God: neither a monism nor a dualism but rather a kind of panentheism ("all in God, God in all"). The tradition also lists as his three long prose prayers: "Taking Refuge with the Lord," "Taking Refuge in Srirangam," and "Taking Refuge in Heaven," which intensely express love of God and heartfelt surrender—something like the Ignatian "Take and Receive."

To study Ramanuja and his writings is to gain a glimpse of a Hindu tradition that is old and deep, learned and pious. Indeed, Christian theologians have written about Ramanuja for many years. Jesuits in early twentieth-century Calcutta included a careful study of him in the "To Christ through the Vedanta" series. In the 1970s, my predecessor at the Center for the Study of World Religions, John Carman, wrote *The Theology of Ramanuja*, a landmark study, while Julius Lipner wrote with great insight and acumen *The Face of Truth*, on Ramanuja's epistemology and theology of language. Recently, Martin Rabindra Ganeri, OP, an Oxford scholar who was prior of the Dominicans in Cambridge and Oxford before becoming the prior provincial of the English province, wrote a splendid comparative study of Ramanuja, *Indian Thought and Western Theism: The Vedanta of Ramanuja*.

Conversely, a scholar of Hindu origins, Chakravarthi Ram-Prasad, a professor at the University of Lancaster and himself of the family lineage of Ramanuja, recently wrote a fine comparative study of

Ramanuja and Shankara (the more well-known radical non-dualist Vedantin), *Divine Self, Human Self: The Philosophy of Being in Two Gita Commentaries.*

As for me, I have studied him on and off for thirty-five years or so, though he has never been at the center of my research. But for a conference in India next month, I have been studying his smallest work, the "Daily Ritual" (the *Nityam*, more literally, the "Always Book" of rites). This is a little ritual book that prescribes the intense and focused prayer and practice of the single-minded and single-hearted devotee, whose dedication is to be reflected in a mix of ritual acts, meditations and visualizations, and remembrances of God's nature, graciousness, and central place in one's life. To my knowledge, it has never been translated into English, so here are some excerpts to give you a feel for it (alternating gender from paragraph to paragraph, to avoid translation contortions in a blog):

> After thoroughly washing his hands and feet and rinsing his mouth, and after choosing space in a pure and very lovely place free of noise, let him purify it too. Then, by remembering the whole succession of teachers, let him approach the highest of teachers, the Lord, and meditate on him as the goal and the means, the remover of all that is undesirable and the acquirer of all that is desirable. Let him meditate on the whole array of the Lord's regalia, his proper form and external forms, his perfections, his glorious states and his play in this world. And then let him approach this Lord as his only refuge, with the words that begin, "His proper form is one and endless, knowledge and bliss, different from all things, his own and other; he is the abode of all that is auspicious and opposed to all that is to be avoided. . . ."
>
> After coming near to this Lord for refuge, with the energies of her mind enhanced by the Lord's grace, and after meditating on that Lord alone, as the Lord of all lords, the Lord of her own self, then let her meditate on his most clear and perceptible form without interruption. For it is exceedingly pleasing. Let her sit in this meditation for some time, and then begin the worship that takes the form of complete service, carried out with an extreme pleasure born of experience of the Lord. . . .
>
> Let him meditate on the Lord, Narayana, who is served by the assembly of guardians, with his royal insignia, with his ornaments and weapons, and who is accompanied by his retinue and his Goddess; on the Lord who holds together and yet distinct the steadfastness and movement and proper form of all the conscious and non-conscious beings depending on him; on the Lord who is untouched by any faults at all, by no afflictions, demerits, etc., who is a great ocean in which streams a host of innumerable auspicious qualities, beginning

with knowledge, strength, lordly power, courage, brightness, etc., all innate, flawless, and abundant. Let him then worship the Lord by offering his own self to the Lord, with the holy mantra. Let him prostrate himself, and with permission begin the full worship of the Lord. . . .

With her whole mind and understanding and sense of self, let her prostrate herself flat on the ground like a tortoise—her arms and legs and head too—paying reverence at all eight points of the body, always in that form making proper worship, paying respect over and over. Let her then sit before the Lord, and make her act of total surrender, and after that, with the Lord's permission, complete her daily worship.

To my tastes, this is wonderful and intense theology, the love of God and surrender to God elegantly—and demandingly—expressed in what is daily worship. Perhaps he inspires me to pray more and better; perhaps he reminds me how often I fall short of simple commands that come to us in the Pauline tradition: "Pray in the Spirit at all times, in every prayer and supplication" (Eph 6:18); "Devote yourselves to prayer, keeping alert in it with thanksgiving" (Col 4:2); "Rejoice always, pray without ceasing, give thanks in all circumstances; for this is the will of God in Christ Jesus for you" (1 Thess 5:16–18). Ramanuja would, I think, perfectly understand these (impossible) exhortations, even the last.

It should not be surprising that I feel it also good that we mark the anniversary year of Ramanuja. Indeed, Ramanuja himself would be the last to wish for a confused mixing together of traditions; he was no syncretist. We must be careful, but we must also be bold. In an age of divisions and forgetting and denial, we must insist on learning from the lives and ideas and prayers of saints and theologians of all traditions, as we move back and forth across borders where no walls can be built. Are not all the saints witnesses to the glory of God?